The Gender Pay Gap and Social Partnership in Europe

T0384485

The gender pay gap (GPG) exists in every European country, but it varies considerably, even in EU member states covered by the same legal principles on pay equality. Part of the variation can be explained by different patterns of social partnership. With current policy pressure to de-centralise collective bargaining and increase the percentage of pay linked to productivity, what role can social partnership play in tackling the GPG?

Reporting on the findings of the European Commission funded research project 'Close the Deal, Fill the Gap', this book uses an interdisciplinary analysis involving legal, economic and sociological expertise, to explore the role of social partnership in GPG in Italy, Poland and the UK. Selected on the basis of their contrasting profiles in terms of legal regulation, industrial relations, systems of collective bargaining, coverage of collective agreements and differing rates of the GPG, the in-depth study provides important insights into the main issues underlying the problem of reducing the GPG which have led to guidelines in the negotiation of arrangements on GPG-related issues.

Based on a unique comparative, interdisciplinary and action-oriented research project, it will be of great interest to all researchers and advanced students with an interest in women's representation in the workforce and the GPG, as well as practitioners and policy makers in organisations such as trade unions and employers' associations.

Hazel Conley is Professor of Human Resource Management at University of the West of England, Bristol, UK. Professor Conley has researched extensively on equality legislation, particularly in relation to gender equality, public services and equal pay. She is the co-editor of *The Gower Handbook of Discrimination at Work* (Gower, 2011) and co-author of *Gender Equality in Public Services: Chasing the Dream* (Routledge, 2015).

Donata Gottardi is Full Professor of Labour Law at the University of Verona. She was Member of the European Parliament, in the Committee on Economic and Monetary Affairs, from 2006 to 2009. Her fields of research include anti-discrimination law, equality and women's rights, European law and industrial relations. She is the coordinator of the project 'Close the Deal, Fill the Gap', concerning the GPG, funded by the European Commission under the Progress Programme. As regards her most recent publications, she is the editor of *La conciliazione delle esigenze di cura, di vita e di lavoro. Il rinnovato T.U. n. 151/ 2001 ai sensi del d. lgs. n. 80/2015* (Giappichelli, 2016) on the Italian legislation on work–life balance and the editor of *L'isola della maternità. Donne lavoratrici di fronte all'esperienza dell'essere madri* (Franco Angeli, 2015) on the protection of mothers at work.

Geraldine Healy is Professor of Employment Relations and in the Centre for Research in Equality and Diversity at the School of Business and Management, Queen Mary University of London. She has published widely in leading journals on gender and ethnicity and trade unions, discrimination and disadvantage, individualism and collectivism, the gendered impact of career breaks and an international study of academic careers. Her recent work has explored the inter-sectionality between gender and ethnicity and the GPG (particularly through the EU project 'Close the Deal, Fill the Gap'. Her recent books include: *Gender and Ethnicity at Work: Inequalities, Career and Employment Relations* (2008) with Harriet Bradley, *Diversity, Ethnicity, Migration and Work: International Perspectives* (2011) with Franklin Oikelome and *Gender and Leadership in Unions* (2013) with Gill Kirton.

Barbara Mikołajczyk is a professor at the Faculty of Law and Administration of the University of Silesia in Katowice, Poland and the head of the Department of International Public Law and European Law. She was also appointed as the ad hoc judge in the European Court of Human Rights (2012–2014). She has authored books and articles dedicated to human rights of various categories of vulnerable persons.

Marco Peruzzi is Associate Professor of Labour Law at the University of Verona, Italy. His fields of research include anti-discrimination law, gender pay equality, European social dialogue and transnational collective bargaining. Among his publications are *La prova del licenziamento ingiustificato e discriminatorio* (Giappichelli, 2017), *L'autonomia nel dialogo sociale europeo* (il Mulino, 2011) and 'Contradictions and Misalignments in the EU Approach Towards the Gender Pay Gap', *Cambridge Journal of Economics*, Special Issue on Equal Pay, 2015, 39 (2), pp. 441–465.

Routledge Research in Employment Relations

Aspects of the employment relationship are central to numerous courses at both undergraduate and postgraduate level. Drawing insights from industrial relations, human resource management and industrial sociology, this series provides an alternative source of research-based materials and texts, reviewing key developments in employment research.

Books published in this series are works of high academic merit, drawn from a wide range of academic studies in the social sciences.

Power at Work
How Employees Reproduce the Corporate Machine
Darren McCabe

Management in the Airline Industry
Geraint Harvey

Towards a European Labour Identity
The Case of the European Works Council
Edited by Michael Whittal, Herman Knudsen and Fred Huijgen

The Internet of People, Things and Services
Workplace Transformations
Edited by Claire A. Simmers and Murugan Anandarajan

Job Quality in an Era of Flexibility
Experiences in a European Context
Edited by Tommy Isidorsson and Julia Kubisa

The Gender Pay Gap and Social Partnership in Europe
Findings from "Close the Deal, Fill the Gap"
Edited by Hazel Conley, Donata Gottardi, Geraldine Healy, Barbara Mikołajczyk and Marco Peruzzi

The Gender Pay Gap and Social Partnership in Europe

Findings from "Close the Deal, Fill the Gap"

Edited by
Hazel Conley, Donata Gottardi,
Geraldine Healy, Barbara Mikołajczyk and
Marco Peruzzi

Routledge
Taylor & Francis Group

LONDON AND NEW YORK

First published 2019 by Routledge

2 Park Square, Milton Park, Abingdon, Oxon, OX14 4RN

605 Third Avenue, New York, NY 10017

Routledge is an imprint of the Taylor & Francis Group, an informa business

First issued in paperback 2020

Copyright © 2019 selection and editorial matter, Hazel Conley, Donata Gottardi, Geraldine Healy, Barbara Mikołajczyk and Marco Peruzzi; individual chapters, the contributors

British Library Cataloguing-in-Publication Data
A catalogue record for this book is available from the British Library

Library of Congress Cataloging-in-Publication Data
Names: Conley, Hazel, editor. | Gottardi, Donata, editor. | Healy, Geraldine (Geraldine Mary), editor. | Miko±ajczyk, Barbara, editor. | Peruzz, Marco, editor.
Title: The gender pay gap and social partnership in Europe : findings from "Close the deal, fill the gap" / edited by Hazel Conley, Donata Gottardi, Geraldine Healy, Barbara Mikolajczyk and Marco Peruzz.
Description: Abingdon, Oxon ; New York, NY : Routledge, 2019. | Includes bibliographical references and index.
Identifiers: LCCN 2018034620| ISBN 9781138738508 (hardback : alk. paper) | ISBN 9781315184715 (ebk)
Subjects: LCSH: Wages–Women–European Union countries. | Pay equity–European Union countries. | Wages–Women–European Union countries–Case studies.
Classification: LCC HD6061.2.E85 G46 2019 | DDC 331.4/294–dc23
LC record available at https://lccn.loc.gov/2018034620

ISBN: 978-1-138-73850-8 (hbk)
ISBN: 978-0-367-73213-4 (pbk)

Typeset in Sabon
by Taylor & Francis Books

We would like to dedicate this book to a united and progressive Europe.

Contents

x   *Contents*

Illustrations

Figures

Tables

Boxes

Acknowledgements

We would like to thank all of the social partners who took part in this project and who generously gave of their time and resources. We would also like to acknowledge the funding we received from the PROGRESS Programme of the European Union (reference no. JUST/2013/PROG/AG/4890/GE), which enabled us to undertake the research for this book.

Contributors

Hazel Conley is Professor of Human Resource Management at University of the West of England, Bristol, UK. Professor Conley has researched extensively on equality legislation, particularly in relation to gender equality, public services and equal pay. She is the co-editor of *The Gower Handbook of Discrimination at Work* (Gower, 2011) and co-author of *Gender Equality in Public Services: Chasing the Dream* (Routledge, 2015).

Mirosław Czerwiński is a doctor of economy and a senior lecturer at the Department of Economics Science at University of Silesia in Katowice, Poland. His research concentrates on the development of the Polish economical thought and on the process of transformation of the Polish economy from centrally planned to market economy. He is the author of *The Socio-economic Views of Ferdinand Zweig* (University of Silesia, 1996) and the editor of *The Civilization of Money* (e-bookowo, 2016). He is also a head of the Postgraduate Studies on Management at the Faculty of Social Sciences.

Donata Favaro is Associate Professor of Economics at the University of Padua, Italy. She has extensively researched on the topic of labour economics from a gender perspective. Among her publications, she is co-author of 'Part-time and Temporary Employment in a Gender Perspective', in T. Addabbo and G. Solinas (eds), *Non Standard Employment and Quality of Work: The Case of Italy*, Chapter 3 (Physica-Verlag, 2012), 'Gender Wage Differentials by Education in Italy', *Applied Economics*, 2011, 43(29), pp. 4589–4605, 'The Flexibility Penalty in a Long-Term Perspective', in S. Davies (ed.), *Gender Gap: Causes, Experiences and Effects* (Nova Science Publishers, 2010) (invited contribution), and 'Gender Differences in Productivity Rewards in Italy: The Role of Human Capital', *International Review of Economics*, 2012, 59 (1), pp. 81–110.

Donata Gottardi is Full Professor of Labour Law at the University of Verona. She was Member of the European Parliament, in the Committee on Economic and Monetary Affairs, from 2006 to 2009. Her fields of research include anti-discrimination law, equality and women's rights, European law and industrial relations. She is the coordinator of the project 'Close the Deal,

Fill the Gap', concerning the GPG, funded by the European Commission under the Progress Programme. As regards her most recent publications, she is the editor of *La conciliazione delle esigenze di cura, di vita e di lavoro. Il rinnovato T.U. n. 151/2001 ai sensi del d. lgs. n. 80/2015* (Giappichelli, 2016) on the Italian legislation on work–life balance, and the editor of *L'isola della maternità. Donne lavoratrici di fronte all'esperienza dell'essere madri* (Franco Angeli, 2015) on the protection of mothers at work.

Geraldine Healy is Professor of Employment Relations and in the Centre for Research in Equality and Diversity at the School of Business and Management, Queen Mary University of London. She has published widely in leading journals on gender and ethnicity and trade unions, discrimination and disadvantage, individualism and collectivism, the gendered impact of career breaks and an international study of academic careers. Her recent work has explored the intersectionality between gender and ethnicity and the GPG (particularly through the EU project 'Close the Deal, Fill the Gap'. Her recent books include: *Gender and Ethnicity at Work: Inequalities, Career and Employment Relations* (2008) with Harriet Bradley, *Diversity, Ethnicity, Migration and Work: International Perspectives* (2011) with Franklin Oikelome and *Gender and Leadership in Unions* (2013) with Gill Kirton.

Pedro Martins is Full Professor of Applied Economics. Professor Martins studies employment and wage dynamics, focusing on some of their key determinants: skills, firm performance, the business cycle, employment laws, industrial relations, FDI and international trade. His research draws on his experience as Secretary of State of Employment in the Government of Portugal (2011–2013) and has been sponsored by the ESRC, the European Commission, the British Academy, IPEA (Brazil) and FCT (Portugal). Professor Martins is also a research fellow of IZA (Bonn) and CEG-IST (Lisbon) and an adviser to EPIS.

Nicoletta Masiero is researcher at the Institute of Economics and Social Research (Ires Veneto – Venice, Italy). She researches job transformation and female employment. Among her latest publications are: 2012, *Tra vulnerabilità e invisibilità. Donne e lavoro nel terziario* (Between Vulnerability and Invisibility: Women and Work in the Tertiary Sector) Ires Working Paper 70; 2015 (with F. Chicchi), 'Incrinature. Posture e linee di fuga del lavoro cognitivo' (Cracks, Postures and Escapes of the Cognitive Labor), *AUT*, 365, pp. 66–83; 2016, 'A Non-Manual of Human Resource Management, or How to Survive to the "Imaginary Humanists"', www.criticalmanagement.org.

Alberto Mattei is Research Fellow in Labour Law at Law Department of University of Verona. His fields of research include collective bargaining, in particular the decentralisation of collective bargaining. He is editor of *Il diritto del lavoro tra decentramento e ricentralizzazione. Il modello trentino nello spazio giuridico europeo* (Editoriale Scientifica, 2014).

Barbara Mikołajczyk is a professor at the Faculty of Law and Administration of the University of Silesia in Katowice, Poland and the head of the Department of International Public Law and European Law. She was also appointed as the ad hoc judge in the European Court of Human Rights (2012–2014). She has authored books and articles dedicated to human rights of various categories of vulnerable persons.

Joanna Nowakowska-Małusecka is Associate Professor in the Department of Public International and European Law at Faculty of Law and Administration, University of Silesia in Katowice, Poland. Her scientific interests concentrate on international humanitarian law, human rights law and children rights in details, international criminal law, especially on the establishment and work of international criminal tribunals, children as victims of genocide, rape and gender related crimes in armed conflicts or in similar situations. She is the author of books and articles on those topics and an editor or co-editor of several publications on different issues on international and European law. She is vice-president of the International Law Association, Polish Branch and a member of International Association of Genocide Scholars.

Marco Peruzzi is Associate Professor of Labour Law at the University of Verona, Italy. His fields of research include anti-discrimination law, gender pay equality, European social dialogue and transnational collective bargaining. Among his publications are *La prova del licenziamento ingiustificato e discriminatorio* (Giappichelli, 2017), *L'autonomia nel dialogo sociale europeo* (il Mulino, 2011) and 'Contradictions and Misalignments in the EU Approach Towards the Gender Pay Gap', *Cambridge Journal of Economics*, Special Issue on Equal Pay, 2015, 39 (2), pp. 441–465.

Magdalena Półtorak is an Assistant Professor of Public International and European Law at the University of Silesia, Poland. Her academic interests concentrate on the issues concerning gender equality in the international, European and national law, focusing particularly on the analysis of legal warranties for equality of women and men in public life (esp. in politics and business), non-legislative solutions facilitating combination of career with family life, empowering women in the decision-making process as well as the legal situation of migrant women in the EU. She is the author of *Women – Quotas – Politics: Warranties of Gender Equality in the European Union* (Parliamentary Publishing, 2015), member of the EuroGender Network and consultant of the local women's organisation.

Ilona Topa is an Assistant Professor in the Department of Public International and European Law at Faculty of Law and Administration, University of Silesia in Katowice, Poland. Her fields of research include international human rights law and international criminal law. Lately, her academic interests concentrate on the rights of vulnerable persons and, particularly, victims of crime.

Urszula Torbus is an Assistant Professor in the Department of Labour Law at Faculty of Law and Administration, University of Silesia in Katowice, Poland. Her fields of research concentrate around individual labour law, including anti-discrimination and equality law, work–life balance and temporary employment. She has published widely on employment rights of workers. Her recent scientific projects concern the equal treatment of workers and precarious workers.

Stella Warren is a Research Associate in the Bristol Leadership and Change Centre at the University of the West of England, Bristol. She has worked on a range of projects for Public Health England and for the Equality Commission for Northern Ireland. She has particular expertise in the areas of gender, diversity and behaviour change and is a founder member of *alta*, a mentoring scheme for professional women in aviation and aerospace.

Introduction

Hazel Conley, Geraldine Healy, Donata Gottardi,
Barbara Mikołajczyk and Marco Peruzzi

There is a gender pay gap (GPG) in every European country, but the size of the gap varies considerably even in EU member states covered by ostensibly the same legal principles on pay equality. Part of the variation in the GPG can be explained by different patterns of social partnership between European countries, but in a time when there is pressure from EU policy to decentralise collective bargaining and increase the percentage of pay linked to productivity, the study considers the role of social partnership in tackling the GPG. Peruzzi (2015) has pointed to the policy contradictions between EU support for the role of the social partners in tackling the GPG and the push for a decentralisation of collective bargaining prompted by the EU policies to address the labour market consequences of the austerity crisis. Cross-national research enables further contradictions to be revealed with respect to the way EU policies are acted out in member state countries thereby demonstrating, not just the national interpretations of EU policies, but also the complex range of responses to subsequent national level regulation, the varied practices in wage-setting at sub-national level and the dynamic changes over time.

Our study is undoubtedly timely given the contemporary focus on the way that women are treated in the workplace and society. The #MeToo and #TimesUp campaigns have vividly demonstrated the most blatant forms of discrimination in the way women are treated and of course how they are paid. However, while the discrimination in the entertainment industry hits the headlines, in other less glamorous sectors the same patterns are repeated time and time again where the consequences for those at the bottom of the pay scale are not only unfair but lead to material disadvantage. At the same time, but less publicised, the EU, trade unions, some national governments and women's organisations are promoting the need for organisations and member states to reduce their GPGs.

The chapters in this book all relate to a single research project on the GPG, the European Commission funded 'Close the Deal, Fill the Gap'. This cross-national research project explores the role of social partners in the context of decentralised and decreasing collective bargaining coverage and the application of EU regulations. It draws on interdisciplinary analysis, involving legal, economic and sociological expertise, developed across three EU countries: Italy, Poland and the UK. The selection of the three countries was made on the basis of their contrasting profiles in terms of models of legal regulation, industrial relations, systems of collective bargaining, extent of decentralisation, coverage of collective agreements and differing rates of the GPG. The comparison of the national frameworks in terms of legal provisions and industrial relations models, coupled with in-depth examination of the topic in specific case studies, provides important insights into within-country differences, shedding light on the underlying complexities of reducing the GPG.

Whilst we acknowledge that the GPG and equal pay are not the same concept, they inevitably overlap and the book attempts to explore the connections between the two. The GPG is by its nature aggregated while equal pay, at its most basic level, involves individuals, regulation and sometimes case law. In Europe, the regulation of both concepts, however, springs from the same well: Article 2 and Article 3(3) of the Treaty on European Union, which enshrine the right to equality between women and men. Article 23 of the Charter of Fundamental Rights of the European Union requires that equality between women and men applies to all areas, including employment, work and pay.

As far as reducing the GPG is concerned, the role of the social partners, either at supra-national or at national level, has been repeatedly emphasised by both the European Commission (Smith, 2012; Peruzzi, 2015) in several communications (e.g. Strategy for Equality between Women and Men 2010–2015, COM (2010)491), and the European Parliament, in its 2008 and 2012 Resolutions in addition to being expressively endorsed by Article 21, dir. 2006/54/EC. At the same time, the austerity measures adopted by the EU as a response to the crisis, from the Euro Plus Pact of March 2011 and additions, repeatedly stress the need for each country to adopt measures to ensure cost developments in line with productivity, including a review of the wage-setting arrangements, and, where necessary, the degree of centralisation in the bargaining process (see, for example, Conclusions of the European Council, 24/25 March 2011). The aim of this book is to assess the interaction and interdependencies between these two different EU policy targets, clarifying the variables and likely gender bias that the social partners need to bear in mind when negotiating collective agreements or adopting other wage-setting instruments at company, sectoral or national level and, in this regard, to propose a set of operating guidelines (see Appendix). In addition, it is hoped that the book will provide an important reference point for the regulatory framework of gender pay equality in the EU prior to 'Brexit'. Moreover, it refutes the argument that the EU leads to uniform conditions and removes national sovereignty.

Existing research suggests that a decentralisation of collective bargaining with related anchoring of wages to productivity (and consequent valorisation of aspects of remuneration such as extra pay, bonuses, payments in kind) may result in a widening of the GPG (e.g. Blau and Kahn, 1992; Machin, 1997; Rubery *et al.*, 2005; Plantenga and Remery, 2006; Gannon *et al.*, 2007). The chapters in the book take an interdisciplinary comparative approach, which analyses the interaction between differences in national legal frameworks, the level of decentralisation in the negotiation of salaries and the rate of the GPG.

The research reported in the book therefore addresses a level of complexity that is often overlooked (O'Reilly *et al.*, 2015). To this purpose, the analysis is developed across three different EU countries, selected to reflect the widest range of diversity in the possible relationships between the legal framework, model of industrial relations and the rate of the GPG. Italy is characterised by a higher percentage of collective bargaining coverage, a national-centred collective bargaining system, and a small GPG, at least according to Eurostat's statistics, which are based on an unadjusted hourly-pay indicator and can therefore fail to give the big and more complex picture of the phenomenon (for example, the small GPG is often considered to relate to women's lower labour market participation, e.g. Blau and Kahn, 2003; Arulampalam *et al.*, 2007). In comparison to Italy, the UK features an individualistic legal framework, much lower percentage of voluntarist collective bargaining coverage, a strongly decentralised collective bargaining system and a much wider GPG rate. However, despite the voluntarist nature of collective bargaining, the law has played an important role in settling equal pay disputes between employers, trade unions and individual employees (Conley, 2014). Interestingly, most of the equal pay legal cases in the UK have been taken in the public sector where collective bargaining has its widest coverage and has sometimes proved problematic for the trade unions involved (Deakin et al., 2015). The relationship between the model of industrial relations and the level of the GPG reveals further complexity in the comparison with the other national context involved in the project: Poland is characterised by a highly centralised legal framework for pay setting but very low trade union density and collective bargaining coverage. Despite the trend towards greater decentralisation of collective bargaining, Poland has one of the smallest GPG rates in the EU-27, which has decreased almost by half since 2009.

To explore these national differences, the analysis combines legal, economic and sociological expertise. In this regard, we note that whilst most of the studies on the GPG come from an economic perspective with some informed by comparative industrial relations structures, few examine comparative legal and welfare structures and how these underpin both industrial relations, sociological and economic analyses. Thus, we build on a comparison between the national systems involved in terms of legal provisions concerning the GPG and how these interact or are held separately from models of industrial relations in order to assess the variables of such systems in meaningful national case studies. Our interdisciplinary investigation therefore offers a critical analysis of the role of social partnership in tackling the GPG and in some ways responds to aspects of O'Reilly *et al.*'s (2015) agenda for future research and policy discourse, in particular, the relationship between litigation and bargaining strategies and the interaction between wage-setting institutions and new organisational practices.

The book is structured to bring together our theoretical analysis, conceptual framework and action/practice research. An important contribution of this book is its attempt to analyse gender pay inequalities by drawing on common multi-disciplinary conceptual frames which will enrich comparative analysis. In particular, the study will identify the importance of both horizontal/vertical segregation and labour market segmentation in understanding pay inequality and importantly the interrelationship between the two. Moreover, the book shows how segregation and segmentation may be used to great effect at an aggregated but also, importantly in the context of decentralisation, a dis-aggregated level. The nature of inequalities is complex and operates at different levels, including the organisation, where inequality regimes (Acker, 1989, 2006) thrive. Introducing the idea of inequality regimes and their different components will alert the reader to an understanding of the mutually con-stituted components that reinforce unfair practices in wage-setting and thereby underpin the GPG. While the book is about tackling the GPG, it makes no assumption that all women are equally disadvantaged. Rather it recognises that disadvantage and discrimination operate in different contexts and are impacted not only by gender but other aspects of inequality including class, ethnicity and age.

Drawing on contextualised comparisons (Locke and Thelen, 1995), Chapter 1 provides the comparative analysis of the relevant legal, industrial relations and economic frameworks of the countries involved. The authors build a picture of the regulatory framework, case law, wage system and tax and social security frameworks in each country, focusing on their impact on the GPG. This chap-ter identifies similarities and differences between the countries that are elabo-rated throughout the book. Complementing this contextual analysis, Chapters 2–4 report on findings from our case studies at national, sectoral and company levels, which are underpinned by the comparative research analysis of the first chapter. Each national case clarifies the main factors that led to gender bias in its collective bargaining and wage-setting, which were influential in the design of the proactive guidelines to support the social partners in the tackling of the GPG (see Appendix).

Chapter 2 contains an interdisciplinary analysis of the influence con-tractual decentralisation has on various factors of GPGs in Italy. Since in Italy the basic wage is elaborated within the centralised system of collective bargaining at the national level, the authors investigate the gaps arising over minimum pay, productivity bonuses, extra allowances, incentive pay or bonuses, including those linked to individual (including gender) needs of the company staff. The authors provide an in-depth analyse of 223 company agreements filed at the Territorial Labour Directorate of Verona in 2014 and of two case studies of companies belonging to the transport and metal-working sectors. Finally, they explore the GPG in the context of corporate welfare in Italy.

The legal, economic and industrial relations research utilised in an empirical investigation of the companies enables the authors to indicate factors of GPG rooted in mechanisms, criteria and terms of determining and redistributing bonuses, horizontal and vertical segregation of the company staff and even the work–life balance arrangements. They also observe some factors that require further research, such as the lower contractual capacity of women and employer attitudes.

Chapter 3 provides the research findings of three case studies relating to the GPG issues in the Polish context. The first was conducted in relation to the collective labour agreements (CLA-s) filed at the District Labour Inspectorate in Katowice and covered 115 companies placed in the Silesian voivodship – a particularly industrialised and unionised region of Poland. The other case studies examine the situation in two very different legal entities – an international shipping company and a university faculty, where the gender ratio among the academic staff is relatively equal.

The outcome of the research confirms that a lower remuneration of women, 'sticky floor' and 'glass ceiling' are universal phenomena and exist despite the type of organisational entity or its activity. Such a situation is an effect of the lack of mechanisms that could balance the negative impact of cultural bias, promote the family as a partnership and enforce the principle of equal treatment in the labour market and society. Moreover, the authors observe that it is difficult to trace the GPG phenomenon in Poland due to a lack of transparency in pay. The authors conclude by arguing that introducing legal requirements for employers to publish reports on gender pay equality could become an efficient tool to combat GPG.

Chapter 4 presents the UK case studies in local government, financial services and the rail sector. The local government and financial sector case studies provide data on particularly influential events in relation to the GPG in the UK. The local government case study examines a controversial national collective agreement that resulted in a large amount of case law. The financial services case study examines the sector with one of the largest GPGs in the UK and a known sexist culture. The rail sector case study examines the attempts of one employer and one trade union to work together to close the GPG. Together the case studies highlight how the decentralised nature of industrial relations in the UK, the uneven trade union coverage in public and private sectors and a quintessentially individualised legal system have coalesced in relation to the GPG and pay inequality.

Chapters 5 and 6 provide an analysis of the main theoretical and conceptual issues raised in our case study analysis. Chapter 5 focuses on the role of social partners in promoting proactive attitudes towards gender representation and raising awareness of the GPG. The main issues explored by the authors refer to under-representation of women at decision-making levels and in negotiation processes, analysing interim measures aimed at achieving parity. Expanding on the guidelines developed in the project, the authors of this chapter examine possible solutions in the negotiation of arrangements on GPG-related topics and consider legal, practical and various 'soft' measures as useful tools for combating vertical and horizontal segregation and help to close the GPG. As part of the analysis, the chapter picks up aspects of the national frameworks outlined in Chapter 1 on conditions for women returning from maternity leave and relates them to the promotion of female representation ratios at higher positions. They indicate work arrangements designed to balance professional and family life, including flexible working hours, as examples of good practice that put more emphasis on task accomplishment rather than on presence at work. In relation to professional development opportunities for women, the authors examine access to training, mentoring and female support networks across Italy, the UK and Poland.

Chapter 6 explores the topical issue of pay transparency in relation to the GPG. Drawing on largely US literature, the chapter explores some of the conceptual issues and models of pay transparency developed by academic lawyers and social scientists following *Lilly Leadbetter* v *Goodyear Tire and Rubber Company* that resulted in the Fair Pay Act 2009, the first bill signed by President Obama. The chapter argues that although pay transparency is the important first step in relation to identifying the GPG, it must be followed by a proactive collective strategy by the social partners to use the data it reveals to close the GPG and vigilance thereafter to ensure it remains closed.

The Conclusion brings together the key themes and findings of the research. It offers insights to social partners on the causes of GPG and provides ideas for its reduction. While collective bargaining is an important solution, the decline in coverage of collective bargaining means it is not the solution for all sectors. Equally important are the decentralised wage-setting systems that are often the outcome of employer discretion rather than negotiation. The Conclusion turns to the value of transparency in the GPG and notes the recent UK legislation on pay reporting. It observes that while this is an important regulatory step forward and provides an opportunity for unions and women's groups to negotiate and challenge the disproportionate number of high GPGs emerging from the reporting exercise, it is not a panacea to solve the GPG. The chapter concludes that social partners and other key actors such as women's groups need to push continually to 'close the deal and fill the gap'. To this end, the project findings have led, in conjunction with national and European social partners, to the development of guidelines for use by trade unions, employers' associations and companies in the negotiation and determination of wage-setting arrangements on GPG-related issues. The guidelines are contained in the Appendix and disseminated through the website www.fillthegap.eu.

References

Acker, J. (1989) *Doing Comparable Worth: Gender, Class and Pay Equity*. Philadelphia: Temple University Press.

Acker, J. (2006) 'Gender Regimes: Gender, Class and Race in Organizations' *Gender and Society* 20(4), pp. 441–464.

Arulampalam, W., Booth, A. L. and Bryan, M. L. (2007) 'Is There a Glass Ceiling over Europe? Exploring the Gender Pay Gap across the Wage Distribution' *ILR Review* 60 (2), pp. 163–186.

Blau, F. D. and Kahn, L. M. (1992) 'The Gender Earnings Gap: Learning from International Comparisons' *American Economic Review* 82, pp. 533–538.

Blau, F. D. and Kahn, L. M. (2003) 'Understanding International Differences in the Gender Pay Gap' *Journal of Labour Economics* 21(1), pp. 106–144.

Conley, H. (2014) 'Trade Unions, Equal Pay and the Law' *Economic and Industrial Democracy* 35(2), pp. 309–323.

Deakin, S., Fraser Butlin, S., McLaughlin, C. and Polanska, A. (2015) 'Are Litigation and Collective Bargaining Complements or Substitutes for Achieving Gender Equality? A Study of the British Equal Pay Act' *Camb. J. Econ* 39(2), pp. 381–403.

Gannon, B., Plasman, R., Ryck, F. and Tojerow, I. (2007) 'Inter-Industry Wage Differentials and the Gender Wage Gap: Evidence from European Countries' *The Economic and Social Review* 38(1), pp. 135–155.

Locke, R. M. and Thelen, K. (1995) 'Apples and Oranges Revisited: Contextualized Comparisons and the Study of Comparative Labor Politics' *Politics and Society* 23(3), pp. 337–367.

O'Reilly, J., Smith, M., Deakin, S. and Burchell, B. (2015) 'Equal Pay as a Moving Target: International Perspectives on Forty-Years of Addressing the Gender Pay Gap' *Camb. J. Econ.* 39(2), pp. 299–317.

Peruzzi, M. (2015) 'Contradictions and Misalignments in the EU Approach towards the Gender Pay Gap' *Camb. J. Econ.* 39(2), pp. 441–465.

Plantenga, J. and Remery, C. (eds) (2006) *The Gender Pay Gap and Policy Responses: Origins and Policy Responses a Comparative Review in 30 European Countries.* Brussels: European Commission DG Employment, Social Affairs and Equal Opportunities.

Rubery, J., Grimshaw, D. and Figueiredo, H. (2005) 'How to Close the Gender Pay Gap in Europe: Towards the Gender Mainstreaming of Pay Policy' *Industrial Relations Journal* 36(3), pp. 184–213.

Smith, M. (2012) 'Social Regulation of the Gender Pay Gap In the EU' *European Journal of Industrial Relations* 18(4), pp. 365–380.

1 National frameworks and the gender pay gap in Italy, Poland and the UK

Comparing oranges with apples?

Hazel Conley, Alberto Mattei, Urszula Torbus and Joanna Nowakowska-Małusecka

Introduction

This chapter considers the legal, economic and industrial relations context with reference to the three countries on which the research focuses: Italy, Poland and the UK. As the title of the chapter suggests, drawing on Locke and Thelen's (1995) seminal article, we adopt a 'contextualised comparisons' approach to our analysis to establish how EU law on pay equality is refracted through different institutional settings. We further use the concept of functional equivalence to identify the specific issues and pressure points that have been instrumental in conceptualising and attempting to achieve equal pay and close the gender pay gap (GPG) in each country. However, to aid a more direct, 'matched comparison' and to provide contextual information important for later chapters in the book, we structure our analysis of each country under common headings covering the basic regulatory framework, case law, wage system and tax and social security frameworks as they impact on pay equality.

Article 157(1) of the TFEU requires each member state to fulfil the principle of equal pay for male and female workers for equal work or work of equal value. It is up to each member state to transpose these concepts into domestic law. Starting from the reconstruction of the principle of equal pay between men and women as stated in EU law, the chapter focuses on the typical aspects of each regulatory system and how EU law has been transposed, highlighting the characteristic features from a comparative perspective. With regard to Italy, the attention focuses on the reconstruction of the concept of equal pay, giving particular attention to the debate within the Italian labour law literature, which has focused, on the one hand, the issue of pay and equal remuneration between men and women and, on the other hand, discrimination and the prohibition of discrimination in remuneration, within the frame of the decentralisation of collective bargaining promoted in legislation in recent years. Regarding Poland, the analysis will focus on the post-communist development of the country, with its high level of statutory regulation and a weakening influence of the trade unions. It will present the necessary legal framework, concerning among others the principle of equal pay for men and women, prohibition of discrimination and regulations on remuneration. For the UK, attention will fall on the peculiarities of the English system, typified by the voluntary and decentralised nature that characterises collective bargaining and the individualistic nature of the legal framework that has resulted in considerable case law. Finally, this chapter will identify the areas of similarities and differences between the systems, starting from the common drive in the EU for the decentralisation of collective bargaining, which has intensified following the most recent economic and financial crisis.

Italian national legal framework

Regulatory framework

In the Italian legal system, the principle of pay equality between men and women at work is enshrined by *Art. 37 of the Constitution*, which states that 'working women are entitled to equal rights and equal pay for equal work'. This article is directly enforceable against both individual employment contracts and collective agreements. The concept of 'equal work' must be interpreted as 'equal job position and tasks' and not 'equal performance'; and the assessment of GPGs needs to take into account the overall compensation, not just the minimum wage granted in accordance with the principles of proportionality and sufficiency set forth by *Art. 36 of the Constitution* (Ballestrero, 1979; Barbera, 1991; Treu, 1979). Italy does not have a minimum wage system, although it has been considered but not implemented for certain types of atypical contracts. The wage system is determined by national collective bargaining.

At the legislative level, the effectiveness of the principle of pay equality is ensured by *Art. 15 Law 300/70*. It contains a general prohibition of discriminations on grounds of different risk factors, gender included, and especially by *Art. 28 Delegated Decree 198/2006* (known as the **Equal Opportunities Act**), which states that any direct or indirect discrimination concerning any pay aspect or condition regarding equal work or work of equal value is forbidden. This text also contains the notions of direct and indirect discrimination (*Art. 25 Delegated Decree 198/ 2006*, already established by *l. 125/1991*) (see Scarponi, 2014).[1] Job classification systems aimed at determining pay are required to adopt common criteria for men and women and be designed so as to remove discrimination. This provision was specifically reinforced by *Delegated Decree 5/10*, aimed at implementing *Directive 2006/54/EC*, which introduced a specific reference to direct and indirect discriminations as well as to any aspect or condition of pay and the need for work responsibilities to enable the removal of pay-related discrimination. It also introduced a specific reference to gender-related pay discrimination in sanction regulations. In case of discrimination, the following sanctions may be applied: withdrawal of public financial supports, incentives or benefits, exclusion from public procurements and financial penalty.

The Italian system is characterised by a multiplicity of institutional players and actions (Guarriello, 2007). The effectiveness of the principle of pay equality is ensured by the promotion of equal opportunities programmes by the National

Committee for the Implementation of Equality Between Men and Women (*Art. 8 Delegated Decree 198/06*). These programmes can also be proposed as a solution for removing collective pay discrimination (*Art. 10, par. 1, let. g*), although such actions are one of the least implemented by the Committee. There is a survey on GPGs carried out by employers (national, regional or provincial) and provided to Equality Counsellors (*Art. 15 par. 1, a*). It must be said, however, that despite the provision provided for this survey by existing Italian law, the survey has turned out to be an ineffective instrument for monitoring the GPG. There is also a specific judicial protection, and public and privately owned companies with more than 100 employees are required to deliver a report on employee conditions, pay included, every two years and send it to the competent Regional Equality Body as well as to the union representatives in the workplace (*Art. 46 amended by Delegated Decree 5/10* with possible financial administrative fines; see Chapter 6). Legislation makes use of reflexive and command-and-control techniques. For example, legislation has fostered company-based self-regulatory solutions by providing financial support to affirmative action programmes (*Articles 43–44–45 Delegated Decree 198/2006*, for further details see Garofalo, 2002).

Other areas of legislation also potentially have a bearing on the GPG in the Italian labour law system. For example, legislation regarding part-time contracts prevents indirect gender discrimination by enshrining a principle of non-discrimination between part-timers and full-timers, in accordance with *Directive 97/81/EC* (*Delegated Decree 81/2015*, which repealed *Delegated Decree 61/00*). This is particularly relevant for women, as it is statistically more probable for a woman to have this type of part-time agreement (Scarponi, 2014). Now the legislation of 2015 (known as the **Jobs Act**) only states that part-timers cannot be treated less favourably than full-time workers and are entitled to the same economic and normative rights as full-timers on a pro rata basis. Moreover, while the previous law specifically enabled individual contracts and collective agreements to provide a more-than-proportioned measurement of performance-related pay elements for part-timers (*Art. 4, par. 2, Delegated Decree 61/00*), such a provision is not provided in the *Delegated Decree 81/2015*.

Regarding collective representation, the legal system recognises and protects unions and collective bargaining at the constitutional level (*Art. 39 Const.*) and collective bargaining can be carried out at both national and decentralised levels. Since the second part of *Art. 39 Const.* was not implemented by the required legislative measures, collective agreements do not have *erga omnes* (agreements cover all workers, not only members of signatory unions) legal effects: on the grounds of established case law, the clauses of (national) collective agreements concerning minimum wages can be judicially applied, even if the employer is not a member of the signatory association. Within the context of litigation, a judge must determine whether a salary is consistent with the principle of sufficiency and proportionality of pay enshrined by *Art. 36 Const.*

In particular, subjects ordinarily covered by collective agreements are: minimum wages, which are set at national level, job classification, use of atypical contracts (such as part-time, fixed-term contracts, etc.), productivity-based bonuses (generally set at a decentralised level), and collective relationships between the signatory parties. Further subjects include company welfare benefits (such as company nursery schools, complementary pension schemes, company health insurance, etc.), work time training, work–life balance arrangements, occupational health and safety, outsourcing and disciplinary sanctions.

Following the policy guidelines set by the Euro Plus Pact in 2011, as reaffirmed by the European Central Bank (ECB) letter to Italy of August 2011, decentralised collective bargaining was strongly fostered and supported by *Art. 8, Law Decree 138/2011*, as converted in *Law 148/2011*, which may have a gender pay impact. Generally, collective agreements cannot derogate *in peius* (that is to say, they cannot be replaced by collective agreements inferior to those which are currently in force) from protective statutory law, but under this provision and on condition that specific conditions (subjects, objectives and negotiating parties) are fulfilled, decentralised collective agreements can derogate from both national collective agreements and legislative regulations and be given *erga omnes* effects. Furthermore, in order to foster collective bargaining of performance-related pay, the legislator introduced a reduction of social-security contributions for collectively negotiated performance-related pay elements and the reduction of tax rates applicable to these pay elements, when negotiated by collective agreements, which have been strongly promoted in 2016 and 2017 (for a detailed summary of the consequences of the above, see Chapter 6).

In the Italian system, collective agreements expressly promote gender equality (Borgogelli, 1992; Recchia, 2002; Ferrara, 2014) and deal with gender-related issues by regulating the protection of maternity with an increase of maternity pay and/or specific training programmes aimed at facilitating return to work, parental leave, paternity leave on the occasion of childbirth, care-giving leaves, work–life balance provisions such as a right to switch from full-time to part-time, and working from home. These are generally guaranteed at a national collective level, however, at the secondary level, many big companies will offer more incentives. Contractual provisions both at the national and decentralised level can also have an indirect gender-related impact. With regards to the GPG, they can have an indirect impact on wage differentials between men and women when dealing with compensation for typically male-dominated job positions (travel allowances, allowances for uncomfortable shifts and/or arduous works) and criteria for measuring productivity and awarding performance-related pay elements based on work attendance (see Chapter 2).

Case law

To put it briefly, it is possible to synthesise the role of case law related to gender pay discrimination into three parts: its handling within national case law; its more recent developments; and the level of consistency of the Italian system regarding the EU principles on the basis of what the ECJ has defined.

First, the case law from Court of Legitimacy has traditionally established that the constitutional principle of equal pay for workers of different genders imposes equal economic treatment on the basis of equal qualifications and duties between men and women without considering the performance of their work, but it must not take into account any extra allowance over minimum pay perceived by individual merits (*Cass. 209/1984; Cass. 2082/1980; Trib. Milano 9.11.1981; Pret. Milano 22.12.1989*, more generally, Treu, 1979). In general, for the case law, *Art. 37 Cost.* is a precept and is a norm of immediate application to individual employment contracts and to collective bargaining if they contain clauses that conflict with the constitutional precept (*Cass. 672/1974*). Classically, in the evaluation of equal remuneration between men and women, it is noted the overall economic treatment and not only the minimum treatment under *Art. 36 Cost* which states, 'the workers have the right to receive a salary commensurate with quality and quantity of their work and otherwise sufficient to ensure a free and dignified life for them and their family' (*Cass. 291/1984*). In each case, the protection provided by law with regard to the abstention or otherwise planned absence (i.e. maternity leave) cannot justify any variation in salary equality (Lassandari, 2018). Again, on the complex relationship between the non-discrimination principle and equal treatment with reference to pay, it should be noted that the Constitutional Court emphasised, although somewhat opaquely, the principle of equal treatment (*103/1989*). However, a few years after, the Supreme Court ruled that there was no principle of equal treatment (*Cass. 6030/1993*) (Barbera, 2011).

Second, there have been a couple of recent rulings concerning gender and incentive pay from the 2011 Florence Tribunal (*n. 179/2011*) and from Padova during 2007 (*no. 762/07* and *Decree 6.4.2007*), which concerned the exclusion of maternity leave, if taken early, from the calculation of attendance as a requirement for access to an incentive plan established by decentralised bargaining in public administration. In 2007, the Prato Tribunal ruled in favour of counting maternity leave and parental leave periods for service and pay. The Tribunal drew on the staffing report published by the bank, which pointed out the high percentage of women taking parental leave, to find indirect discrimination (*Trib. Prato 263/2007*, confirmed in 2009 by the Florence Appeals Court). Lastly, in 2016, the Turin Tribunal ruled that the counting of maternity, parental and sick leave as absences from work (within the scope of attendance-based bonuses) to be discriminatory against the workers who took advantage of them. Statistical data gathered by the company in question (GTT) highlighted that sick leave was used by women eight times more than men, and thereby becoming a criterion of indirect gender discrimination (*Trib. Torino 1858/2016*, see Peruzzi, 2017). The latest ruling of the Venice Court of Appeal established that any impediment to advancement of one's career which is based on absences accrued as a result of taking maternity or parental leave is considered to be discriminatory (*n. 841/2018*).

Third, Italy has influenced the case law of the European Court of Justice. Recently the ECJ declared, on the basis of a wide concept of pay and including pension schemes, that by maintaining the provisions under which the eligible retirement age for public employees varies between men and women, the Italian

Republic failed to fulfil its obligations under *Article 141 EC (Case C-46/07)*. In 2012, in a case concerning Italy, once more the ECJ stated that *Article 15* of *Directive 2006/54/EC* must be interpreted as precluding national legislation which, on grounds relating to the public interest, excludes a woman on mater-nity leave from a vocational training course which forms an integral part of her employment. If the training is compulsory in order to be able to be appointed definitively to a post as a civil servant, in order to benefit from an improvement in her employment conditions, the woman must be guaranteed the right to participate in the next organised training course, even if the date of which is uncertain (*Case C-595/12*).

Wage system

Despite the promotion of collective bargaining decentralisation, salary struc-tures in Italy are centralised and are guaranteed by freedom of trade unions and collective bargaining under *Art. 39 Const.*, without any legislative provision of a minimum wage. In fact, *Art. 36 Const.* enshrines the principles of sufficiency and proportionality of pay with regard to dependent labour and represents the constitutional parameter to which collective bargaining must conform: mini-mum wages are set by national collective agreements, while performance-rela-ted pay elements are set by decentralised agreements (company or territorial agreements) according to the rules set by national agreements. In detail, the pay is composed of: minimum wage, length of service bonus, collective interim pay guarantee, allowances depending on the type/nature of the job, remuneration for overtime/holiday working hours (at a higher rate), and individual bonuses/performance-related pay elements awarded by the employer unilaterally or in accordance with a collective agreement (Gragnoli and Corti, 2012).

With regard to gender-specific aspects of pay, in the Italian system there is maternity leave pay that covers a compulsory period of leave from work for pregnant workers. It consists of 80% of pay based on the last pay period, plus possible additional voluntary contributions granted by the employer unilaterally or in accordance with a company agreement (**Single Act on Maternity and Paternity**, changed over the years, see Gottardi, 2016). There is also parental leave pay, which is optionally available to both parents to take care of a child in their infant years. Paternity leave provides 30% of pay based on the last pay period, for a period of ten months and to be divided between both parents, which can be voluntarily uprated by employers. The **Jobs Act of 2015** also provides that dependent workers, in the absence of collective bargaining at the company level, may also benefit from parental leave on an hourly basis (see Nunin, 2016). Paternity leave pay can be extended in two cases: in the case of death or infirmity of the mother, paternity pay can be remunerated at the same rate as maternity leave pay. Introduced in 2017, two days of paternity leave taken within the first five months of life can be remunerated at full pay. Col-lective bargaining, especially in some large companies, may include an extension of the leave as part of a work–life balance policy (Treu, 2016).

Tax and social security framework

The Italian system of social security law is characterised by a measure designed to protect families whose total income falls below certain limits, which varies according to the number of family members in a particular household and their combined total income called 'family unit allowances' (Cinelli, 2016). The allowance is usually paid to supplement part-time work and is based on the organisation of the work. 'Horizontal' part-time contracts are based on consistent daily working hours for the entire workweek, i.e. five hours per day, Monday to Friday, whereas a 'vertical' part-time contract could provide the same requisite hours per week as exemplified above but spread over three eight-hour days. This can imply possible indirect gender discrimination and widen the GPG because the amount can be reduced in cases of low hours part-time work. If part-time work is longer than 24 hours a week, the family unit allowance is received in its entirety; if lower, the family allowance is equal to the number of days worked, regardless of the hours worked each day. This system is favourable to those with a 'horizontal' part-time contract, compared to those who have mixed or 'vertical' part-time (*Art. 11, par. 2 Delegated Decree 81/ 2015* known as the **Jobs Act**). The possibility for indirect gender discrimination and widening of the GPG is greater between men and women and may arise because more women than men are generally involved in part-time contracts, meaning that family unit allowances are likely to be primarily requested by men, since they are more frequently entitled to access their full weekly amount of hours (Eurostat, 2017).

One can find, even in the most recent social security measures, certain legislation aimed at promoting the use of company welfare through collective bargaining (*l. 208/15* and *l. 232/16*): corporate welfare (i.e. day-care services, etc.) is tax-free and contribution-free, and, if measures are directed towards female employees to promote the work–life balance, may result in a future loss of social security contributions thus potentially increasing the GPG and gender pension gap (for a further explanation, see Chapter 2).

Furthermore, the latest data from the National Social Security Institute indicates an interesting and worrying aspect. The 'cost of maternity' is largely considered to be due to leaving the labour market after the birth of the child. The new data indicate that even mothers who return to the labour market suffer a loss of wages. Typically, 24 months after maternity leave their salary is less than 10% than what they would earn if they had not had their child (INPS, 2016).

Lastly, regarding the tax aspects, there are fiscal allowances for family burdens that are generally shared equally between the parents. However, the law allows the parents to concentrate all these fiscal allowances on the parent with the higher income when the other cannot take full advantage of such fiscal benefits due to insufficient income. In this sense, the gender implication for pay can, therefore, become a concentration of fiscal benefits for men, possibly at the expense of women. Furthermore, the absence of family allowances in the pay slip can play a critical role in case of redundancy, since family commitments are one of the selection criteria that employers are required to apply in a collective redundancy situation.

UK national legal framework

Regulatory framework

The majority of UK equality legislation has developed since the 1970s and was, therefore, influenced by membership of the European Union. However, the strategy of successive UK governments was to implement equality law in a minimalist way and, on a number of occasions considered in more detail below, the UK has been required to amend legislation because it was not considered to be compliant with European directives and principles (Deakin and Morris, 2005; Dickens, 2007). The main provisions for equal pay between men and women in the UK are now contained within the **Equality Act 2010** (EqA 2010) under 'Equality of Terms' (Chapter 3 ss 64–80). The Act entitles women doing work of equal value with a man in the same employment to equality in pay and other terms and conditions. The Act implies an equality clause into the employment contract meaning that contractual terms can be no less favourable on the grounds of sex (s 66). To enforce the equal pay provisions women and men must compare themselves to one or more employees of the opposite sex (s 79) doing the same work, like work or work rated as equivalent (s 65) with the same employer to establish pay inequality exists. The burden of proof then switches to the employer to show that the difference in pay is not directly or indirectly the result of sex discrimination.

It is important to note that the equal pay legislation only applies to employees.[2] Collective agreements in the UK are not, of themselves, legally binding (**Trade Union and Labour Relations (Consolidation) Act 1992 s.179**). However, the terms of a collective agreement can be inserted into employment contracts to make them legally enforceable. Where this happens, it will be applied to all workers in the bargaining unit covered by the collective agreement and not just trade union members.

The EqA 2010 introduced a new concept in relation to GPG reporting. Section 78 of the Act included provisions for secondary legislation to require private and voluntary sector organisations with 250 or more employees to publish information on their GPG. The regulations were not brought into effect until April 2017 but do provide detailed instructions on how the gap should be calculated (see Chapter 6 for a detailed analysis).

Other areas of statute also potentially have a bearing on the GPG in the UK. The gendered nature of part-time work means that the **Part-time Workers (Prevention of Less Favourable Treatment) Regulations 2000** should be particularly important in reducing the GPG. However, the statistical data suggest that the pay gap for part-time women workers has closed little since the introduction of the Regulations (see also Manning and Petrongolo, 2008).

One area of legislation outside of the EqA 2010 that does seem to have had an impact on the GPG is the **National Minimum Wage Act 1998**. The Act came into law in April 1999. Although there was some concern that the minimum wage rates had been set too low to affect low-paid women working in the public sector (Thornley and Coffey, 1999), the Low Pay Commission estimated that the introduction of the national minimum wage would increase the pay of 0.5 million men and 1.5 million women. Part-time men (26%) and women (22%) were likely to benefit more since their hourly pay rates were the lowest (Dex *et al.*, 2000). There is general agreement that the national minimum wage benefits low-paid, particularly part-time workers, but because the legislation affects both low-paid men and women the impact on the GPG is muted (Dex *et al.*, 2000; Robinson, 2002; Connolly and Gregory, 2002; Butcher, 2005; Manning and Petrongolo, 2008).

There is some provision for gender pay equality in the **Public Sector Equality Duty (s 149 of the EqA 2010)**. The Public Sector Equality Duty (PSED) is 'soft' or 'reflexive' legislation, but, unlike the legislation summarised above, it is 'proactive' legislation and has the potential to have some collective applications (Conley, 2014). The PSED has two provisions – a general duty and specific duties. The provision for specific duties requires secondary legislation and is devolved to the Scottish Parliament and the Welsh Assembly for public authorities in those regions.

The specific duties for Wales provide extensive requirements for public authorities to address pay gaps for all protected groups and specifically GPGs. The Welsh regulations require public authorities to collect data and address the causes of GPGs by setting objectives and drawing up an action plan. The Scottish regulations focus largely on the publication of data and are not as proactive as the Welsh regulations. The regulations originally placed a limit of 150 employees required before public authorities should take action, which reduced in 2017 to 20. The Scottish regulations include analysis for disabled and Black, Asian and Minority Ethnic (BAME) groups as well as men and women. The specific duties in England did not have any direct provisions for equal pay or the GPG until s.78 of the EqA 2010 was brought into force for private and voluntary sector employers. To ensure consistency across the sectors, a specific duty was added in 2017 for English public authorities that introduced the same requirements as s.78 with a slight difference in the cut-off dates. There is, as yet, no research to assess how the differences in approach between the three regions are being used by the trade unions or the impact of the differences in relation to the GPG.

Case law

The EqA 2010 was preceded by the **Equal Pay Act 1970** (EPA 1970) and numerous amendments following challenges to the ECJ and rulings that the Act did not meet the requirement of European Community law (see Deakin and Morris, 2005). Much of the pressure to review the equality law prior to the EqA 2010 was driven by the argument that the law had become too complex and cumbersome. The EPA 1970, the Equality of Terms legislation in the EqA 2010, the **Part-Time Workers' Regulations** and the **National Minimum Wage Act** were/are enforceable only by individual workers. There is no provision for 'class actions' in UK equality law. There was an attempt in the EPA 1970 to provide a mechanism for collective resolution of disputes concerning equal pay by establishing the Central Arbitration Committee (CAC). However, the powers of the CAC were limited in 1979 by a ruling in the *Hy-Mac* case to cover only cases of direct discrimination (see Deakin and Morris, 2005) meaning that collective resolution of equal pay disputes is weak in the UK (Dickens, 2007). There have been occasions, however, when trade unions have brought a large number of individual cases (many thousands in some cases) against the same employer, and in one notable case, *Preston and Ors* v *Wolverhampton Healthcare Trust and Ors*, in relation to 60,000 cases concerning pension arrangements for part-time workers (see Heery, 1998; Conley, 2014) against a group of employers, to be heard at the same time.

The individualistic nature of the law coupled with increasingly decentralised collective bargaining and the limited inclusion of equal pay in collective agreements means the equal pay legislation has largely been tested and enforced via a massive and complex set of case law in the UK. As in the *Hy-Mac* case, some of these cases have brought into question the application of collective bargaining to equal pay. For example, in *Enderby* v *Frenchay Health Authority* the employers claimed as a material defence factor that differences between speech therapists (largely female) and pharmacists and clinical psychologists (largely male) were due to different collective bargaining structures for the two groups. However, the ECJ ruled that this was not an adequate defence, over-ruling the UK courts (see Fredman, 1994). Another case, which has had a direct and dramatic impact on collective bargaining and equal pay, is *Allen and Ors* v *GMB* (Conley, 2014; Deakin *et al.*, 2015). This case resulted from the Single Status collective agreement in local government and is covered in depth in the case study in Chapter 4.

Employment tribunal issues affecting equal pay cases

Three recent issues have had a direct impact on the ability of workers to take equal pay cases to an employment tribunal and on employers who lose an equal pay case. The first relates to the UK government's decision to require claimants applying after 29 July 2013 to pay a fee to take a case to employment tribunal (**Employment Tribunals and Employment Appeal Tribunal Order 2013 (SI 2013/1892)**). The fees fell into two bands (Type A and Type B[3]). Equal pay claims fall in to the more expensive Type B. The introduction of these fees had a dramatic effect on the number of equal pay cases being submitted to employment tribunal with a 75% drop in the first year (Ford, 2014). The trade union Unison and the Equalities and Human Rights Commission (EHRC) instigated a legal challenge, using the EU principle on effectiveness, claiming that the fees were making it impossible for some workers to exercise their employment rights (*Unison and Equality and Human Rights Commission* v *Lord Chancellor*). After three attempts the challenge succeeded in overturning this legislation. The government has removed fees for future cases and is required to refund fees that have been charged.

The second issue relates to an amendment the government made to the EqA 2010 (**Equality Act 2010 (Equal Pay Audits) Regulations 2014**) which states where a complaint presented on or after 1 October 2014 and where a tribunal finds that there has been an equal pay breach, the tribunal must order the respondent to carry out an audit. There are, as yet, no examples of where these regulations have been put into practice.

The third relates to **s.77 of the EqA 2010** which prevents employers from inserting a pay secrecy clause in contracts of employment or preventing in any other way employees discussing their pay with each other. This clause also covers workers seeking to find a comparator for an equal pay claim and should, in theory, make finding an actual comparator easier (see Chapter 6 for a detailed analysis).

Wage system

Salary structures in the UK are largely decentralised to the level of the organisation and are voluntarist, only subject to legal constraints in the statutes considered above. The exceptions are public sector, military and other state employment. Some aspects of the EqA 2010 do cover universal minimum gender specific elements such as maternity pay and maternity leave. Sections 72 to 76 of the Act cover pregnancy and maternity equality. Section 74 covers the Maternity Equality Clause in relation to pay and s.75 covers the Maternity Equality Rule in relation to pensions. The legislation in relation to bonuses (variable pay) paid during maternity leave is complex and depends on whether the bonus is contractual or discretionary. Pay rises during pregnancy and maternity leave are protected and membership of a pension scheme is not affected by pregnancy or maternity leave.

A pregnant worker has the right to paid time off for antenatal care (**Employment Rights Act 1996 (as amended)**). The UK has a system of statutory maternity leave and pay. Pregnant employees have the right to 52 weeks' maternity leave and some have the right to 39 weeks' statutory maternity pay. Similar arrangements exist for adoption leave and pay. The first six weeks is paid at 90% of the employee's average weekly earnings. The remaining 33 weeks is paid at a statutorily set amount. A woman is not obliged to take all of her statutory maternity or adoption leave (only the first two weeks is compulsory or four weeks for factory workers). A system of shared parental leave was introduced for children born on or after April 2015. A mother can decide whether to convert her statutory maternity leave into shared parental leave allowing leave not taken by the mother to be taken by the father or eligible partner. However the government reported in 2018 that the take-up of shared parental leave could be as low as 2%.[4] There is also a system of rights to unpaid time off for employees, providing up to four weeks per year per child capped at 18 weeks to be used within the first five years of the child's life, or up to the age of 18 for children adopted at a later age or for a disabled child. There is provision for either one or two consecutive weeks' statutory paternity leave for the partner of a woman on maternity leave, the biological father, the child's adopter or the partner of the child's adopter. The person taking paternity leave must have been employed for at least 26 weeks by the 15th week before the baby is due, subject to having made enough National Insurance contributions. Statutory paternity pay is paid by the employer at the same rate as statutory maternity pay. The leave must be taken within the first eight weeks of the birth. The employment contract may improve upon the statutory provisions for maternity/adoption/parental pay and leave.

Tax and social security framework

UK social policy is historically underpinned by a strong breadwinner model characterised by a conception of a family unit that was based on heterosexual marriage and in which the male head of the household worked full-time and earned enough to keep a wife and family. How far this model existed outside of a white, middle-class ideal has been challenged by a number of feminist academics (for example, Lewis, 1992; Mama, 1984). The social security and taxation systems have historically reflected the breadwinner model by defining women's access to benefits and tax allowances in relation to their husband's income and, as in the Italian case, conferring family tax incentives on higher earning fathers. However in 2013, child benefit was withdrawn for families where one parent earns more than £50,000 in the UK.

Childcare costs in the UK are reported to be the highest in Europe (OECD, 2016), meaning that for many women working full-time is not an option. The state does provide some minimal support as a recognition of the important economic role played by working women. From 2017 the amount of free childcare that working parents can get for three- and four-year-olds doubled from 15 to 30 hours per week. However, there is some evidence that this is being recouped through indirect charges to parents because of insufficient government funding (Pre-School Learning Alliance, 2017). Another scheme launched in 2017, Tax-Free Childcare, means the government will refund £2 of every £8 spent on childcare up to a maximum of £2,000 per annum for working parents earning under £100,000, subject to eligibility.

Despite these limited attempts to encourage women to enter and stay in the labour market, the historical sex bias in social policy is still shaping women's life-long incomes. For example, even by 2006, only 13% of women qualified for the full basic state pensions compared with 92% of men (Thane, 2006). Although most of the most blatant aspects of sex discriminatory social policy were removed following the **Sex Discrimination Act 1975**, their removal has been slow, incremental and often made only after legal challenges that UK law was incompatible with European law. For example in *Regina* v *Secretary of*

State for Employment ex parte Equal Opportunities Commission and Another the extended qualifying period for unfair dismissal for part-time workers in the **Employment Protection Act 1975** was successfully challenged. In 1994 the House of Lords ruled that this law amounted to indirect discrimination against women as so many more women than men work part-time and was, therefore, incompatible with European law. The *Preston* case considered above highlights that similar discriminatory practices in relation to part-time women workers were evident in company pension schemes, but again, only after a ruling by the ECJ. Furthermore, the discrepancy in retirement ages for men and women in relation to state pensions was only rectified in the **Pensions Act 2011**. After pressure from Europe, the government agreed in 1995 to equalise the retirement ages for men and women but this will not take full effect until 2018 when the retirement age for women will be raised to meet that of men. These changes are argued to be of detriment for women born in the 1950s who have had little chance to compensate for a state-imposed extended working life (WASPI, 2015). In effect, the British state has equalised pension arrangements between men and women in one generation to the detriment of women but pay equality has not been secured for women after 50 years of legislation.

The impact of austerity and Brexit

Austerity measures taken by the government in relation to the 2008 financial crisis have rekindled the debates about gender-biased social policy. The Conservative/Liberal Democrat coalition government that took office in 2010 introduced a raft of public spending cuts and public sector pay was frozen for all but the lowest paid for three years, followed by an indefinite 1% cap on pay increases. Since approximately 65% of public sector workers are women and most of the higher paid jobs for women are in the public sector, it is anticipated that these measures will have an impact on the GPG.

The emergency budget was challenged by the Fawcett Society, a women's organisation dating back to the women's suffrage movement of the nineteenth century (Conley, 2012). The Fawcett challenge was built on data that was collected largely by the Women's Budget Group (WBG),[5] a collective of feminist economists, researchers, policy experts and activists, who often work closely with trade unions. One of the main arguments of these groups is that changes being made to the social security and taxation framework in the name of austerity are eroding the improvements made since the **Sex Discrimination Act**. For example, marriage has been given a higher profile in the latest changes to the taxation system with a system of transferable allowances for married couples coming into effect in 2015. The WBG (2013) has argued that this infringes a system of independent taxation that does not financially tie a wife to her husband.

On 23 June 2016, the British people voted by 52% (with 48% against) in a national referendum to leave the EU. Since the referendum, women's groups have claimed that the gendered impact of a decision to leave the EU did not form any significant part of the campaigning undertaken by either the 'remain' or 'leave' lobby groups, who were dominated by men (Guerrina and Murphy, 2016). The cost to women of a vote to leave was not calculated, which represents a failure to gender mainstream one of the most crucial political decisions to be taken for decades. The UK government has stated that it intends to transpose all European law into UK law but it is, as yet, unclear how past and future European case law will be assimilated following Brexit. Moreover, there is a genuine fear that current rights will be watered down during the assimilation process.[6]

Polish national legal framework

Regulatory framework

In the Polish legal system, similar to the Italian system, the principles of equality and non-discrimination are embedded in the **Constitution of 1997**. It provides that all persons shall be equal before the law and no one shall be discriminated against in political, social or economic life for any reason whatsoever (*Art. 32*). The ban on discrimination because of one's gender is covered by the wording 'any reason whatsoever'. The Constitution also underlines equal rights of men and women in family, political, social and economic life. It proclaims that men and women shall have equal rights, in particular regarding education, employment and promotion, and shall have the right to equal compensation for work of similar value (*Art. 33*), therefore, the position of men and women in the Polish society is formally equal. The prohibition of the differentiation of the legal position of individuals due to their gender can be perceived as one of fundamental principles of the Polish legal system (Borysiak, 2016).

At the legislative level, similar to the UK, the majority of the Polish equality legislation was strongly influenced by membership of the European Union. After the political and economic transition in 1989, the first equality regulations were introduced into the **Labour Code** (LC) in 1996, however, it is the pre-accession (2002–2003) period that brought the extension of equality regulations. The main provisions concerning equal pay between men and women are now contained within the **Labour Code 1975 (as amended)**. The principles of equal treatment and of non-discrimination are fundamental principles of Polish labour law (*Art. 11^2 and Art. 11^3 LC*). The equal pay principle is perceived as the development of general prohibition of discrimination (Supreme Court, SC_ 2012). Those principles are developed in Chapter IIa, added to the LC in 2003. It provides that employees should be treated equally in relation to establishing and terminating an employment relationship, employment conditions, promotion conditions, and access to training, in particular regardless of sex and other criteria, as well as regardless of employment for a definite or indefinite period of time or full-time or part-time employment (*Art. 18^{3a} LC*). Further transposition of the Directive 2006/54/EC, introduced by the Act of 3 December 2010 on the implementation of certain provisions of the EU on equal treatment (**Equal Treatment Act 2010**) brought the extension of the equal treatment principle. It widened the obligation of equal treatment and non-discrimination to other than labour relationship spheres, in particular undertaking and performing economic or professional activity, vocational training, the access and activity in trade unions, the access to instruments and labour market services, social security, health care, and services offered in the public. Both the **Labour Code** and **Equal Treatment Act** (ETA) prohibit any direct or indirect discrimination.

The LC refers also expressly to equal pay (*Art. 18³ᶜ LC*). It states that employees, regardless of their sex, have the right to equal remuneration for the same work, or for work of equal value. The notion of remuneration includes all components, regardless of their name or characteristic, as well as other work-related benefits granted to employees in cash or non-cash form. Work of equal value means work that demands from employees not only comparable professional qualifications, certified by documents set forth in separate provisions of the law or by practice and professional experience, but also comparable responsibility and effort.

The violation of equal treatment principle entitles both employees (*Art. 18³ᵈ LC*) and other workers (*Art. 13 ETA*) to compensation. Both acts introduce a reversed burden of proof. Therefore, the employee who alleges the breach of the principle of equal treatment must establish unequal pay by comparing to another employee of the opposite sex doing the same work or work of equal value with the same employer. Then the employer is obliged to prove that they have not violated LC provision. Claims arising out of the breach of equal pay principle are barred by a limitation of three years (*Art. 291 LC*).

The protection is also granted in the areas that usually have an impact on the GPG. As noted above, the LC, in accordance with the Directive 97/81/EC, protects part-time workers against discrimination as it is regarded as a forbidden criterion of workers' differentiation. However, although part-time employment is usually more often performed by women, it does not have that much impact on the GPG in Poland. Due to relatively low pay levels, both parents are usually full-time workers, and part-time work is rarely chosen by female workers. According to the Central Statistics Office (GUS) only 10.7% of women work part-time, comparing to 4.7% of men (CSO, 2016).

The other area that can potentially impact on the GPG is a minimum wage. In Poland, similar to the UK and in contrast to Italy, there is a statutory regulation on minimum wages provided by the **Minimum Wage Act 2002** (MWA). The obligation is to ensure at least the minimum wage applies to all employees, regardless of sector of industry. The minimum wage increases every year (on 1 January) and its amount is the subject of negotiations between social partners on a national level (within the Social Dialogue Council). When there is a lack of consensus, it is determined by the Councils of Ministers. The minimum wage since 1 January 2018 is 2100 PLN per month, which is equal to approximately 500 euro.

Similar to the UK, in Poland the equal pay legislation applies only to employees. It does not apply to over two million people performing the work under civil contracts or the self-employed. Collective agreements may also cover people working on a basis other than an employment relationship (*Art.*

239 § 2 LC), but they rarely do in practice. However, since 1 January 2016, workers who are not employees are protected under the MWA that introduced a minimum hourly rate applying to persons performing work under the civil law contracts and self-employed. The minimum hourly rate is linked to the minimum wage (*Art. 8a-8e MWA*).

The equal pay principle in the Polish legal system is set in an individualistic context. Despite its introduction into the LC, there are no legal obligations for employers to review the remuneration pay systems for compliance with the equal pay principle, nor do employers undertake this voluntarily. The survey on the collective agreements concluded in 2009–2015 in the Silesian district in Poland which was performed for the purposes of 'Close the Deal, Fill the Gap' project, showed that none of over 100 agreements contained such a clause (see Chapter 3). Furthermore, there are no legal requirements for any employers to publish reports on the GPG, and MWA is silent about equal pay or the GPG.

On the collective level, similar to Italy, the legal system recognises and protects unions and collective bargaining on the constitutional level (*Art. 59 Const.*). Collective bargaining can be conducted both at single-establishment level (plant level) or multi-establishment level (supra-plant level) that can apply to the regional or national level. In practice, the collective bargaining take place mostly at an establishment level. Collective agreements cover all employees whose employers are covered by their provisions, with exceptions concerning some public sector employees (*Art. 239 LC*), regardless of their membership to trade unions.

Generally collective agreements cannot derogate *in peius* (to the disadvantage of employees) from protective statutory law, with some very minor exceptions set by the LC. If provisions of collective labour agreements and other collective agreements violate the principle of equal treatment in employment they are not binding (*Art. 9 LC*). Collective agreements enter into force after registration (by the labour inspectorate or by the labour minister), who examine their compliance with law. It is worth underlining that there are no legal initiatives to foster collective bargaining, which stays at a relatively low level, mostly due to a high and developed statutory level of protection, and the prohibition to derogate *in peius*. According to the European Participation Index (EPI), collective bargaining coverage in Poland was estimated at 35% (Vitols, 2010; EPI, 2009). In 2016 it was only 15% (see Table 1.1).

Case law

The enforcement of the equal pay principle is left to individuals. As noted above, equal pay is not the subject of collective negotiations. The **Collective Disputes Resolution Act 1991** provides that collective dispute between employees and an employer or employers may concern wages. However, a collective dispute may not be entered to support individual claims that may be settled in proceedings before the competent body for settling disputes concerning individual employees (*Art. 4*).

Cases concerning unequal pay are not often brought before the court. One explanation for the limited case law might be because the equal pay principle was introduced to the LC in 2002. According to data provided by Ministry of Justice, only about 1% of all labour law cases in Polish courts at any level was connected to different forms of discrimination in employment (not only pay discrimination), with 60.8% initiated by female plaintiffs (Ministry of Justice, 2014). The redress of claims is difficult due to relatively low legal consciousness (Mania, 2010) and a particular culture of secrecy in relation to pay (see Chapter 6). Employers do not have an obligation to conduct job evaluation (Walczak, 2004), which makes the comparison between work of equal value difficult. Furthermore, despite the legal framework, there is no practice of bringing or supporting individual cases by trade unions or labour inspectors.

The jurisprudence may also be a cause of the limited amount of case law. First of all, the reversed burden of proof principle begins with the role of plaintiff who alleges the breach of equal treatment. They are obliged to indicate better remunerated workers and indicate that the differentiation is based on forbidden criterion, and then the burden of proof shifts on the employer (*SC 2016*). The issue of transparency, required for the initiation of equal pay claims is discussed in Chapter 6. Second, the interpretation of the notions 'same work' or 'work of equal value' can be problematic. In general, equal works means the same work in terms of type, qualifications, performance, conditions, work available, and the quantity and quality of work. Therefore, subjective perceptions of differences in quality or quantity of work can justify different remuneration (*SC 2013; SC 2012*).

However, the jurisprudence does confirm a very wide notion of remuneration for the purposes of the equal pay legislation. It includes additional annual salary, severance payments, bonuses and rewards. In particular, excluding the maternity leave period when calculating additional annual salary is regarded as discrimination. Furthermore, the access to benefits such as a company car, business phone or apartment are taken into account in pay discrimination cases (*SC 2012*).

Wage system

Remuneration systems in Poland are introduced by either collective agreement or regulation on remuneration (in the absence of a collective agreement). As noted above, according to *Art. 9 LC*, the provisions of collective labour agreements and other collective agreements, regulations and statutes based on the law, determining the rights and duties of the parties to an employment relationship, are not binding if they violate the principle of equal treatment in employment. However, since 1 January 2017, where there is no collective agreement, regulations on remuneration are obligatory only for employers employing over 50 employees rather than the previously lower limit of 20 employees. Employers employing less than 50 employees include pay details in individual employment contracts to comply with pay confidentiality to the detriment of pay transparency (see Chapter 6).

Wages for state employees are determined by law. This includes persons employed in state budgetary units, state budgetary enterprises, state universities, as well as professional soldiers and officers specified by the law (**Wages in Budgetary Sector Act 1999**). The conditions of remuneration and granting other work-related benefits for employees employed in entities of the state budget sector, provided the employees are not covered by a collective labour agreement, are specified in an executive regulation issued by the minister (*Art 77³ LC*). Negotiations concerning the wages in the public sector are limited (*Art. 239 § 3 LC*). Interestingly, less discretion in relation to pay setting in the public sector might be related to the difference in GPG indicators – according to the CSO, in the public sector, where there is a noticeably smaller employers' discretionary margin, the GPG level reaches 3.8%, while in the private sector it grows up to 17% (CSO, 2014).

Tax and social security framework

The Polish tax and social security system has always been characterised by a high level of female full-time employment. Historically this was driven by low wages, the ideology of centrally planned economy, and a full employment policy. However, it was also underpinned by a well-developed system of child and elderly care. Political and economic transformation in 1989 brought changes to those principles, but the demands of the labour markets and changes in society maintained the level of female employment. In the early 1970s the percentage of women employees in Poland exceeded 40% and in 2014 it approached 49% (CSO, 2016). The tax system reflects the formally equal position of working men and women.

Fiscal tax deduction can apply to either working men or women, so, similar to the Italian system, they are generally shared equally between the parents. The **Natural Persons Income Tax Act 1991** (NPIT) introduces, for example, advantages for single parents, or tax exemptions for family allowances or child tax credits. They have no gender connotations. However, the NPIT allows the joint taxation of married taxpayers, which most often puts women at the position of secondary earner and can bring adverse results (Gunnarsson, 2016; Gunnarsson *et al.*, 2017).

The Polish social security system explicitly introduces the equal treatment principle. The **Social Insurance System 1999** states that it is based on the principle of equal treatment of all insured, regardless of their gender, marital status or family status (*Art. 2a*). This principle refers in particular to requirements to participate in the social insurance system, the duty to pay and calculate the amount of contributions for social insurance, calculation of the amount of benefits, the period of benefit payment and the maintenance of the right to benefits. In addition, the **Illness and Maternity Benefits Act 1999** provides high statutory benefits, reaching 80% of salary during maternity and parental leaves up to one year (see Chapter 6), which minimises the adverse impact of a break in work on female remunerations.

Equality is contravened by a discrepancy in retirement ages for men and women. It was estimated that female pensions were up to 30% lower than male pensions (World Bank, 2004). Due to financial and EU pressure (European Council recommendation 2012) the amendment in 2012 of **Retirements and Disability Pensions Act 1999** (RDPA) was introduced on 1 January 2013, increasing the equal statutory retirement age for both men and women to 67. It was supposed to be reached by 2020 by men and 2040 for women, growing slowly one month per each quarter of a year. This change was reversed from 1 October 2017 by the amendment in 2016 of RDPA following presidential election promises which met with the wide approval of society. As a result, with the retirement age of 60 years for women and 65 for men, the Polish pension system again impairs the position of women and is obviously to the detriment of female pensions. Lowered retirement age is not compulsory, but there is labour market pressure to terminate the employment contract at this lowered age, reinforced by poor elderly and childcare systems. Moreover, women who reached the lowered retirement age are not protected against dismissal. It is reinforced by the jurisprudence. Although SC treats the termination of employment contract because of reaching the retirement age as age discrimination (*SC 2009*), it admits that the right to pension benefits can be a justified criterion of collective redundancy (*SC 2016; SC 2011*).

The impact on women's pensions is confirmed by the State Social Security Institution (Zakład Ubezpieczeń Społecznych), which released the first press information on pensions under the new regulations. It indicated the differences in medium pensions of men and women to the detriment of women, reaching as high as 80% in the mining sector.

Pregnancy, maternity leave and parental leave

Under Polish law, pregnancy and maternity leave are subject to protection, which means that a woman's contract of employment cannot be terminated by her employer during this period, 'unless there are reasons justifying termination without notice through her fault, and an enterprise trade union representing the employee has consented to the termination of the employment contract' (*Art. 177.1 of the LC*). This provision does not apply to a female employee on a trial period not exceeding one month, or a female employee working on the basis of a replacement employment contract. The termination of a contract of employment with notice by an employer during this period of protection against dismissal may occur only in the event of the declaration of bankruptcy or liquidation of the employer. These regulations also provide the female employee with financial entitlements, especially the right to remuneration. If providing her with other employment is not possible, the female employee is entitled to receive benefits as specified in separate provisions. The period during which such benefits are received is counted into the period of employment on which the employee's rights are based. At the same time, it must be stressed, that these provisions also apply accordingly to a male employee raising his child while on paternity leave (*Art. 177.4 and 177.5 of the LC*).

During pregnancy, which must be attested by a medical certificate, a female employee retains the right to remuneration for periods of absence from work caused by medical examinations, if they cannot be performed outside the working hours (*Art. 185 of the LC*). Additionally *Art. 92 of the LC* provides that, in case of sickness during pregnancy, the employee retains the right to 100% remuneration, regardless of whether the sickness is connected with pregnancy.

The above-mentioned general provisions have been complemented and laid down in more detail in the Act on social security cash benefits in case of sickness and maternity, as is evident from *Art. 184 of the LC* with regard to a maternity allowance that is due for maternity leave, additional leave on the terms of maternity leave, parental leave, and paternity leave. It must be stressed that leave entitlements are vested not only in the female employee, but also in the father/ employee. However, in reality, these rights are exercised predominantly by women, which later on translates into their work-related benefits.

It is also worth drawing attention to provisions of *Art. 187 of the LC*, pursuant to which, a female employee who is nursing a child has the right to two half-hour breaks from work calculated into the working time. An employee who is nursing more than one child has the right to two 45-minute breaks from work, which may, at the employee's request, be granted at one time. However, if the employee's working time is shorter than four hours per day, the employee is not entitled to breaks for nursing, and if the working time does not exceed six hours per day, the employee is entitled to one nursing break. According to the National Labour Inspectorate, a female employee is eligible to the break as long as she is nursing a baby and the Labour Code does not contain any provisions on time limits. It is enough to deliver a certificate of lactation signed by a medical doctor.

The Labour Code also provides that an employee raising at least one child up to the age of 14 is entitled to be released from work at their request for two days or 16 hours in a calendar year, while retaining the right to remuneration (*Art. 188 of the LC*). While provisions of the Code do not grant this right to leave just to mothers, but to employees in general, in reality – as already mentioned – it is mostly exercised by women. This applies equally to allowances for absences from work caused by having to take personal care of a child. Detailed rules governing this have been laid down in separate provisions of the law, namely in the aforementioned **Act of 1999**.

Sickness benefit

From the point of view of the issues discussed in this chapter, attention must be drawn to provisions of the aforementioned **Act of 1999** on social security cash benefits in case of sickness and maternity. The Act provides for, among others, a sickness benefit, maternity benefit, and guardianship allowance, all of which are of interest given the subject matter of this chapter. The sickness benefit is payable to a female employee who, while pregnant, was incapable of work for a period no longer than 270 days (*Art. 8 of the Act of 1999*). The monthly sickness benefit amounts to 100% of the benefit assessment basis (*Art. 11.2 of the Act of 1999*).

Maternity benefit

The maternity benefit is a special right, granted under *Art. 29 of the Act of 1999* to an insured woman who, while covered by sick leave, insurance, or during parental leave:

- gave birth to a child;
- accepted a child less than seven years old for upbringing, and, in case of a child who had a deferred school entry decision issued, a child less than ten years old, and applied to a guardianship court with a motion for instituting proceedings for an adoption; or
- accepted for upbringing as a foster family, with the exception of a professional foster family, a child less than seven years old, and in case of a child who had a deferred school entry decision issued, a child less than ten years old.

The above-mentioned provisions apply respectively to an insured man. Moreover, the maternity benefit is payable to an insured man – the child's father, who obtained the right to paternity leave or interrupted employment in order to care for a child, when the insured mother resigned from collecting maternity benefit after having used it for a period of at least 14 weeks following the birth of the child.

A woman may also claim maternity benefit in the event of giving birth to a child after the expiry of insurance, provided that the insurance expired during pregnancy in either of the two cases discussed below. First of all, as a result of a declaration of bankruptcy or liquidation of the employer, and second, in the event of a violation of the law, established by a judicial decision (*Art. 30 (1) of the Act of 1999*). If, in the situation referred to above, a female employee was not provided with other employment, she is entitled, until childbirth, to an allowance in an amount equal to the maternity benefit (*Art. 30 (3) of the Act of 1999*).

The monthly maternity benefit due during the period determined by provisions of the Labour Code as the period of maternity leave and period of paternity leave amounts to 100% of the benefit assessment basis. On the other hand, the monthly maternity benefit due during the period determined as the period of parental leave amounts to 100% of the benefit assessment basis for a period no longer than eight weeks, and for a period exceeding eight weeks – 60% of the benefit assessment basis (*Art. 31 (1)* and *(2) of the Act of 1999*). The amount of the maternity benefit payable to an insured female employee who submitted an application for full-time parental leave immediately after the maternity leave is different, though. It amounts to 80% of the benefit payable during the entire period of maternity leave, additional leave on the terms of maternity leave, and parental leave (*Art. 31 (3) of the Act of 1999*). The same amount of maternity benefit is payable to an insured woman who is not an employee and who submitted an application for the payment of the maternity benefit for a period corresponding to the period of maternity leave, additional leave on the terms of maternity leave, and full-term parental leave no later than 21 days following the birth of the child. These provisions apply accordingly to an insured male employee and an insured male who is not an employee.

Guardianship allowance

Another benefit that concerns a significant number of women is the guardian-ship allowance. As a general rule, it is women who interrupt employment to care for a small or sick child. Under the **Act of 1999**, the guardianship allow-ance is due to an insured person who is released from the execution of work on account of having to take personal care of a child who is less than eight years old, when it is otherwise not possible to provide the child with care, for example, in case of an unforeseeable closure of the nursery school frequented by the child. The allowance is also payable to an insured person taking personal care of a child less than 14 years old (*Art. 31 (1) of the Act of 1999*). The allowance is payable for a period of maximum 60 days in a calendar year (*Art. 33 (1) of the Act of 1999*). However, if besides the insured there are other family members able to care for a child over two years old, the guardianship allowance is not payable (*Art. 34*). The monthly guardianship allowance amounts to 80% of the benefit assessment basis (*Art. 53 (1) of the Act of 1999*).

Single payment childbirth grant and allowance

The childbirth grant is one of the additional payments to the family allowance that is provided for by the **Act on Family Benefits of 2003**. It is payable to a mother, father or legal custodian of a child as a one-off payment of 1,000 PLN for each child, if more than one child is born (*Art. 9 of the Act of 2003*). The payment of the allowance is subject to the condition that a woman must have been placed under medical care from the tenth week of pregnancy at the latest to the date of birth (*Art. 9 (6) of the Act of 2003*).

At the same time, *Art. 15b of the Act* provides that a one-time benefit (newborn allowance) of 1,000 PLN per child be payable upon the birth of a live child. The actual payment of the allowance is contingent on the family income per person, which must not exceed the amount of 1,922 PLN. The payment is also subject to the condition that a woman must have been placed under medical care from the tenth week of pregnancy at the latest to the date of birth.

Care allowance

The Act also provides for a childcare allowance of 400 PLN per month, payable during the parental leave. It may be granted to a child's mother, father or actual caretaker for a period of 24, 36 or 72 months, depending on whether care is provided to one or more than one child born at one birth, or whether the child is disabled (*Art. 10 (1) of the Act of 2003*). Nevertheless, the Act indicates a number of circumstances under which the allowance cannot be claimed. The care allowance cannot be granted to a person who:

- immediately before acquiring the right to parental leave had been employed for a period of time shorter than six months;
- had taken up or continued employment or other gainful activity which made it impossible to take personal care of the child during parental leave;
- the child was placed in a facility providing round-the-clock care, such as special school and education centre, with the exception of a facility providing treatment activity, and receives the round-the-clock care there for more than five days per week, as well as in other cases of ceasing to take personal care of the child;
- the person receives maternity benefit during the parental leave; or
- the person receives parental allowance (*Art. 10 (5) of the Act of 2003*).

Parental allowance

Under *Art. 17c of the Act*, this allowance is payable, for example, to a mother from the day of birth in the amount of 1,000 PLN per month for a period of 52 to 71 weeks, depending on the number of children born at one birth. The person entitled to claim the allowance receives one parental allowance at a time, regardless of how many children they are raising. Furthermore, pursuant to *Art. 17c (9) of the Act*, the allowance cannot be granted if at least one of the child's parents receives maternity benefit or other compensation during the period of maternity leave, additional leave on the terms of maternity leave, or parental leave, or does not have actual custody of the child, or if the right to parental allowance, additional payment to the family allowance, care allowance (for caring for a disabled child), special attendance allowance, or carer's allowance has already been established. The underlying principle is that it is not possible to accumulate benefits.

Additional annual salary and bonuses

Public sector employees are eligible to receive an additional annual salary under the **Act of 1997**. It is paid in the full amount to employees who have worked with their employer throughout the calendar year (*Art. 2 (1) of the Act*). An employee who has not worked with the employer throughout the calendar year also acquires the right to the additional annual salary, provided that they have worked with the employer for at least six months. In this case, the amount to be paid is calculated in proportion to the length of time actually worked. Furthermore, the Act provides that, in case of employees on parental leave, maternity leave, paternity leave, or additional leave on the terms of maternity leave or parental leave, the requirement of having worked for at least six months in order to qualify for the additional annual salary does not apply. Where this is the case, the actual amount to be paid is calculated in proportion to the length of time worked with the employer. It must be remembered though, that the right to the aforementioned leaves is usually exercised by women, which results in their 13th month salary being significantly lower that the additional salary received by male employees.

It is also worth drawing attention to rules that govern the awarding of bonuses, especially the so-called appreciation bonuses. The analysis of collective labour agreements, carried out by the Polish project team (see Chapter 3), has shown that bonuses are awarded to employees who show initiative and are available and ready to take on extra tasks to substitute for their colleagues. It is difficult to expect this degree of availability of a female employee who is caring for a small child, or of an employee who is pregnant. Moreover, bonuses are frequently calculated based on the base salary minus any periods of temporary incapacity to work for which an employee received sick pay or sickness benefit. What follows is that any absences from work, including absences caused by maternity or having to care for a child for which an employee receives a social insurance benefit in case of maternity, are excluded from the days eligible for bonus. Worded this way, provisions laid down in the collective labour agreements not only refer to the existing Labour Code provisions, but often in fact repeat them.

Additional rights granted to women in relation to pregnancy and maternity, while beneficial, entail certain consequences for the amount of salary, especially the additional annual salary (available to public sector employees), and bonuses. It must be stressed, however, that some of the rights related to leave connected with the birth and upbringing of a child, and thus rights related to the respective bonuses and allowances, are available to both women and men. In reality, these rights are mostly exercised by female employees, which means that pay gaps still exist.

Comparing key variables to the GPG in Italy, Poland and the UK

From the above country analyses, it is clear that each country has different institutional contexts which we have summarised in Table 1.1 shows sharp differences between public and private sectors in Italy and Poland with the GPG significantly lower in the public sector than the private sector. This was not the case in the public sector in the UK, where the GPG was marginally higher and where the public sector GPG was the highest in the EU-28. The differences may be accounted for by the high proportion of men working at senior levels in the UK public sector and the experience of austerity which has hit the public sector and women hardest. Nevertheless, it may be considered surprising since the public sector has some of the most progressive equality policies, a high proportion of highly qualified women, has high trade union representation and collective bargaining coverage. Nevertheless, as research has indicated, policies do not always lead to equality practices (Healy *et al.*, 2011). A further curious difference that Eurostat data (although unadjusted) reveal is in relation to age. In Italy, the GPG progressively declines with age, whereas in Poland, the GPG rises to age 35–44 age band and then declines leaving a negative GPG at 65+. In contrast, in the UK, the GPG progressively increases at

Table 1.1 Key aspects of employment relationship in Italy, Poland and the UK

	Italy (%)	Poland (%)	UK (%)	EU-28 average
GPG	5	8	21	16
Public	4.4	2.8	24.4	
Private	17.9	16.1	22.2	
TU density 2016	20–30[a]	11.8[b]	23.5[c]	
Collective bargaining coverage	80[d]	15[e]	26.3[f]	60[g]
Legally binding collective bargaining	yes	yes	no	
Mandatory GPG reporting	no	no	yes	
Centralised bargaining	yes	no	no	
GPG full-time	0.1	6	9.4[h]	
GPG part-time	11	10	-6.1[i]	
Gendered pensions gap	37.1	22.5	39	38.6

Sources: http://ec.europa.eu/eurostat/statistics-explained/index.php/Gender_pay_gap_statistics, accessed 20 April 2018 unless otherwise indicated.

a https://read.oecd-ilibrary.org/employment/oecd-employment-outlook-2017_empl_outlook-2017-en# page1 accessed 11.05.18.
b https://stat.gov.pl/files/gfx/portalinformacyjny/pl/defaultaktualnosci/5821/10/2/1/wskazniki_jakosci _pracy__21_03_2018_pl.pdf, accessed 30.04.18.
c Trade Union Membership Statistical Bulletin (DBEIS, 2017).
d http://www.worker-participation.eu/National-Industrial-Relations/Across-Europe/Collective-Barga ining2 accessed 20.4.18.
e http://www.solidarnosc.org.pl/aktualnosci/wiadomosci/zagranica/item/17633-raport-etui-niepokoja cy-obraz-rokowan-zbiorowych-w-ue-polska-w-ogonie, accessed 30.4.18.
f Trade Union Membership Statistical Bulletin (DBEIS, 2017).
g http://www.worker-participation.eu/National-Industrial-Relations/Across-Europe/Collective-Barga ining2.
h https://www.ons.gov.uk/employmentandlabourmarket/peopleinwork/earningsandworkinghours/bul letins/annualsurveyofhoursandearnings/2017provisionaland2016revisedresults#gender-pay-differences.
i www.ons.gov.uk/employmentandlabourmarket/peopleinwork/earningsandworkinghours/bulletins/a nnualsurveyofhoursandearnings/2017provisionaland2016revisedresults#gender-pay-differences.

each age band from 4.5 for under 25s to 26.8 for 65+. Most worrying is the very high pensions gap, where again the UK has the highest pensions gap. One caveat that we must make is that data collection methods vary even within countries and thus may give different results, but the general patterns normally remain constant. These differences in patterns raise many questions which we shall mainly seek to address in our remaining chapters.

Conclusions

In line with Locke and Thelen (1995) this chapter identifies that, whilst employers in Italy, Poland and the UK are regulated by the same EU law in relation to pay equality, the application of the law is refracted through different institutional arrangements and historical traditions (Maurice and Sellier, 1979). This is coupled with different 'identities' of key actors that shape their frames of reference in relation to pay equality. The result is that, whilst the influence of common EU law is clear in each of the three countries, there is very different practice in relation to equal pay and wide differences in the GPG in each country.

Particularly stark is the difference between the collectivist approach of Italy and to the largely individualist approaches that the regulatory framework forces upon Polish and UK trade unions. An interesting example of this is in relation to the concept of equal value, which considering its basis in EU law, is treated very differently in our three countries. Equal value is explored in more detail throughout the rest of the book, but it is clear that in Italy the more centralised collective bargaining system means that equal value is assumed to be achieved through setting non-discriminatory pay rates for jobs, which has not been challenged to any great extent by case law. By comparison, equal value in the UK has been far more problematic in relation to both collective bargaining and case law (see Chapter 4) and in Poland (see Chapter 3).

Although there are clear institutional differences between the three countries, particularly in relation to collective bargaining arrangements, there are also some key similarities. Two of these are in relation to variable aspects of pay (performance-related pay and bonuses) and deferred pay (pensions), where time away from the labour market for care-related reasons means that women's overall and lifetime pay is likely to be severely negatively impacted and are not accurately reflected in most calculations of the GPG. We explore these issues in greater detail in our case study chapters (2, 3 and 4). The role of the state in perpetuating gender bias in tax and social security payments is evident in all three countries. Whilst all have taken steps to mitigate institutional gender bias since the introduction of EU anti-discrimination legislation, the historical legacy means that mothers are still more likely to rely on the 'social wage' than fathers, with consequences for the GPG.

A Table of cases

Italy

Const. Court 103/1989
   Cass. 209/1984
   Cass. 2082/1980
   Cass. 6030/93
   Cass. Trib. Milano 9.11.1981
   Pret. Milano 22.12.1989
   C-46/07
   C-595/12

Trib. Torino 1858/2016
Trib. Prato 263/2007, confirmed in 2009 by the Florence Appeals Court
Trib. Florence n. 179/2011

UK

R v CAC *ex parte Hymac Ltd.* 1979 IRLR 461
   Enderby v *Frenchay Health Authority* 1993 IRLR 591
   Regina v Secretary of State for Employment ex parte Equal Opportunities Commission and Another 1994 IRLR 176 (HL)
   Preston v *Wolverhampton Healthcare Trust.* 2000 ECR1–320 (ECJ)
   Allen and others v *GMB* 2008 EWCA Civ 810
   Unison and Equality and Human Rights Commission v Lord Chancellor 2014 EWHC 218 (Admin)

Poland

SC 09.06.2016 r. III PK 116/5, Lex no 2057629
   SC 26.01.2016 r. II PK 303/14, Lex no 2019532
   SC 19.01.2016 r. I PK 72/15, Lex no 2005653
   SC 03.06.2014 r. III PK 126/13, Lex no 2487089
   SC 22.11.2012 r. I PK 100/12, Lex no 1277639
   SC 10.10.2012 r. I PK 82/12, Lex no 1267069
   SC 29.11.2012 r. II PK 112/12, Lex no 1294658
   SC (7 j.) 21.01.2009 r. II PZP 13/08, Lex no 475297
   SC 25.01.2012 r. II PK 104/11, Lex no 1162675
   SC 7.04.2011 r. I PK 323/10, Lex no 1165751

Notes

1 According to *Art. 2 Directive 2006/54*, direct discrimination means 'where one person is treated less favourably on grounds of sex than another is, has been or would be treated in a comparable situation' and indirect discrimination means 'where an apparently neutral provision, criterion or practice would put persons of one sex at a particular disadvantage compared with persons of the other sex, unless that provision, criterion or practice is objectively justified by a legitimate aim, and the means of achieving that aim are appropriate and necessary'.
2 Sex and race discrimination legislation can apply to contracts for services. Note also that the Part-Time Workers (Prevention of Less Favourable Treatment) Regulations has the broader applications to workers, whereas the Fixed-Term Employees Regulations (Prevention of Less Favourable Treatment) Regulations contain the narrower definition of employee.
3 Type A fees: £160 to lodge a case; £250 for a hearing; £100 for a reconsideration of a decision.
     Type B fees: £250 to lodge a case; £950 for a hearing; £350 for a reconsideration of a decision.
4 www.gov.uk/government/news/new-share-the-joy-campaign-promotes-shared-parental -leave-rights-for-parents.

5 The Women's Budget Group: http://wbg.org.uk/about-us/.
6 www.equalityhumanrights.com/en/our-work/news/queens-speech-2017-equality-laws-m
ust-not-be-watered-down-brexit.

References

Ballestrero, M. V. (1979) *Dalla tutela alla parità: la legislazione italiana sul lavoro delle donne*. Bologna: Il Mulino.
Barbera, M. (1991) *Discriminazioni ed eguaglianza nel rapporto di lavoro*. Milan: Giuffrè.
Barbera, M. (2011) *L'eguaglianza e il diritto del lavoro, Studi in onore di Tiziano Treu*. Jovene.
Borgogelli, F. (1992) 'Autonomia collettiva e parità uomo-donna: una lettura della legge n.125/1991' *Lavoro e diritto* 1, pp. 139–161.
Borysiak, W. (2016) in: Konstytucja, R.P. [Constitution of Republic of Poland], red. M. Safjan, L. Bosek.
Butcher, T. (2005) 'The Hourly Earnings Distribution Before and After the National Minimum Wage' *Labour Market Trends* Office for National Statistics Special Feature, October. Available from: www.ons.gov.uk/ons/rel/lms/labour-market-trends–discontinue d-/volume-113–no–10/the-hourly-earnings-distribution-before-and-after-the-national-min imum-wage.pdf?format=hi-vis (accessed 5 September 2018).
Central Statistic Office (CSO) (2014) *Różnice w wynagrodzeniach kobiet i mężczyzn w Polsce* [*Differences in Remunerations of Men and Women in Poland*]. Warsaw.
Central Statistic Office (CSO) (2016) *Kobiety i mężczyźni na rynku pracy* [*Women and Men in the Labour Market*]. Warsaw.
Cinelli, M. (2016) *Diritto della previdenza sociale*. Turin: Giappichelli.
Conley, H. (2012) 'Using Equality to Challenge Austerity: New Actors, Old Problems' *Work, Employment and Society* 26(2), pp. 353–363.
Conley, H. (2014) 'Trade Unions, Equal Pay and the Law' *Economic and Industrial Democracy* 35(2), pp. 309–323.
Connolly, S. and Gregory, M. (2002) 'The National Minimum Wage and Hours of Work: Implications for Low Paid Women' *Oxford Bulletin of Economics and Statistics* 64(supplement), pp. 607–631.
Deakin, S. and Morris, G. (2005) *Labour Law 4th. ed*. Oxford: Hart Publishing.
Deakin, S., Fraser Butlin, S., McLaughlin, C. and Polanska, A. (2015) 'Are Litigation and Collective Bargaining Complements or Substitutes for Achieving Gender Equality? A Study of the British Equal Pay Act' *Cambridge Journal of Economics* 39(2), pp. 381–403.
Dex, S., Sutherland, H. and Joshi, H. (2000) 'Effects of Minimum Wages on the Gender Pay Gap' *National Institute Economic Review* 173, pp. 80–88.
Dickens, L. (2007) 'The Road is Long: Thirty Years of Equality Legislation in Britain' *British Journal of Industrial Relations* 45(3), pp. 463–494.
EPI (2009) 'Benchmarking Working Europe' Brussels: ETUC. Available from: www.etui. org/Publications2/Benchmarking-Working-Europe-2009 (accessed 25 September 2018).
Eurostat (2017) *Statistiche dell'occupazione* [*Statistics Explained*]. Available from: http:// ec.europa.eu/eurostat/statistics-explained/index.php/Employment_statistics/it (accessed 21 March 2018).
Ferrara, M. D. (2014) 'Il gender mainstreaming nei contratti collettivi: tendenze della contrattazione di genere' *Diritti Lavori Mercati* 2, pp. 1–19.
Ford, M. (2014) 'The Impact of Fees in the Tribunal' OxHRH Blog, 22 September. Available from: http://ohrh.law.ox.ac.uk/the-impact-of-fees-in-the-tribunal/ (accessed 21 March 2018).

Fredman, S. (1994) 'Equal Pay and Justification' *Industrial Law Journal* 23(1), pp. 37–41.

Garofalo, M. G. (ed.) (2002) *Lavoro delle donne e azioni positive. L'esperienza giuridica italiana*. Bari: Cacucci.

Gottardi, D. (ed.) (2016) *La conciliazione delle esigenze di cura, di vita e di lavoro*. Turin: Giappichelli.

Gragnoli, E. and Corti, M. (2012) 'La retribuzione' in Marazza (a cura di), Contratto di lavoro e organizzazione, in Persiani, Carinci (diretto da), *Trattato di diritto del lavoro*, Volume IV, Cedam: 1375–1488.

Guarriello, F. (2007) 'Il ruolo delle istituzioni e della società civile' in M. Barbera (ed.), *Il nuovo diritto antidiscriminatorio*. Milan: Giuffrè, pp. 467–527.

Guerrina, R. and Murphy, H. (2016) 'Strategic Silences in the Brexit Debate: Gender, Marginality and Governance' *Journal of Contemporary European Research* 12(4), pp. 872–880.

Gunnarsson, Å. (2016) 'Introducing Independent Income Taxation in Sweden in 1971' FairTax Working Paper Series No. 2.

Gunnarsson, Å., Schratzenstaller, M. and Spangenberg, U. (2017) *Gender Equality and Taxation in the European Union*. Study for the FEMM Committee, European Parliament. Available from: www.europarl.europa.eu/RegData/etudes/STUD/2017/583138/IPOL_STU(2017)583138_EN.pdf (accessed 21 March 2018).

Healy, G., Bradley, H. and Forson, C. (2011). 'Intersectional Sensibilities in Analysing Inequality Regimes in Public Sector Organizations' *Gender, Work & Organization* 18 (5), pp. 467–487.

Heery, E. (1998) 'Campaigning for Part-Time Workers' *Work, Employment and Society* 12(2), pp. 351–366.

INPS (2016) 'Istituto Nazionale di Previdenza Sociale', *XV Rapporto Annuale*. Available from: www.inps.it (accessed 5 September 2018).

Lassandari, A. (2018) 'Art. 37, De Luca Tamajo R., Mazzotta O. (a cura di)', *Commentario breve alle leggi sul lavoro*, Wolters Kluwer: Cedam, Milano, p. 54ss.

Lewis, J. (1992) 'Gender and the Development of Welfare Regimes' *Journal of European Social Policy* 2(3), pp. 159–173.

Locke, R. M. and Thelen, K. (1995) 'Apples and Oranges Revisited: Contextualized Comparisons and the Study of Comparative Labor Politics' *Politics and Society* 23(3), pp. 337–367.

Mama, A. (1984) 'Black Women, the Economic Crisis and the British State' *Feminist Review* 17, pp. 29–32.

Mania, K. (2010) 'Dostęp do wymiaru sprawiedliwości w Polsce – wybrane zagadnienia' [Access to Justice in Poland – Selected Issues], *Kwartalnik ADR* 3(11), pp. 65–70.

Manning, A. and Petrongolo, B. (2008) 'The Part-Time Pay Penalty for Women in Britain' *Economic Journal* 118(526), pp. F28–F51.

Maurice, M. and Sellier, F. (1979) 'Societal Analysis of Industrial Relations: A Comparison between France and West Germany' *British Journal of Industrial Relations* 17(3), pp. 322–336.

Ministry of Justice (2014) 'Dyskryminacja, mobbing i molestowanie seksualne w miejscu pracy' [Discrimination, Mobbing and Sexual Harassment in a Workplace]. Edited by K. Orowiecka and J. Kowalczyk.

Nunin, R. (2016) 'Il congedo parentale: nuovi limiti temporali dopo il d.lgs. n. 80/2015' in D. Gottardi (ed.), *La conciliazione delle esigenze di cura, di vita e di lavoro*. Turin: Giappichelli, pp. 63–69.

OECD (2016) *Society at a Glance 2016: OECD Social Indicators, a Spotlight on Youth*. Available from: www.oecd-ilibrary.org/docserver/9789264261488-en.pdf?expires=1526

479999&id=id&accname=guest&checksum=AD7BBA74CB4425D6AC6B2A8D0B6B18
8E (accessed 16 May 2018).

Peruzzi, M. (2017) 'Criteri di distribuzione dei premi di risultato e possibili discriminazioni retributive di genere' *Rivista Italiana di Diritto del Lavoro* 2, pp. 286–294.

Pre-School Learning Alliance (2017) Available from: www.pre-school.org.uk/parents-fa cing-childcare-place-shortages-and-extra-costs-under-30-hour-offer-new-survey-reveals (accessed 16 May 2018).

Recchia, G. A. (2002) 'Le azioni positive nella contrattazione collettiva privata' in M. G. Garofalo (ed.), *Lavoro delle donne e azioni positive. L'esperienza giuridica italiana.* Bari: Cacucci.

Robinson, H. (2002) 'The Wrong Side of the Tracks? The Impact of the Minimum Wage on Gender Pay Gaps in Britain' *Oxford Bulletin of Economics and Statistics* 64(5), pp. 417–448.

Scarponi, S. (2014) 'Il principio di eguaglianza uomo/donna fra divieti di discriminazione e promozione delle pari opportunità' in S. Scarponi (ed.), *Diritto e genere. Analisi interdisciplinare e comparata*. Padua: Cedam, pp. 63–113.

Thane, P. (2006) 'The Scandal of Women's Pensions in Britain: How Did It Come About?' History and Policy: Policy Papers. Available from: www.historyandpolicy. org/policy-papers/papers/the-scandal-of-womens-pensions-in-britain-how-did-it-come-about (accessed 21 March 2018).

Thornley, C. and Coffey, D. (1999) 'The Low Pay Commission in Context' *Work Employment and Society* 13(3), pp. 525–538.

Treu, T. (1979) 'Art. 37' in G. Branca (ed.), *Commentario della Costituzione*. Rapporti economici, I. Bologna: Zanichelli, p. 146ss.

Treu, T. (2016) 'Il welfare aziendale: problemi, opportunità, strumenti' in T. Treu, *Welfare aziendale 2.0*. Milan: Wolters Kluwer, p. 3ss.

Vitols, S. (2010) 'The European Participation Index (EPI): A Tool for Cross-National Quantitative Comparison'. Available from: www.worker-participation.eu/.../EPI-ba ckground-paper.pdf (accessed 21 March 2018).

Walczak, K. (2004) 'Wartościowanie stanowisk pracy ustawowym obowiązkiem praco-dawcy?' [Job Evaluation as a Statutory Obligation of an Employer?], *Monitor Prawa Pracy* 9.

WASPI (2015) *Women Against State Pension Inequality*. Available from: www.waspi.co. uk/ (accessed 5 September 2018).

WBG (2013) 'Recognising Marriage in the Tax System will not Benefit Women'. Women's Budget Group Briefing. Available from: http://wbg.org.uk/wp-content/uploa ds/2013/10/WBG-briefing-on-TTAs-final.pdf (accessed 21 March 2018).

World Bank (2004) *Report no 29205, Płeć a możliwości ekonomiczne w Polsce: czy kobiety straciły na transformacji?* [*Gender and Economic Possibilities in Poland: Have Women Lost on Transformation?*]. Available from: http://siteresources.worldbank. org/INTPOLAND/Resources/Gender_report_pl.pdf (accessed 21 March 2018).

2 Decentralisation and the gender pay gap in the Italian context

Case studies

Donata Favaro, Donata Gottardi, Nicoletta Masiero, Alberto Mattei and Marco Peruzzi

Introduction

The case studies presented in this chapter are intended to identify the impact, limits and potential of contractual decentralisation with respect to the factors triggering gender pay gaps (GPGs) in a context, such as the Italian one, where basic wages are determined at the national level on the basis of a centralised system of collective bargaining.

The target of investigation is the gaps observed over the basic wage threshold – especially in the awarding of *superminimi* (monthly bonuses over minimum pay) and in the distribution, also regulated by company collective agreements, of incentive pay, in particular, of productivity bonuses – as well as those linked to the phenomena of horizontal and vertical segregation.

The analysis approach is multidisciplinary and interdisciplinary: it combines a legal perspective aimed at highlighting the critical issues in the formulation of the regulations, based on a reading of the regulatory contractual data offered by a reliable sample of company collective agreements, and an economic analysis, designed to measure the impact of the regulations – but also of the non-negotiated and unwritten employer practices – on the pay levels of men and women in specific company contexts. The depth of the investigation, made possible by observing the real-life situation of one of the companies concerned, enabled us to integrate our observations with a sociological analysis, allowing us to show, in particular, the impact of the phenomena of horizontal and vertical segregation on the development of the GPG.

Complementing the case studies are some observations on the Italian experience of instruments of corporate welfare, regulated through second-level collective bargaining, which are increasingly encouraged by the national legislation in the perspective of decentralisation and significant for their multiple interconnections, more or less visible, with the issue of pay equality for male and female workers.

The regulations

Gender discrimination and criteria for awarding productivity bonuses negotiated in second-level collective agreements: Case Study 1

In accordance with the target of the project 'Close the Deal, Fill the Gap' – the need to assess the interaction and interdependencies between the involvement of the social partners in the reduction of the GPG, on the one hand, and the prompting of a higher level of decentralisation in the bargaining process with an anchoring of the setting of pay to productivity, on the other – the research focused on the choice of criteria for awarding performance-related pay elements at the company level.

This aspect is crucial in the fight against the GPG: if workers' performance is measured and performance-related pay elements are awarded on the basis of work attendance, this can have relevant gender bias and eventually result in a widening of the GPG. Because of a persistent uneven distribution of family and caring burdens, women are less available than men to work long hours or are more absent than men are from work because of their use of maternity or parental leave. Therefore, the way such criteria are negotiated at the company level and established in company agreements can have a pivotal impact on the reduction of, or rather, the worsening of the GPG.

To assess the main practices negotiated by the social partners at the company level in this field, a sample of company agreements was analysed. The company agreements were selected according to criteria that could provide a reliable section of the agreements concluded by the companies in a given territory, independently of their industry sector, their size, or the types and names of trade unions involved.

To meet these requirements, the analysis focused on the company agreements filed at the Territorial Labour Inspectorate to access specific social security and tax credits provided by the law.[1] To access these reductions of tax rates and social security contributions, employers need to file their relevant company agreements at the Territorial Labour Directorate.[2] The analysis focused on the company agreements filed at the Territorial Labour Directorate of Verona in 2014.

The empirical research of this first case study followed a strictly legal approach, based on the reconstruction, reading and interpretation of regulatory contractual data provided by the second-level agreements filed. In this way, the research sought to verify the potentially discriminatory aspects present in the regulations, aside from a concrete measure of the GPGs resulting from their application, which is fully possible only when disaggregated micro-data on wages are available and through interdisciplinary and multidisciplinary analysis. This type of investigation is instead conducted on the company case studies presented in the following sections.

The research conducted in the first case study pursued two main questions. First, what criteria are used to determine productivity bonuses? Second, if attendance at work is the only or is one of the criteria used for determining the bonus, not so much as an indicator of the bonus as in terms of the criterion on the basis of which to redistribute it, are gender adjustments provided for within the same decentralised agreements?

To begin with, in terms of methodology, the investigation needed to take into account some aspects of interpretation of the contractual documents that required both further verification consisting of an additional collection of contractual sources related to the analysed agreements (for example, relevant national collective agreements, collective agreements previously concluded), and further investigation aimed at having direct verification with the signatory trade unions, in order to resolve the interpretive doubts, also linked to ambiguity, that emerged from the first reading of the document, of some of the wording used.[3]

With regard to the content, the empirical analysis was conducted by carrying out a classification by quantity of contracts, taking into consideration 223 agreements. Of the 145 specifically involving the productivity bonus, 79% (115) regulated it in a specific manner and not by merely following a programme.[4]

Further sub-analyses followed this first classification. The distinction by sector showed that under the 13 sectors relevant to the agreements, the criterion of attendance at work was present regardless of the sector concerned or whether or not it was a male-dominated sector. The reading for the contractual types involved revealed that most of the agreements provided a bonus for all employees (77%), while only some also extended this possibility to temporary workers (15%). Specifically regarding part-time work, which usually pertains more to female staff, the majority of the agreements (66%) stipulated that the bonus be reapportioned based on work hours.

With regard to the method used to determine the bonus, the analysis found that an overwhelming majority of the agreements used attendance at work as the only criterion or as one of the criteria for such an allocation (75%). Only 2% of the agreements stipulated that the bonus could be assigned based on specific criteria that did not include attendance, while 23% of the contracts, with no explicit reference to attendance at work, provided for an all-round distribution of the bonus.

With reference to aspects of gender, the analysis revealed that, while 33% of the agreements did not provide any adjustment for gender in calculating attendance, 66% established that in some cases only statutory maternity leave was excluded from the calculation of absences (36%), while other agreements also excluded parental leave (28%), which is principally used by female employees, as shown in other investigations.[5]

In more general terms, the analysis of the agreements raised a series of questions, both concerning the legal certainty of their content and in terms of their legal validity, as well as questions of policy on more strictly political and trade union terms.

First of all, a question about the legal certainty of the regulations arose. The empirical examination revealed, in addition to a lack of attention paid to the questions of gender in the drafting of the rules, the possibility that the written data are supplemented by unwritten practice that cannot be derived from the contractual document; ambiguity in the use of terms that required a direct verification with the trade union (for example, the concept of effectiveness at work in order to redistribute the bonus that may or may not require a calculation of work attendance); and finally, again, incorrect use of legal terminology (for example, the use of the phrase 'statutory parental leave').

Second, questions arose around doubts on the legal validity of the agreements. The possible invalidity of certain contractual clauses became evident with respect to the European and national framework regarding the right to non-discrimination between standard workers and non-standard workers (for example, the determination of the bonus with a reduction based on attendance only for part-time workers, without any gender adjustment, thus potentially resulting in indirect gender discrimination).

As the third important aspect, questions more strictly to do with policy surfaced for the unions called to negotiate the productivity bonus. Three particularly significant aspects emerged from the empirical analysis. First of all, for the top positions at the company level, there is usually an individual negotiation for this bonus that is not negotiated at the collective level through the union filter. Second, it emerged that the criterion of attendance at work is often requested by the employees themselves as a tool, considered objective and impartial, to measure performance. Third, there is an additional concern at the union level about the singling out of different criteria from the attendance that can be used at the employer level without collective mediation and that can potentially have an even more discriminatory impact on the employees.

Finally, we need to take into consideration that the potentially discriminatory impact of the criteria for distributing productivity bonuses on the gaps is strengthened and magnified through the application of tax relief and reductions concerning the sums paid out by way of productivity bonuses and possible conversion to company benefits.

Therefore, in this respect, we might ask whether such magnification could actually be made worse by the incentive to convert, at the worker's request, from a monetary bonus to corporate welfare benefits, provided for by the most recent financial laws.[6]

In particular, with the conversion of the bonus into a benefit, a full tax exemption is applied, and thus it is even more favourable than the tax levy subsidised by the 10% provided by the bonuses. Referring back to the further depth offered in the last case study, the one relating to the Italian experience on the topic of corporate welfare, it seems opportune to anticipate here that the fungibility between bonus and benefit, to be able to gain access to tax exemption, should be determined by the collective productivity agreements, at the territorial or company level, and not only by an individual agreement, as it is an option that also has repercussions for the worker at the contribution level.[7] Moreover, the regulation requires that the staff benefits affected by the conversion consist of a sum of money or have a value that can be determined in money within the meaning of art. 9 of the Italian Consolidated Law on Income Tax (TUIR).

Therefore, regardless of a hypothetical greater tendency of workers to take advantage of expense reimbursements or payments for services related to education or training (for example, baby-sitting services, art. 51, para. 2, f-*bis* TUIR) or assistance for elderly or care-dependent family members (art. 51, para. 2, f-*ter* TUIR), in lieu, in full, or in part of the monetary bonus, more than a question of a pay gap, the question posed in this case is an econometric one detected within it, as a result of the 'stripping' of some elements, even though they are perceived and valued economically, from the wages (or salary) being compared.

However, the risk of twisting the problem further in the classic vicious circle that links the GPG with the working hours gap and settlements rejected only for women can be seen with more clarity in the company experiences that provide for the possibility (allegedly favouring women and appreciated by them) to exchange individual incentive wage bonuses with 'flexible/smart' work arrangements, or with those forms of corporate welfare related to the flexible organisation of time and place of work, intended to facilitate the work–life balance, arrangements that are also subject to fiscal incentives provided for by the legislation.[8]

Not only can this model widen the gap in pay elements linked to merit, it risks reinforcing a stereotyped approach to the work–life balance, which crystallises, if not progressively widens, the abovementioned gap. This is even more paradoxical, if it is true that smart or tele-working arrangements are presented at the legislative level as a factor of growth in competitiveness and productivity,[9] while these practices are proposed as a compensatory measure of pay for the productivity itself.

The impact of the regulations: analysis of the company case studies

After having examined the possible difficulties detected in the formulation of the regulations on the awarding of productivity bonuses determined within the company collective agreement, the investigation focused on the analysis of the practical and effective impact of the regulations within two specific company situations.

With regard to methodology, there are three factors that justify the choice of these company contexts.

First of all, these are companies that are particularly sensitive to the issue of equality between men and women: they both have specific arrangements concerning work–life balance and the fight against gender discrimination in their company agreements. Second, from a geographical point of view, they are located in the same Italian region, namely Veneto. Third, despite belonging to two different industry sectors – namely, transport and engineering – their company agreements provide for a distribution of productivity bonuses that are not based on the criterion of work attendance or at least only to a small extent.

In both the company case studies, the analysis combined a legal approach with an economic one. The context and data offered by the case study of the company from the transport sector enabled us to also integrate a sociological perspective into the investigation.

Transport sector company: Case Study 2

The subject of this case study is a company from the transport sector that consisted of 4,300 employees in Italy, 270 of whom were employed in the Region of Veneto, which is the territory covered in the economic analysis of the micro-data, and 159 were employed in the call centre of the plant in Marcon, Venice, Region of Veneto, which is covered in the sociological analysis.

The legal analysis focused on the company agreement concluded by this company with the national transport federations of Italy's three most representative unions (FILT CGIL, FIT CISL and UIL TRASPORTI), together with union representatives at the territorial and company levels. The agreement was signed on 27 June 2014.

The analysis specifically examined the part of the agreement regulating performance-related pay elements and determining the criteria for awarding such bonuses.

Before investigating this aspect, it is worth highlighting that the company agreement paid specific attention to work–life balance arrangements and anti-discrimination practices (for example, flexible starting times; the possibility for full-time permanent workers to request a temporary reduction of their working hours in order to take care of a child not older than age three; support of a working environment characterised by the protection and promotion of diversity).

When analysing a company agreement regulating performance-related pay elements, it is necessary to distinguish the criteria used to determine the overall amount of the productivity bonus to be distributed to the company employees in a certain year, and the criteria used to award such bonuses pro rata to each single employee. This distinction is key for our analysis: only the latter can specifically affect the GPG and possibly imply gender bias. This is the case of company agreements using work attendance as the sole criterion or one of the criteria for awarding productivity bonuses.

From this perspective, as far as the determination of the overall amount of the productivity bonus was concerned, the company agreement concluded in 2014 referred to a variety of criteria. Among these criteria (such as profitability, quality, efficiency and innovation), the relevance of work attendance (meant as the average work attendance of the company employees, taking into account the entire Italian territory), was considerably scant. It could affect the full amount of the bonus up to 5% at the most. Moreover, the only absences taken into consideration were those related to sick leave, which supposedly implies a full inclusion of maternity and parental leave in the measurement of work attendance.

However, as mentioned above, this provision concerns the determination of the overall amount of the bonus, not the awarding of such bonuses pro rata to each single employee. As far as this last aspect is concerned, the company agreement (apparently) provided an all-round distribution of the bonus, which amounted to 750 euro (as at 2014) if all goals were accomplished at 100% and was reduced pro rata in the case of part-time workers in accordance with their reduced contractual working time. However, the grid with micro-data that the company gave us for further economic analysis explicitly mentioned a reduction of the bonus awarded to a single employee also in the case of 'optional maternity leave' (which should be called 'parental leave': as mentioned in Case Study 1, this mistake not only raises a question of legal correctness but unconsciously reveals the hidden assumption underlying the provision of work–life balance measures), of unpaid leave and of events lasting more than ten consecutive working days in a month. This raises a significant question about the choice of the criteria for awarding the bonus: they were only partly defined in the company agreement, but were determined by the company unilaterally on the basis of unwritten practices with regard to aspects that are very significant for the purpose of our research.

This confirms what the interviews with the social partners highlighted in Case Study 1, examined in the previous section: hidden gender bias can be found even when company agreements provide for an all-round awarding of performance-related pay elements, as unwritten company policies can imply a reduction of such bonuses in the case of parental leave.

The data made available by the company motivated us to carry out an empirical analysis. The data covered all the workers of the regional unit. This was a total of 270 workers, 175 (65%) of whom were women. The data included, for every worker, information on the type of occupation, tenure at the company, total annual earnings and fixed and variable components of the earnings, hourly earnings (determined by the National Collective Labour Agreement), annual hours of work, working hours (part-time or full-time), contractual classification level, and annual earnings and productivity bonus.

The aim of the empirical analysis was to verify, at different levels, the presence of factors that fuel the pay differences between women and men. An initial examination of the contractual classification levels of the workers immediately found the vertical segregation that female workers experience. In contrast to 41% of the men, 72% of the women were classified at the lowest contractual level. Only 4% of the women attained the highest classification (compared with 13% of the men) and barely 3% of the women held managerial roles; this percentage rose to 13% for men. This vertical segregation affected earnings and the GPG. For the same working hours (only full-time workers), the women received a lower median pay annually than that of their male colleagues by about 15% (see Figure 2.1, solid line). This difference reduced and almost disappeared when we considered women and men with lower earnings, but rose exponentially when we considered workers with incomes higher than the median income. The glass ceiling reached levels greater than 50% in the range of the last decile of the distribution of the annual earnings. These results confirmed at the company level what has already been revealed in the literature on the GPG: a glass ceiling prevents women from attaining occupations with roles of responsibility, at the apex of the hierarchical pyramid.

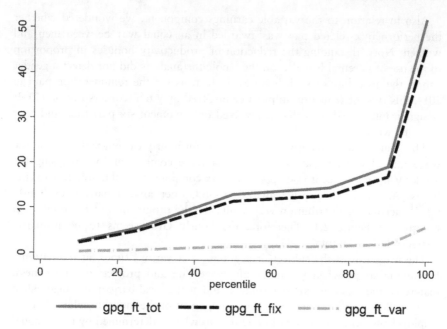

Figure 2.1 Total gender pay gap (GPG) and its fixed and variable components: full-time workers only

Continuing to observe the annual earnings of full-time workers, we wondered what percentage of the GPG could be ascribed to the variable components of the salary, including performance-related pay. The literature that has tried to assess the effect of performance-related pay on the GPG has not achieved unanimous results. However, De la Rica *et al.* (2010) showed that 'despite women's increasing effort to signal job attachment through higher human capital accumulation ... there is a "penalty" for women even in those components of the wage that should respond more to workers' performance and less to job characteristics'.

In Figure 2.1 we report the total GPG (gpg_ft_tot, solid line) and the proportion of this gap that refers to fixed components (gpg_ft_fix) and variable components (gpg_ft_var) of the earnings.[10] The values are calculated in line with the different proportions of distribution of the workers' income. As can be deduced from the figure, the fixed components of the earnings are responsible for almost the entire pay gap, with the exception of earnings at the top of the distribution, in line with the last decile. Only in line with these earnings does the GPG attributable to the variable components reach a significant proportion of approximately 5%. The glass ceiling pattern is confirmed for both pay components. In our specific case, therefore, we cannot affirm that the variable parts of the earnings contribute in general to fuelling the GPG. We can say, however, that these income components have a certain weight on the pay gap in proximity to the highest incomes.

Also in relation to the variable earnings component, we wondered whether the performance-related pay was awarded in an equal way between men and women. Notwithstanding the reduction of productivity bonuses in proportion to the use of parental leave[11], on the whole the analysis did not detect a gender gap in the awarding of such bonuses. In fact, as for the remuneration paid in 2014, this type of reduction in practice involved only ten workers out of 270. It is significant nevertheless that it involved only women: six part-time and four full-time workers.

The analysis subsequently led us to focus on hourly earnings, that is, on the wage rate. The wage rate is the most suitable component for analysing the gender wage gap since it is stripped of every component attributable to working hours. An initial descriptive analysis found, inter alia, a pattern of hourly GPG[12] across the distribution very similar to the progression of the total GPG reported in Figure 2.1. Therefore, the hourly GPG seems to be primarily responsible for the total GPG.

The wage rate is the subject of negotiation at various times: at the national bargaining stage, when the minimum wage rate and protection for sickness, maternity and paternity are determined, and at the local bargaining stage, when the so-called *superminimi*, that is, the component of the monthly salary that the employer provides to workers in addition to what is determined by the national agreement. The opportunity to work on data at the single-firm level enabled us to attempt an evaluation of the effect of these *superminimi* on the GPG. In fact, our data allowed us to observe with precision the workers' contractual levels and to evaluate during the empirical analysis the average contribution of every contractual level to the hourly salary. The analysis used the methodology of an econometric estimation of the hourly salary logarithm, using a simple multivariate linear regression model. This methodology allowed us to quantify the average effect of individual and occupational characteristics on the hourly earnings of the male and female workers considered separately (Oaxaca, 1973; Blinder, 1973). The model includes the following covariates: the years of experience in the company (tenure), a dichotomous variable for every contractual level, a control variable for part-time work and one for the category 'workers' and controls for the workplace. The individual and working characteristics that we included in the regression are those used generally in the literature on the subject, with the addition of control variables for the contractual levels. This allowed us to demonstrate possible gender gaps in the economic progression identified in changes in contractual level and also to evaluate the effect of the components of salary determined locally, namely the *superminimi*. In Table 2.1 we report the estimate results.

The results of the regression model demonstrate a remuneration model that differs considerably between men and women. In particular, length of service is a reward factor only for women. In this case, one more year of tenure than the average tenure guarantees a statistically significant remuneration increment for women but not for men. However, part-time work has significant negative effects on salaries for men, of approximately −7%.

Table 2.1 OLS estimates of log hourly wages: Company 1

	Women	Men
Tenure	0.012*	0.003
Part-time	0.000	−0.069*
Contractual level. Base category: Level 3J		
Level 3S	0.035*	0.071
Level 2	0.196*	0.254*
Level 1	0.281*	0.449*
R^2	0.91	0.90
Observations	175	95

Note: Our elaborations on company data. Covariates include blue/white collar, place of work. *Significance at the 5% level.

Important differences between female and male workers are observed in the changes in contractual classification level. Level 3J, the lowest, is the base contractual level against which the coefficients of the highest levels are interpreted. The highest contractual levels (Levels 2 and 1) reward men to a greater extent. Moving from Level 3S to Level 2 increases the hourly salary of men by almost 6% more than the increase observed for women. The gap increases with movement from Level 2 to Level 1, a step that rewards men with an increase of about 20% and women with a little more than 8%. These differences in economic recognition at each change in level, in our opinion, are due to the components of *superminimi* determined at the local level, or more precisely, at the individual level. This result could be caused by various factors (lower contractual capacity of the female workers or discriminatory attitude of the employer), however, we cannot verify this with the information in our possession.

Our results enable us to conclude that the remuneration model, in the company investigated, differs between men and women. Company 'loyalty' rewards women, guaranteeing salary increases that are not found for men. In contrast, we identified an economic progression for men greater than the rise in classification level. In fact, with the same contractual classification, women receive lower rates than men and this difference increases with the rise in classification level.

As expected, the context and the data offered by the case study under investigation enabled us – albeit within the limits of a plant situated in the Province of Venice engaged in call centre activities – to carry out further analysis from a sociological perspective.

Specifically, in order to identify possible forms of *indirect* and *involuntary* gender discrimination or segregation that contribute to the GPG, a qualitative investigation of the staff employed in the call centre was conducted, based on the material acquired from the union and the company as well as interviews with the workers.

The population of the call centre comprised 129 employees as follows:

Table 2.2 Gender and part-time contracts in transport sector company, Case Study 2

	Full-time	Part-time	Total
Male	15	1	16
Female	32	81	113
	47	82	129

The only man who had a part-time job worked at 94% of full-time hours. In other words, 20% of women worked full-time compared with 95% of men. The job titles of the part-time workers corresponded almost exclusively to the lowest, namely customer service advisor (CSA); only one part-time woman at 75% was a customer service supervisor (CSS).

Among the 129 employees, there were:

- One customer service manager (CSM) in charge of the entire call centre, who in this case, in contrast to other Italian call centres, was a woman aged 54, at the company for 28 years, whose educational qualification was equal to a secondary school diploma, with a full-time contract; as the CSM, classified as manager, she was in charge of:

  a   One CS operations manager classified as a middle manager, male with university degree age 48, at the company for more than 23 years, full-time.

  b   One customer service facilitator from the Business Optimisation and Development department, classified as a white-collar worker, a woman with a university degree age 36, with approximately seven years of service, full-time.

  c   Eight CSSs aged between 35 and 59 years, two men with secondary school diplomas, and six women (two with university degrees, one with a secondary school diploma and one whose educational qualifications were not indicated), classified as white-collar workers, the CSSs were all full-time except for one of the two women with university degrees who was part-time at 75%; each CSS was in charge of one of the eight teams in which the remaining population of the call centre was distributed.

  d   The remaining population of 118 CSAs comprised 105 women, of whom 80 are part-time, and 13 men, all full-time (except one who was part-time at 94%); of the 23 university graduates, 20 were CSAs with part-time contracts.

The average age of the employees was around 44 and the average length of service was about 16 years, thus quite a loyal population.

Taken together, the evidence provides a positive picture of the company policy towards a balance between work life and private life. The willingness they showed towards flexibility arrangements in terms of granting part-time work (in various proportions) was also confirmed by the union, which maintained excellent relations with the company. In fact, the management chose to adapt to changes in employees' needs and to obviate turnover by adopting a loyalty policy intended to improve the quality of service through optimising (not exactly in salary terms) know-how.

Flexibility on start and finish times and the granting of part-time working hours were the key factors of this employee management policy.

In the previous two years, the company, a leader in this sector in Italy, decided to build further client loyalty by adopting, as a specific objective, excellence (from good to great) in the services offered. The employees' professionalism was recognised as essential for attaining this objective and the state of excellence was pursued through a systematic evaluation of their performance. In the pursuit of excellence and attainment of the objectives, according to the human resources (HR) manager interviewed, it was crucial to optimise and motivate the staff by following the manual, whose principles were based on both result and respect. In fact, the HR manager insisted that, for the company, the 'result' was not sufficient and the management must collectively demonstrate they followed the principles of 'respect'. The management's adherence to this policy appeared absolute, pursued with conviction and enthusiasm and, it could be said, a morally responsible leadership. The consequence was an amalgam of the culture, vision and mission of the company and the employees, who enabled attainment of the result by demonstrating autonomy, initiative and motivation through participation in team work, but also dedication and enthusiasm through drawing on all their aptitudes and skills.

The call centre does not present a range of particularly varied positions, but on the professional level, the CSAs interviewed recognise that employment in this company constituted a vital working experience and they claimed to be satisfied with respect to both the company policy on training and updating and the internal recruiting systems for potential career advancements. Indeed, the company offered opportunities for advancement by periodically informing the employees about vacant positions. In fact, the internal selection process corresponded to a rather complex company philosophy and the career opportunities did not always coincide with the need for balance, since they required a willingness to move and were not particularly feasible for those with part-time contracts. For example, the CSS interviewed was a 35-year-old woman with no children who worked fulltime. Moreover, the two CSAs interviewed were representative of the company population in claiming not to be interested in career advancements, despite possessing educational qualifications.

In addition, the satisfaction of the employees was strongly motivated by the culture and climate of the company, which was defined by them as open and informal, attentive to differences, not only in gender, but also in ethnicity and sexual orientation. The relationships between colleagues and with superiors were judged positively and the lack of opportunities for growth did not seem to be viewed as horizontal or vertical segregation, because the environment was perceived as dynamic and stimulating, contrary to the common perception about working in a call centre.

In this regard, however, the CSA who was the company's union delegate, while recognising the continuing opportunities for skill innovation and learning new professional competencies offered by the management, expressed a more complex point of view, calling attention to the uniqueness of the call centre within a male-dominated sector. From this perspective, in fact, the attention documented by the company agreements towards part-time work and the flexibility in start and finish times had a special value, since the second-level bargaining demonstrated sensitivity towards needs that are ignored in other companies in the sector, which has a clear dominance of male staff. At the same time, the contextualisation confirms that discontinuing full-time work interested the female members of staff of a predominantly male sector, such as that of logistics, freight transport and shipping, confirming the priority of family care over work commitments for women. Moreover, the concentration of female staff in the call centre confirms the professional stereotype of patience and courtesy, but above all, the female voice as an indispensable asset for customer satisfaction. The work of the CSA was defined by the union delegate, in essence, as care work, comparable to that of a nurse or teacher, entrusted to women who are recognised for their irreplaceable soft skills, which are considered crucial for the quality of service, even if not always valued in terms of pay and role.

In summary, the case examined seems to exemplify multiple concurrent causes of segregation, both horizontal and vertical.

Indeed, the company is characterised by an unquestionable attention to the needs of their female staff, but this can be read from a horizontal segregation perspective. The so-called female skills, traditionally attributed to the psychology and behaviour of women, are in other words an unspoken requisite for the type of service requested, but as often happens, they are sanctioned, or in any case not fully recognised, especially at the CSA level. In the professional skills of the CSA, helpfulness and attention to the customers appear to be essential, along with the ability to solve problems in the least time possible, and it is the performance and achievement of standardised objectives that undergo systematic checks, while the qualifications, skills or potential do not appear to be evaluated, except for management. In the case of highly educated staff who have robust company know-how, it cannot be ruled out that this leads to a certain penalisation and vertical segregation. The greatest dissatisfaction or frustration of the CSAs is actually attributed by the union delegate to the lowest classification level. Further, the possession of higher formal qualifications is not as critical as fidelity: the two managers interviewed did not have degrees, but had always worked full-time, moved to other cities for long periods, and did not have children. In this regard, the trade unions did not pursue the questions relating to evaluation of staff in the devaluation of skills considered as female, nor have they until recently shown particular attention to the classification problem. Moreover, at the bargaining tables, the male unionists prevail (as observed by the female union delegate, with a certain bitterness).

Company from the metalworking sector: Case Study 3

The subject of this case study is a company from the metalworking sector that comprised 503 employees (all included in the economic analysis of micro-data), distributed across two different plants: one based in Bassano (Vicenza, Veneto Region), where the company's white-collar workers were employed, and the other based in Feltre (Belluno), with the blue-collar workers.

The legal analysis focused specifically on the company agreement signed by the company on 5 June 2013 with the workers' representatives at the company level, together with union representatives at the territorial level of only one of the most representative federations in the engineering sector (FIM-CISL).

Before investigating the part of the agreement regulating performance-related pay elements, it is worth highlighting that the agreement gave specific attention to work–life balance arrangements, affirmative action, the promotion of equal opportunities and anti-discrimination practices.

Regarding the part of the agreement on productivity bonuses, again there is a need to distinguish the criteria used to determine the overall amount of the productivity bonus to be distributed to the company employees in a certain year, and the criteria used to award such bonuses pro rata to each employee.

When dealing with the determination of the overall amount of the productivity bonus, the company agreement referred to a variety of criteria. Specifically, the overall amount of the bonus was meant to vary according to four different indices. Each index affected a different specific percentage of the bonus. The bonus was therefore to be composed of four different parts, defined according to the following parameters: target performance index, value-added performance index, quality performance index and contribution performance index.

With respect to the awarding of the bonus, except for the part deriving from the application of the contribution performance index, all other parts of the bonus were predetermined and awarded to the employees on the basis of an individual index, which varied according to the individual work attendance of each employee. In the measurement of work attendance, only sick leave and unpaid leave were taken into account. This meant that neither maternity leave nor parental leave implied any reduction of the bonus.

The contribution performance index measured the rate of sickness absenteeism in the company. The target in 2013 was 4% (resulting in a bonus of 300 euro), measuring the ratio between the number of hours of sickness absence taken by all the employees of the company and the number of workable hours. In contrast to the others, this part of the bonus was awarded to the employees on an all-round basis.

In general, the bonus (all parts considered) was awarded pro rata according to the reduced working hours for part-time workers, and according to the reduced number of months of service in the case of fixed-term contracts and agency workers, and in the case of termination of the contract during the year.

The company allowed us to assess the actual impact of this method of awarding performance-related pay elements by giving us micro-data on all the employees' wages for 2014.

Before beginning this part of the analysis, it is important to clarify that for employees with managerial tasks, the productivity bonus regulated in the company agreement was substituted by individual bonuses awarded on the basis of a skill or performance evaluation procedure (validated by the trade union, but not negotiated with it). In this regard, it is interesting to note that the company enabled the employees to trade these individual bonuses for work–life balance measures, such as teleworking. This could be considered quite alarming and paradoxical. On the one hand, if work–life balance arrangements are persistently viewed as a way for women to both work and take care of children, this exchange can lead to a double discriminatory effect: an increase in the GPG, stemming from a gap in the awarding of bonuses, and a crystallisation of the uneven distribution of family burdens between men and women, which determines a gender time gap and consequently a further GPG. On the other hand, it is paradoxical, especially if one considers that the Italian legislation is promoting 'smart working' and teleworking as a means of increasing work productivity.

The company provided us with a very rich database of detailed information on all the workers. In this case, in addition to the data on the type of contract, total annual earnings and fixed and variable components of earnings, annual hours of work, hourly and annual earnings, years of tenure at the company, contract classification level and whether employed full-time or part-time, the company provided information on the education qualifications of each individual.

The proportion of women and men differed from that of the previous case study. In this case, of a total of 503 workers, 171 (34%) were women and 332 were men. Further, part-time work was not very widespread: 73% of the women and all the men worked full-time. The contract classification level in this case is very complex. Workers were classified according to their type of work – blue-collar, intermediate, or white-collar – and for every type of work in a classification level. The middle managers and managers, as is the norm, were distinct from the other work types.

Distribution by gender, type of work and classification level reiterated what was observed in the previous case study: the women were concentrated in the medium–low contractual levels, in contrast to the men, who achieved medium–high classifications more easily. Exemplifying this distribution is the imbalance between the number of male and female managers: the ratio was 12:1. Internal advancement at the firm was more difficult and less frequent for women, even when they were employed full-time. Also observed in this company was a vertical segregation in which the women remained classified at the lowest levels. As in the previous company case, this vertical segregation had repercussions on pay.

Figure 2.2 depicts the gender gap calculated by the annual full-time earnings calculated in line with various percentiles of earnings (the same measurement calculated in Figure 2.1 for the first company case).

As can be deduced from Figure 2.2, the gender gap calculated on the annual earnings follows a trend very similar to that of the first company (Figure 2.1). The gap rises consistently with the rise in pay, taking on negative value in line with the lowest pay and reaching approximately 20% in line with the 90th percentile. The gap rises continuously with the rise in salaries, with an acceleration in line with the highest decile. The gap increases exponentially in line with the last decile of distribution, reaching a value of 70% in line with the greatest pay values. This demonstrates, as in the previous case, the presence of a definite glass ceiling that prevents women from reaching pay levels equal to those of men.

Since the data at our disposal are only partial on the variable parts of pay, we will not dwell on the analysis of the various components of the total earnings (as done for the previous company case) and will move on to the examination of the hourly pay gap. In Figure 2.3 we report the distribution of the hourly pay gap for full-time workers.

The hourly pay gap almost entirely overlaps with the total gap, supporting the fact that the GPG arises at the salary bargaining phase when the hourly pay is negotiated. This company case is unique in that the hourly gap is negative in line with the lowest deciles, to be specific, between the first and the second decile. We searched for the reasons for this gap in favour of women, analysing the productive characteristics of the female and male workers that can be found in this pay decile. What distinguishes the two groups is the company tenure: the average tenure of the women is 11 years in contrast with an average tenure of seven years

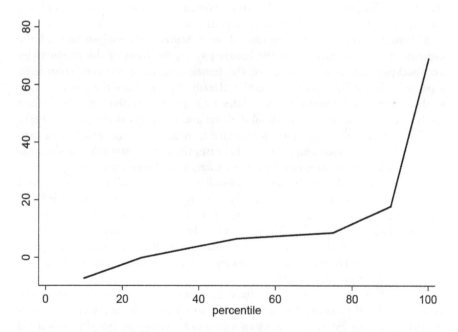

Figure 2.2 Total GPG: full-time workers only

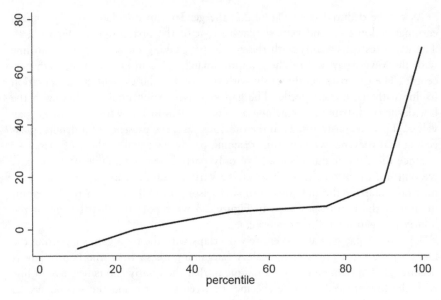

Figure 2.3 Hourly GPG

for the men. This suggests that the women remain longer in very low-level roles, but with the recognition of tenure they manage to obtain greater pay than that of their male colleagues. The gap in favour of women in the lowest deciles would be a consequence, therefore, of the vertical segregation.

As before, in this case we also carried out a multivariate analysis through the estimation of the logarithm of the hourly pay on the basis of the productivity and occupational characteristics of the female and male workers considered separately. In addition to the variables already discussed for the previous case study, we included among the covariates two control variables for the highest levels of education: secondary school diploma and university degree. As far as the level of contractual classification is concerned, things are more complicated than we saw in the previous company. In this case, there were multiple classification levels, which were distinguished by work categories. There were five work categories and they included the usual blue-collar and white-collar workers and a work category called 'intermediate' that distinguished those who carried out functions partway between the functions of the blue-collar workers and those of the white-collar workers. In addition to these three was the category of manager, as well as that of the *quadri* (middle managers), who are company figures partway between the white-collar workers and the managers. In Table 2.3 we summarise the regression results.

The results of the previous case study are partly confirmed by this case study. However, the differences between female and male workers were less pronounced. In contrast to the previous case study, company 'loyalty' rewarded both women and men, with 0.6% more for every year of tenure above the

Table 2.3 OLS estimates of log hourly wages: company 2

	Women	Men
Tenure	0.006*	0.006*
Part-time	0.002	−0.006
Education. Base category:		
Lower secondary school diploma		
Upper secondary school diploma	0.007	−0.000
University degree	−0.022	−0.098*
Contractual level. Base category:		
Level 3		
Blue-collar Level 4	0.042*	0.082
Blue-collar Level 5	-	0.082*
Blue-collar Level 5s	-	0.215*
Intermediate Level 5	-	0.360*
Intermediate Level 5s	-	0.445*
White-collar Level 4	0.072	0.115*
White-collar Level 5	0.258*	0.335*
White-collar Level 5s	0.372*	0.471*
White-collar Level 6	0.578*	0.610*
White-collar Level 7	0.706*	0.842*
Quadro	0.910*	1.091*
Manager	1.577*	1.551*
R^2	0.85	0.87
Observations	171	332

average tenure. The highest education levels did not guarantee pay increases. In particular, workers with university qualifications were penalised financially.

Some interesting points emerged from the comparison of female and male workers in the classification levels. Blue-collar workers and white-collar workers actually presented very diverse situations. In the case of blue-collar workers, an unequivocal vertical segregation emerged. No woman blue-collar worker was classified at the highest levels (Levels 5 and 5s) or at the intermediate levels, which remained the prerogative of men only. This indicated a pay gap that reached almost 40 percentage points – the difference between the increase in pay for men classified at the 'intermediate 5s' level and the pay for women classified as blue-collar workers at Level 4. In this case, therefore, the women blue-collar workers suffered a definite glass ceiling. This segregation was much more evident than it is in the company in the previous case study.

With respect to the white-collar category, we found a less segregated model in which the women also reached the highest classification. The pay gap was particularly high when the classification level was low (Levels 5, 5s and 6) but reduced with the move to the highest classification levels. At the managerial level, a gap slightly in favour of women became evident. It is worth remembering, however, that the company had 12 male managers and only one woman manager.

Our results appear to suggest that the pay model of this company from the metalworking sector is a model in which the occupational type (blue-collar versus white-collar) makes a difference. Women classified as blue-collar workers experienced a strong vertical segregation and a distinct pay penalty in comparison with their male colleagues. In contrast, the women classified in white-collar roles were able to advance in contractual level and this advancement enabled a reduction in the pay gap.

The gender pay gap and corporate welfare: some reflections on the Italian experience

The Italian experience, with welfare instruments in the workplace as regulated by collective bargaining, is of major significance within any reflection of gender pay differentials and the guarantee of equal pay for men and women.

This study is of particular importance given the central role played by such arrangements along with the changes expected in future. Moreover, it is important if one moves beyond the confines of a mere illustration of the phenomenon and the rules applicable to it – which would however be of scant benefit within the context of this publication – and rather questions the implications for the rights and expectations of working people from a gender perspective.

The following discussion will address the issue from this specific perspective, which is normally disregarded by commentators, who almost always limit themselves to taking note of the situation whilst not however inquiring into the consequences, adopting a critical approach that is capable both of appreciating positive aspects and of revealing potential pitfalls.

It must be recalled as a preliminary matter that this issue concerns a dynamic that has evolved over a long period of time, but which has become a significant topical issue above all over the last years, having been promoted and sustained by the possibility for workers and undertakings to obtain tax and pension benefits.

Evolutionary stages

Workplace welfare practices have a long history, which may be summarised here and broken down into three interconnected phases.

The first may in turn be further subdivided into two tendencies: one involving the forms of 'industrial paternalism' that developed during the 1950s in several important companies, and the other emerging in some of the major sectors, including in particular the banking sector, with the introduction of pension and healthcare funds.[13]

The next phase, which occurred during the first decade of the twenty-first century, developed closely in line with the previous phase as many of the undertakings involved were the same as those that had introduced pension and social benefit funds, thereby adopting a Corporate Social Responsibility (CSR) approach, following policies that focused not only on economic factors but also social and environmental issues. CSR has been visibly receding in recent years with the global economic and financial crisis, resulting in both falling staffing levels as well as disappointment at the lack of resistance displayed.

The third phase has inherited and in part maintained the same structure,[14] whilst, however, promoting the move beyond voluntary, unilateral choices by employers by establishing a basket of incentives for bilateral regulation through collective bargaining.

Whilst nobody questions the direct link between the reduction in resources available for social spending, and hence for public welfare, and the development of 'secondary welfare', the promotion of policies that involve the social partners and encourage them to pay attention to the needs and welfare of individuals whilst engaging in bargaining must be assessed positively.

However, one must not underestimate the significance of the other side of the question, which attempts to find ways of reducing the tax and social security burden on salaries. This is a long-standing unresolved problem. It was addressed by the Inter-Confederal Agreement of 1990, which called upon the government to reduce the burdens imposed on the cost of labour, which were defined as 'improper'; however, it had also been considered earlier still by the first triangular agreement between the government and the social partners in 1983 during a period of galloping inflation, allowing for the recovery of fiscal drag (even though this never occurred).

The issue is beset with difficulties:

> amplified by the lack of methodological instruments, not to speak of operational instruments, that are capable of reconciling the new forms of the secondary welfare ... with the traditional content of the employment relationship, passing from remuneration through the criteria used for measuring and classifying labour to the dynamic of the relationship over time and throughout the various lifecycles.
>
> (Treu, 2016: 3, 6)

Terminology

The doubts start with the decision as to which adjective should be used in relation to non-public welfare.

One proposal suggests that it should be defined as 'secondary welfare' (Maino and Ferrara, 2015) in order to stress from the outset its parallels with primary welfare, which delineates the field of action of the welfare state, and in order to follow the identification of one of its more traditional institutes: complementary pension schemes, namely the 'second' pillar of pensions.

Whilst the terminology used has not been set in stone,[15] the expression 'contractual welfare' is becoming increasingly widespread, as it covers collective bargaining on national, company and local levels. This in actual fact tends to reach beyond the confines of the company and to reach out towards the reference community and its public and social representatives. Let us consider, for example, childcare services: the creation or incentivisation of nursery places may be used as a network instrument both internally (company) and externally (local territory).

In view of the objective of this chapter, the term 'corporate welfare' will be used: goods and services made available by the employer for its own employees. Amongst company law specialists, these are considered to be 'mechanisms for incentivising employees to achieve higher performance levels' (Gatti and Iannotta, 2014: 57), with the aim of 'increasing the wellbeing of the worker and his or her family' (Gatti and Iannotta, 2014: 62).

However, it is also important to note the observation that 'conceptual clarity within the notion of corporate welfare is inversely proportionate to its diffusive and evocative capacity' (Tursi, 2012: 213).

Parameters of the areas covered

Difficulties are thus encountered also where attempts are made to classify and identify the object of inquiry, which proves to be broad and located within shifting boundaries. This is demonstrated by the need of all those who deal with such matters – above all within the sociological and organisational economics literature – to dedicate a preliminary analysis to listing and cataloguing institutes.

One possible framework involves a distinction between supplementary welfare, loyalty-enhancing welfare, measures intended to reconcile work and family life, and those aimed at promoting individual wellbeing.

The following list can be provided solely as a guideline and in order to enable the breadth of the phenomenon to be better understood: pension funds and complementary pension schemes, healthcare funds and healthcare assistance, childcare services, extension of parental leave or leave to care for disabled persons, flexible working hours, expansion of grounds for eligibility for advances on end of service payments, expenses for care for relatives who are elderly or not self-sufficient, spa treatments, subsidised loans, canteens and lunch vouchers, fuel vouchers, discount agreements with shops, consumer incentives, study grants and contributions to schooling costs, summer and recreational camps, transport, laundry services.

However, this list is based on empirical data, and the fact remains that only limited parts of it have been applied to individual workplaces under collective bargaining arrangements. This is not all. The provisions dedicated to welfare within corporate collective contracts often reflect previous negotiations concerning this issue, with the result that the very fact as to whether or not certain institutes are included is dependent upon the choices made by the parties to the agreement rather than on objective criteria.

For example, corporate contracts within sectors that have a long tradition in this area that incorporate into the provisions on welfare only the new extensions to its scope, exert a restrictive effect in drawing a form of distinction between previously acquired entitlements and substantive innovation.

This is counteracted by contracts that include benefits such as those available to student workers, study leave and part-time work, which can only be considered to be inherent within a workplace welfare system if the parameters of welfare are expanded to its fullest extent with the aim of achieving economic benefits.

It is a risky venture to confuse the area of benefits made available in order to promote worker wellbeing with the general principle that competence to lay down the terms for improving benefits lies with collective bargaining, as it involves dispensing with the need to identify its boundaries.

It must also be considered that errors in drafting the terms of collective contracts as a result of inaccuracies may also be significant, as these may even result in a reduction in the threshold of rights and protection available under legislation. Moreover, in spite of the fact that precise and complete monitoring of collective bargaining is not possible, it is apparent that in most cases the provision of care is regarded as equivalent to caring for young, ill or disabled children. It appears that it is always the relationship between parent and child that prevails, also due to cost containment requirements, as if Italy were not already a country with a low birth rate and a rapidly ageing population.

For our present purposes, it would in any case be a vain exercise to attempt to resolve the question of what falls within the, as yet, imprecisely defined scope of this 'secondary welfare', just as we take for granted the impact of salary bonuses on the GPG (regarding which, see the case studies analysed above). It is of greater interest to consider which and how many arrangements that can normally be classified under corporate welfare may be regarded as gender-friendly or gender-oriented.

Italian legislation

The objective of this analysis, as was recalled at the start of this chapter, is the impact of so-called corporate welfare on gender-related pay differentials as viewed through the specific lens of the structure put in place by Italian law which, over the last two years, has been pursuing its own development by establishing a direct link with variable remuneration (productivity bonuses and profit shares) and the decentralisation of collective bargaining. The twofold link with the objective of the study, which is to inquire into the roots of the GPG and how to reduce if not eliminate the gap, is thus fully evident.

It may suffice in this context to present a summary account of the Italian legislation in this area. The Stability Law for 2016[16] enacted a legislative provision allowing workers the possibility to choose between earning (in cash) a results bonus, or requesting that it be converted in full or in part into welfare goods and services, thereby receiving benefits in kind or in the form of reimbursed expenses, with an economic benefit consisting in the exemption of those amounts from the employee's taxable income. The employer also obtains economic benefits, consisting in the tax deductibility of the costs incurred and an exemption from the requirement to pay social security contributions. On both sides of the employment relationship the direct benefit achieved is predominantly economic in nature.

With the stroke of a pen, the legislation on tax relief for employment income for goods and services provided by the employer has been significantly changed, if not turned on its head. Before the Stability Law for 2016 was enacted, the exemption was not recognised when these benefits constituted a 'replacement for amounts consisting in cash remuneration (fixed or variable)' (Brenna and Munno, 2016: 178). As of 2016, an exemption is available, albeit subject to the requirement of consent by the employee, precisely for benefits provided in place of variable remuneration (productivity, profit or result bonuses).

This is not all. The exemption was previously recognised for welfare measures that constituted a *quid pluris* provided by the employer in addition to, and not instead of, fixed or variable salary elements. As of 2016, the tax relief has been extended also to 'replacements' and, in this case, is no longer determined unilaterally by the employer but rather stipulated within collective bargaining. The corporate welfare measures that are becoming established in Italy thus move beyond the outlook of 'giving something extra', that is the lynchpin of CSR, and have turned into one of the principal objects of collective bargaining.

This demonstrates once again the ability of legislation to impact upon existing factual situations, above all when introducing tax breaks or contribution holidays, thereby altering the balance of convenience. In effect, the institutes involved are classified by the law with reference to their tax position. This is one of the (many) cases in which legislation is derived from various sources, such as tax law, even where it concerns aspects related to work, its performance and its remuneration.

This tax relief, and thus the removal of the benefits from taxable income, raises the spending power of workers and also increases sales on the market for goods and services. Corporate welfare thus turns into a form of remuneration in kind, which makes sense due to the associated tax benefits. However, it must not be forgotten that the choices made by Italian lawmakers in recent years have provided for incentives and tax breaks that risk becoming a kind of drug for the market and preventing effective, innovative and coordinated actions on system-wide level.

Corporate welfare and the reconciliation between work and family life

Another positive aspect is that the issue of reconciling work and family life has ventured out of the corner to which it is usually confined and has become a core element of contractual renewals. Paying heed to the needs of working people is becoming a core element of promoting the development of the company contractual level. Scholars who deal with the issue are noting with increasing frequency that corporate welfare should be considered to pursue the aim of improving both the 'work and private life' of employees (Maino and Mallone, 2016: 78), turning it into an instrument for reconciling work, family and personal life.

This has the effect of achieving two objectives, both of which receive strong support from the European institutions: the dissemination in Italy of decentralised collective bargaining and paying attention to the needs for flexibility on the part of workers.

It must not be forgotten that the system of trade union relations in Italy has always been characterised by a high degree of centralisation and that the recommendations issued by the European Commission have, for some time, been calling for greater delegation to corporate and local level, which has to date been hampered by a productive system that is splintered into a myriad of micro-enterprises coupled with the sparse benefit for employers in unionising employment relations.

As regards the focus on the provision of care, it is sufficient to refer to the recent Resolution of the European Parliament of 13 September 2016 on creating labour market conditions favourable for work–life balance, which dedicates an entire paragraph to 'Women and men as equal earners and equal carers' which, alongside the role of states, refers to the benefits of involving the social partners and civil society in policies to combat discrimination and to promote gender equality at work (European Commission, 2016: para. 25).

The removal of trade union hostility

A number of elements, starting from those referred to above, have led trade unions to endorse the choices made in the legislation.

This is demonstrated by the documents signed jointly by the CGIL [Italian General Confederation of Labour], CISL [Italian Confederation of Workers' Trade Unions] and UIL [Italian Labour Union] on 14 January 2016 for 'A modern system of industrial relations, for a developmental model based on innovation and equality employment', which contains a specific paragraph dedicated to contractual welfare, to be developed on national, company and local level as 'a basis for nurturing "organisational wellbeing" and reconciling work with family life as part of an overall improvement in productivity and working conditions'.

This is confirmed by the agreements concluded during the summer of 2016, starting with that applicable to industrial enterprises,[17] which attempted to simplify and disseminate local bargaining and put in place, albeit generically, the conditions for 'identifying the services and corporate welfare benefits to be offered to workers', should they choose this solution as an alternative to the payment of cash bonuses.

However, the positions of the various trade unions have not always been so unified. Criticisms have been made based on the risk of an increase in inequality. This was the main objection brought by the CGIL, which focused both on the differences in treatment resulting from the fact that benefits are offered only to staff employed within enterprises as well as the schemes available, which could only be used by some employees.

Although resistance has been overcome, the underlying question remains unresolved: 'corporate benefits are in themselves exposed to the risk of pursuing partial objectives and favouring trends towards the sectoralisation of supply' (Treu, 2016: 9).

We therefore now move on to the part of the investigation that seeks to identify potentially critical aspects within the legislative framework.

The interface with the logic of bonuses

According to the mechanism provided for under applicable legislation, the approach rooted in solidarity of most corporate welfare schemes is incorporated into a system centred on bonuses. Although it is not yet clear what the actual ramifications of this change in focus will be (see De Colle and Feltrin, 2016: 213), it has given rise to doubts and perplexities.

The main difference compared to past experience – based largely on similar institutes – appears to consist precisely in the acceleration of the link with the improvement in results in terms of quality, productivity, profitability, efficiency and innovation in the workplace. Swapping a bonus in return for goods and services thereby ends up affecting the variable element of remuneration.

As one would expect that this choice would be made above all by female workers, considering their greater propensity to access services that promote reconciliation between work and family life, it is highly likely that this may result in an increase in the pay gap.

A further form of linkage must also be pointed out. Most analyses include amongst the objectives of corporate welfare the reduction of absenteeism by linking up with the criterion of presence in the workplace in order to receive productivity and result bonuses (regarding which see the analysis provided above).

If these are to bear fruit, they will not be immediate but will occur over the medium term, promoted by a positive feedback loop whereby the services intended to reconcile work and family life are capable of reducing absences and periods of leave which – according to current arrangements – lead to a reduction in the amount of result-based bonuses.

Adapting the organisation of work

A further aspect of integration between welfare arrangements may be found within the provisions of the Stability Law for 2016, which increases the tax benefit where the enterprise establishes forms of worker participation in the organisation of work (as pointed out by Caruso, 2016: 192). This is the aspect that has to date developed the least, considering the long-standing resistance within the Italian system of industrial relations, but which research has indicated could be particularly worth investigating.

In this case the linkage consists in the possibility for workers to propose organisational changes, which may concern not only the production process but also to the spatial and temporal dimension. This may include flexitime or teleworking, along with its replacement of 'smart' or 'agile' work, which attracted a blaze of interest within collective bargaining, even before a legislative definition and regulatory framework were introduced (Law No. 81/17).

On a methodological level, it is necessary to highlight the importance of distinguishing between arrangements and considering on an equal footing both changes to the place of work and working hours as well as the provision or grant of subsidised access to services. It is this logic which underlies the guidelines issued by the Italian Revenue Agency,[18] which require that both the object and value of such services be determined.

In particular, forms of flexibility that are favourable to individuals must be embraced wholeheartedly, although they must not leave open the risk of 'improper' exchanges.

The exchange and related critical issues

The more one moves away from the benevolent and enlightened unilateral philanthropy of the employer towards the sphere of collective bargaining, the greater attention must be paid to the risk of 'improper' exchanges, which may result as such from bargaining between opposing positions.

In reality, the logic of the exchange is incorporated, as noted above, into the very text of the legislation.

Certain forward-looking observations (Stendardi and Munno, 2016: 145) have noted 'the dual benefit in reducing the costs of the aggregate acquisition of services (and the resulting increased objective value and perceived value for the employer) along with increased productivity achieved within the context of the enterprise' (Stendardi and Munno, 2016: 152). 'The provision of welfare services may supplement/replace salary payments and, if done properly, guarantee greater real and perceived value.' The authors go on to provide an example, which it is appropriate to repeat in full:

> When confronted with a company's need for flexibility, one can envisage welfare payments that allow the worker to engage with commitments from his or her private life, making him of her more open to different ways of working and flexibility. This could not be resolved by providing financial compensation: this is the 'excess perceived value' of welfare, this is one of the possible ways of dealing with the issue of 'reconciling work and family life'.
>
> (Stendardi and Munno, 2016: 153)

This is the position established under the legislation contained in the Stability Laws for 2016 and for 2017. It is no coincidence that the authors cited above welcome the possibility of

> 'welfarising' all or part of the result bonus, resulting in a complete exemption from taxation of the cost of the benefits in question, broadening

the scope for targeted contractual provision, thereby opening up new space for the development of contractual arrangements that are focused on participation, productivity and the organisational wellbeing of employees within the company.

(Stendardi and Munno, 2016: 157)

However, there is a question as to whether it is always a genuine exchange. An analysis of the practice of businesses and the literature in this area does not dispel all doubts.

The following citation is enlightening: 'according to an initial analysis, it is apparent that smart working is regarded by employees as a benefit: it in fact allows them to have more time for themselves and for meaningful relationships, to reduce stress levels, to increase self-efficacy, to achieve greater satisfaction and also to reduce perceived problems associated with the management of their dual role' (Mazzucchelli, 2014: 91).

The ability to manage work flexibly and the ability to negotiate one's own requirements enables workers to maintain the right level of concentration, reducing the impact of personal/family concerns on their performance at work; the working climate, which is characterised by reciprocal trust within an informal negotiational perspective, enables people to look to the future without concerns, being certain of unconditional support from the company.

(Mazzucchelli, 2014: 105)

In other words: the employer grants flexibility to workers, regarding it as benefit constituting a corporate welfare arrangement, which may be used by workers as an alternative to receiving a result bonus.

This perspective opens up numerous critical aspects, given that the financial bonus is waived in return for a benefit that has 'zero cost' (or almost)[19] for the employer. It would be too simplistic to limit ourselves to noting that this constitutes a violation of the provisions of the legislation referred to above: Italy is not a country with a consolidated and widespread system of public controls and the form that has been drawn up for monitoring the experiences of the various actors is extremely generic.

The doubts were moreover confirmed in the ISTAT (Italian National Institute for Statistics) 2015 annual report (cited above), which takes account of the results of a random sampling of initiatives carried out in the area of corporate welfare, from which it is apparent that 'protection of a healthy workplace and worker safety is the most widespread practice: more than 80% of manufacturing and service companies and 65% from the trading sector'. The report feels the need in relation to this issue to specify, albeit in passing, that statutory obligations moreover apply in this area.

It is in fact one thing to note how applicable legislation ensures that 'assuming identical costs for the employer, the net benefit for the worker resulting from the provision of compensation in the form of benefits is far greater than that generated by the payment of the corresponding amount as salary' (Carniol, 2013), yet quite another to purport to classify as benefits certain goods and services provided to employees – largely provided as alternatives to result bonuses – which however are mandatory statutory requirements, such as guarantees of workplace health and safety or organisational changes allowing workers to benefit from flexitime.

The question of equality and affirmative action

It is now necessary to return to a general observation: if it cannot be doubted that the redistribution of resources in order to achieve the objective of substantive equality is the linchpin of the public policies of the welfare state, the same cannot however be asserted for corporate welfare. However, as is known it is not uniform treatment that guarantees substantive equality – which is required under Article 3(2) of the Constitution. Protection must be tailored to needs: 'not "the same for everyone" ... but "equal treatment for equal needs"' (Ferrera, 2015: 7).

Furthermore, some institutes of corporate welfare may be regarded as forms of affirmative action, i.e. instruments for overcoming discrimination and achieving equal opportunities between male and female workers. For this reason, affirmative action is not neutral but may apply to either male or female workers.

However, the care sector has more female than male workers, despite the generic nature of job adverts and skills required. For this reason also, it would be preferable to replace the albeit neutral phrase of 'reconciling work with family life' with 'redistributing care work', which engages more directly and expressly with the issue.

It is also for this reason that, whilst positively assessing the requirements of working people, the Italian legislation contained in the two most recent stability laws risks opening up a deep fissure which may widen yet further the GPG. At the same time, it is important not to overlook the scale of the impact of the transformation of variable remuneration into services or other benefits in kind and to be mindful of the concerns that it raises due to its impact on the pension system, which will have the result of exacerbating rather than reducing the already alarming gender pension gap.

In conclusion, as is often the case, access to forms of corporate welfare may serve both to remove discrimination and also as a source itself of discrimination.

According to an initial analysis, the outcome in workplaces appears to be the dedication of greater attention to the needs of individuals, with express reference to reconciling work and family life, resulting in a reduction in inequality.

However, inequality may also proliferate, resulting in deep-seated differences: between those in work, and who thus also become eligible for corporate welfare benefits, and those not in work; between those who work as employees and those who are self-employed or work according to atypical contracts; and, within the same company, between those whose needs coincide with the benefits available and those who do not find these to be of any use.

In a country like Italy, many commentators have also reported the risks of geographical disparities (see Ferrera and Maino, 2014) whilst overlooking disparities that exacerbate the gender gap.

Given that 'corporate welfare plans are becoming increasingly important within the remuneration policies of companies' (Carniol, 2013), it is essential to analyse them from the gender perspective which, as noted above, can enable us to verify both the negative aspects as well as the risks of negative ramifications and unjustified manipulation.

As we are still in the initial phase of application of the legislation in this area, the social partners should be invited to assess carefully the contents of and choices made within collective bargaining and to ensure that they are aware of any potential negative implications.

Conclusions

The analysis of the case studies presented in this chapter highlighted that in a context, such as the Italian one, where basic wages are determined at the national level on the basis of a centralised system of collective bargaining, GPGs are mainly determined by the awarding of performance-related bonuses, individually negotiated (so-called *superminimi*), collectively negotiated (for example, the productivity bonus) or paid on the basis of a unilateral decision-making process of the employer.

From this perspective, the role of the social partners becomes key to reduce arbitrary discretion and lack of transparency in the allocation of bonuses as well as to avoid gender bias in the choice of criteria for the awarding of bonuses in company agreements. However, if the criterion of work attendance shows to be controversial as it can imply indirect discrimination to the detriment of women, the choice of alternative criteria might be a challenging task for the social partners to fulfil in the negotiation process, as it requires to design a gender-neutral system of skills and productivity evaluation.

The analysis of the case studies also highlighted the typical link between the GPG and horizontal and/or vertical segregation. Specifically, it showed how working time flexibility and the granting of part-time working can sometime work against women if supervisory positions are assigned only to full-time workers and the career development of women is, therefore, jeopardised. The hidden link between work-life balance arrangements and the GPG becomes apparent also in the case of company practices enabling the employees to trade productivity bonuses for those forms of corporate welfare related to the flexible organisation of time and place of work. In fact, if these arrangements are persistently viewed as a way for women to both work and take care of children, this exchange can lead to a double discriminatory effect: an increase in the GPG, stemming from a gap in the awarding of bonuses, and a crystallisation of the uneven distribution of family burdens between men and women, which determines a gender time gap and consequently a further GPG. This is even more paradoxical if one considers that smart or tele-working arrangements are presented at the Italian legislative level as a factor of growth in competitiveness and productivity, while the abovementioned practice of exchange propose them as a compensatory measure of pay for the productivity itself.

The multiple links between the GPG and the issues of productivity rewarding, work–life balance arrangements, and corporate welfare benefits show the challenges but also the opportunities that the social partners need to take in a context pushing towards an increase of decentralisation in collective bargaining.

Notes

1 In particular: (i) A reduction of tax rates applicable to performance-related pay elements is granted on condition that such elements are regulated and set by collective agreements, concluded with the social partners, in accordance with the Programmatic Guidelines on Productivity of 21 November 2012 and the Intersectoral Agreement on Productivity of 24 April 2013, as well as Law No. 228/12. Specifically, the employee is granted a 10% tax rate instead of the ordinary one. Such reduction is applicable to all the pay elements linked to interventions aimed at increasing and enhancing company productivity, meaning not only performance-related awards, but also those pay elements related to an introduction of flexible working time schedules, new technologies and functional flexibility. This explains why a first preliminary phase of the analysis was dedicated to picking out the company agreements that specifically regulated performance-related pay elements. (ii) A reduction of social security contributions (a 25% reduction of those at the expense of the employer; a total 100% exemption from those at the expense of the employee) applicable to performance-related pay elements as long as they are set by collective agreements (Law No. 247/07 and Law No. 92/12).
2 Since 24 September 2015 this requirement is generally stated at the legislative level by art. 14, Legislative Decree No. 151/2015, one of the decrees from the Italian Jobs Act.
3 In this respect, the objective of 'certainty', in terms of reliability, of the sample selected in a particular territorial context, regardless of the relevant industry sector, from the size of the company and/or the type of trade union concerned, needed to be balanced, practically and effectively, with a problem of 'fragmentation' inherent in the agreements themselves that, to be overcome, required this additional investigation.
4 The remaining part was concerned with other types of provisions (e.g. hours of work), not necessarily connected with productivity, despite falling under, in terms of the law in force at the time, the distinctive, complex meaning of 'productivity wages'.
5 As in, for example, the widespread use by female employees of parental leave and leave for a child's illness, shown in the sustainability reports used in the dispute *S. M. and A. v GTT S.p.A.* decided by the Court of Turin on 26 October 2016, No. 1858; for detail, see Peruzzi (2017).
6 By Law No. 208 of 28 December 2015, art. 1, para. 182–190 (Stability Act 2016), Law No. 232 of 11 December 2016, art. 1, para. 160–162 (Stability Law 2017) and additional tax relief by Law No. 50 of 24 April 2017, art. 55, converted into law 21 June 2017, Law No. 96 (Corrective Action 2017), and more recently by Law No. 205 of 27 December 2017, art. 1, para. 28 and 161 (Stability Law 2018).
7 See Revenue Agency Circular of 15 June 2016, No. 28/E, para. 1.3.
8 Interministerial Decree 25 March 2106.
9 Article 2 of the interministerial decree of 25 March 2016, pursuant to art. 1, para. 188, Law No. 208/15 to regulate the implementing procedures of the system of tax benefits credited for productivity bonuses. disbursed in execution of company or territorial agreements, identifies the use of flexible labour as a means of increasing productivity, profitability, quality, efficiency and innovation. Article 18 of Law No. 81/17 specifies that agile working is encouraged also 'for the purpose of increasing competitiveness'.

10 In this analysis context, for the fixed part of the earnings we mean the part of the earnings not linked to productivity bonuses, inclusive of base salary, fixed by the national collective agreement and thus necessarily equal for men and women who carry out the same duties; length-of-service allowances, determined by the national collective agreement and variable according to the length of service of the employee in the company; and *superminimi* (extra allowances over minimum pay), individually negotiated and differing according to the employee. However, for the variable part of the earnings we mean the part of the earnings closely linked to the productivity bonus, as regulated by the company collective agreement.

11 As shown above, the grid given to us by the company showed the presence of a unilateral unwritten practice on the basis of which the productivity bonus was reduced in proportion to the absences linked to the use of parental leave.

12 Always for the only full-time female workers.

13 In actual fact, at some banks these funds date back to the Fascist corporative period.

14 It should be noted that in the most recent report by ISTAT [Italian National Statistics Institute] (*Rapporto annuale 2015, La situazione del paese*, www.istat.it), the analysis of the 'benefits and services offered by enterprises to employees' is carried out in a section entitled 'Corporate welfare practices and corporate social responsibility' (section 4.1.4).

15 Others also refer to occupational welfare, with a curious and imprecise mixing of terminology (see Caruso, 2016: 177).

16 Article 1(182) to (191) of Italian Law no. 208 of 28 December 2015, along with the amendments introduced by Article 1(160) of Italian Law no. 232 of 11 December 2016. On an administrative level, reference should be made to the inter-ministerial decree of 29 April 2016 and Italian Revenue Agency Circular no. 28/E of 15 June 2016.

17 Inter-confederal agreement of 14 July 2016 between Confindustria and the CGIL, CISL and UIL trade unions concerning tax relief, points 5 and 6.

18 Italian Revenue Agency, Circular no. 28/E of 15 June 2016.

19 It is necessary to take account of the 'effort at internal reorganisation of operations and staff' by the employer, as recalled by Mallone (2015: 45).

References

Blinder, A. S. (1973) 'Wage Discrimination: Reduced Form and Structural Estimates' *Journal of Human Resources* 8(4), pp. 436–453.

Brenna, R. and Munno, R. (2016) 'Il Welfare aziendale: aspetti fiscali' in T. Treu (ed.), *Welfare aziendale 2.0. Nuovo welfare, vantaggi contributivi e fiscali*. Milan: Wolters Kluwer.

Carniol, F. (2013) 'Il welfare aziendale nel sistema del total reward'. Available from: www.benessereorg.it/il-welfare-aziendale-nel-sistema-del-total-reward/ (accessed 18 April 2018).

Caruso, S. B. (2016) 'The Bright Side of the Moon: politiche del lavoro personalizzate e promozione del welfare occupazionale' *Rivista Italiana di Diritto del Lavoro* 35(2), pp. 177–207.

De Colle, M. and Feltrin, P. (2016) 'Che me ne viene? Il Welfare aziendale visto dai lavoratori' in T. Treu (ed.), *Welfare aziendale 2.0. Nuovo welfare, vantaggi contributivi e fiscali*. Milan: Wolters Kluwer.

De la Rica, S., Dolado, J. J. and Vegas, R. (2010) 'Performance Pay and the Gender Wage Gap: Evidence from Spain', CEPR Discussion Paper No. DP7936.

European Commission (2016) 'European Parliament Resolution of 13 September 2016 on Creating Labour Market Conditions Favourable for Work-Life Balance'. Available from:

www.europarl.europa.eu/sides/getDoc.do?type=TA&reference=P8-TA-2016-0338&lang uage=EN (accessed 18 April 2018).

Ferrera, M. (2015) 'Introduzione' in F. Maino and M. Ferrera (eds), *Secondo rapporto sul secondo welfare in Italia 2015*. Turin: Centro di Ricerca e Documentazione Luigi Einaudi.

Ferrera, M. and Maino, F. (2014) *Social Innovation Beyond the State: Italy's Second Welfare in a European Perspective*, Centro di Ricerca e Documentazione Einaudi, Working Paper 2WEL, n. 2.

Gatti, M. and Iannotta, M. (2014) 'Lo sviluppo dei modelli di Welfare aziendale nell'e-sperienza italiana' in M. Gatti (ed.), *La risposta organizzativa ai bisogni delle persone*. Milan: Libri Este.

Maino, F. and Ferrara, M. (eds) (2015) *Secondo Rapporto sul secondo welfare in Italia, 2015*. Turin: Centro di Ricerca e Documentazione Luigi Einaudi.

Maino, F. and Mallone, G. (2016) 'Welfare aziendale, contrattuale e territoriale: tras-formazioni in atto e prospettive di sviluppo' in T. Treu (ed.), *Welfare aziendale 2.0. Nuovo welfare, vantaggi contributivi e fiscali*. Milan: Wolters Kluwer.

Mallone, G. (2015) 'Il Welfare aziendale in Italia: tempo di una riflessione organica' in F. Maino and M. Ferrera (eds), *Secondo rapporto sul secondo welfare in Italia 2015*. Turin: Centro di Ricerca e Documentazione Luigi Einaudi.

Mazzucchelli, S. (2014) 'Lo smart working come benefit: pratiche innovative di Welfare aziendale' in M. Gatti (ed.), *La risposta organizzativa ai bisogni delle persone*. Milan: Libri Este.

Oaxaca, R. (1973) 'Male-Female Wage Differentials in Urban Labour Markets' *International Economic Review* 14(3), pp. 693–709.

Peruzzi, M. (2017) 'La parità retributiva di genere nello specchio della decentralizzazione contrattuale. Problemi e soluzioni in una prospettiva di analisi comparata' *Rivista Italiana di Diritto del Lavoro* 36(2), pp. 241–273.

Stendardi, U. and Munno, A. R. (2016) 'Il Welfare contrattuale: un nuovo orizzonte strategico' in T. Treu (ed.), *Welfare aziendale 2.0. Nuovo welfare, vantaggi contributivi e fiscali*. Milan: Wolters Kluwer.

Treu, T. (2016) 'Introduzione' in T. Treu (ed.), *Welfare aziendale 2.0. Nuovo welfare, vantaggi contributivi e fiscali*. Milan: Wolters Kluwer.

Tursi, A. (2012) 'Il "Welfare aziendale": profili istituzionali' *Rivista delle politiche sociali* 4, pp. 213–238.

3 Decentralisation and the gender pay gap in the Polish context

Case studies

Mirosław Czerwiński and Ilona Topa

Introduction

This chapter presents the research findings of three case studies relating to the GPG issues in the Polish context, taking into account provisions of the collective labour agreements (CLAs), private (a shipping company) and public (a university's faculty) sectors. Directed by the aims of the 'Close the Deal, Fill the Gap' project, this chapter considers the factors that impact on the level of the GPG in Poland. It has turned out that doing research in this sphere faces many obstacles. It appears that, apart from an awareness deficit about the GPG among the labour market stakeholders, there is a general secrecy around pay policy and general reluctance of entities to provide data referring to remuneration. These were key stumbling blocks in obtaining the relevant materials to elaborate on the Polish GPG. Moreover, secrecy of pay policy[1] and lack of awareness are closely linked. Without the possibility to compare wages, employees are not able to contest payment schemes. Given these barriers, the data referring to remuneration collected in this chapter are rare and somewhat unique in the Polish context. The provisions of the CLAs are one of the sources of information on the general attitude towards the problem of discrimination based on gender and the first case study analyses how they address this issue. The CLAs are filed at the District Labour Inspectorate in Katowice and cover the agreements concluded by companies that have their seat in the Silesian voivodship – a particularly unionised region of Poland with a comparatively high number of CLAs registered. One of the criteria used for awarding additional components of payment is work attendance, which can imply a gender indirect discrimination. Therefore the chapter also examines the issue of corrective provisions in CLAs – minimising the negative impact the absences resulting from child care have on the level of payment.

The second and third case studies examine the situation in two different legal entities (a company and a university faculty) to verify if on the micro-level the issue of gender discrimination is of relevance, how it is addressed and of course the actual impact of gender on the level of remuneration. The second case study relates to the division of the international shipping company in order to establish how the problem of GPG is dealt with in the private sector. To compare the attitudes, the third case study contains the analysis of this issue in the public sector.

Case Study 1: collective labour agreements registered at the District Labour Inspectorate in Katowice in 2009–2015

The provisions contained in the CLAs reflect the general attitude towards the problem of discrimination based on gender. Undoubtedly, the anti-discriminatory provisions in the CLAs are the first element that can play an important role in the fight against the GPG. Also, the inclusion of specific provisions (of correctional character) relating to establishing the additional components of remuneration can have an impact on the reduction or, on the contrary, on the worsening of the GPG.

This case study aims at analysing the registered CLAs to establish if (and to what extent) they contain provisions relevant for the question of the GPG. Specifically, we ask are there any references to the equal treatment requirement?[2] What are the additional elements of remuneration, and what are the criteria used for awarding them? Does gender play any role in their redistribution? Are there any corrective provisions particularly with respect to the traditional distribution of family and caring burdens?

The analysis covers all 115 CLAs filed at the District Labour Inspectorate in Katowice between 2009 and 2015. These are all agreements concluded by companies that have their seat in the Silesia voivodship (one of 16 Polish voivodships or provinces), regardless of any specific criteria (such as the size, sector or type of trade unions involved). The results of the research are presented in the context of specific supplementary normative sources (such as the Teachers' Charter, the Miners' Charter and the Foundry Workers' Charter) and other relevant law provisions. It is important to mention that the Silesia voivoidship has a long-term trade union tradition and is the region of the highest level of unionisation in Poland, understood as the percent of adult inhabitants in each voivodship that are trade union members (see Figure 3.1). This includes also mining and quarrying industry where the percentage of trade unions' members is the highest (Central Statistical Office of Poland Information, 2015).

Polish labour law requires a wide protection of employees' remuneration, which is applicable also to additional elements of pay. It is crucial to note that even if particular legal provisions relating to remuneration are not directly introduced into CLAs (or regulations on remuneration), they are legally binding and can be claimed by employees. Before analysing provisions of CLAs, two important assumptions must be invoked. First, the legal principle that collective agreements may not contain any provisions less favourable to employees than the provisions of the Labour Code (LC).[3] Second, before entering into force, CLAs shall be registered and their legality is examined by the labour inspectorate.[4] CLAs will not be registered if they do not comply with the law.

To provide a comprehensive overview of the legal situation of employees relating to additional elements of pay and to allow us to make an assessment of the examined CLAs, it must be underlined that Polish labour law

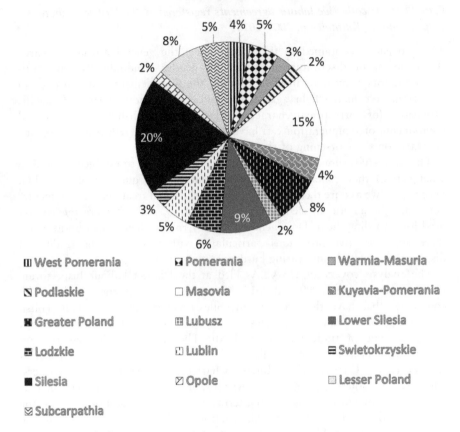

III West Pomerania   ⊠ Pomerania   ▦ Warmia-Masuria

◩ Podlaskie   □ Masovia   ▧ Kuyavia-Pomerania

▨ Greater Poland   ▤ Lubusz   ■ Lower Silesia

▥ Lodzkie   ⊡ Lublin   ≡ Swietokrzyskie

■ Silesia   ⊠ Opole   □ Lesser Poland

⊠ Subcarpathia

Figure 3.1 Level of unionisation in Poland
Source: Central Statistical Office of Poland, Information of 13 July 2015: Trade Unions
in Poland in 2014.

provides for many additional elements of pay that are of obligatory
character.

These include:

1 Compensation due to overtime work

For overtime work a bonus is due in the amount of 100% of remuneration for
overtime work at night, on Sundays and public holidays, on a day off granted to
an employee in exchange for work on a Sunday or on a public holiday, in
accordance with the established work schedule. An employee is entitled to 50%
of remuneration for overtime work falling on any other day. The bonus of
100% of remuneration is also due for each hour of overtime work on the
grounds of exceeding the average weekly standard working time in the
applicable reference period.

2 Compensation for night-time work

A night worker is entitled to a bonus to remuneration for each hour of work at night, amounting to 20% of the hourly rate applicable to the minimum remuneration for work, determined under separate provisions (in relation to employees who provide work at night outside of the work establishment on a regular basis, the bonus may be replaced by a lump sum equivalent to the expected length of work at night).

3 Remuneration for the period of incapacity for work

While an employee is unable to work because of an illness or isolation due to a contagious disease lasting in total up to 33 days in a calendar year (an employee who has reached 50 years of age lasting in total up to 14 days), he/she retains the right to 80% of remuneration (unless the specific provisions of labour law provide for higher remuneration). In the case of an accident on the way to work or from work, or illness during pregnancy, an employee retains the right to 100% of his/her remuneration. Also, the employee absent from work because of necessary medical examinations provided for candidates for donors of cells, tissues and organs, or undergoing an operation of gathering cells, tissues and organs retains the right to 100% of the remuneration.

4 Disability or retirement

An employee who meets the criteria for a disability or retirement pension, and whose employment relationship is terminated due to having qualified for a disability or retirement pension, is entitled to a cash severance allowance amounting to one month's remuneration.

5 Bereavement payment

If an employee dies during an employment relationship or while collecting benefits due to incapacity to work in respect of illness after the termination of the employment relationship, the family is entitled to a bereavement payment. The amount of the payment depends on the employment period of the employee with a given employer and amounts to:

- one month's remuneration if the employee was employed for less than ten years;
- three months' remuneration if the employee was employed for at least ten years;
- six months' remuneration if the employee was employed for at least 15 years.

6 Work stoppage

If an employee is ready to perform work but is unable to, due to reasons concerning the employer, the employee is entitled to remuneration resulting from the personal remuneration grade setting out an hourly or monthly rate, and if this component of remuneration was not established – 60% of the employee's remuneration. In any case, this remuneration may not be lower than the amount of the minimum remuneration for work. The remuneration is due to an employee for the duration of a work stoppage for which the employee is not responsible. If a work stoppage is the responsibility of the employee, the employee is not entitled to the remuneration.

7 Severance pay in case of redundancy[5]

The amount of severance pay depends on the employee's employment record at a given employer and is:

- one month's salary, if the employee has worked for less than two years;
- two months' salary, if the employee has worked for at least two but not more than eight years;
- three months' salary, if the employment record exceeds eight years.

The amount of severance pay cannot be more than 15 times the size of the minimum wage.

8 Additional year salary for employees of public sector

Public sector employees are entitled to an additional annual salary amounting to 8.5% of the annual remuneration[6] (including salary and other benefits related to work taken into consideration while calculating a cash equivalent for the leave not used prior to the termination or expiry of the employment relationship).

All the obligatory elements of pay listed above relate to each employee, regardless of her/his gender or any other criteria (in accordance with LC principle that the employees, regardless of their sex, have the right to equal remuneration for the same work or for work of identical value (article 18[c] of the LC)). In addition, remuneration includes all components of pay, notwithstanding their specific name or characteristic, as well as other work-related benefits granted to employees in cash or non-cash form. LC does not contain further provisions specifying any other additional elements of remuneration. In consequence, they can be without any restrictions established by subsidiary sources of labour law (such as collective agreements or regulations on remuneration).

The situation of employees differs if comparing public sector employees and private sector workers (Grotkowska and Wincenciak, 2014). The latter's wages are determined by specific laws while the wages of private sector employees are generally freely established in the employment contracts (of course, respecting the norms relating to minimal wages that are established by law).

Also, for some particular groups of employees – miners, foundry workers and teachers – there are special legal regulations that contain certain provisions on their remunerations: the Teachers' Charter,[7] the Miners' Charter[8] and the Foundry Workers' Charter.[9] Their analysis has not revealed any discriminatory provisions.

However, it must be underlined that, traditionally, the education sector is dominated by women, while the mining and foundry industries are dominated by men. In addition, of relevance for the differentiation of wages in the mining sector were the provisions that provide special financial bonuses for underground mineworkers (in practice mainly male workers[10]).

The information on CLAs by type of activity is presented in accordance with the Polish Business Activity Classification (Polska Klasyfikacja Działaności, PKD)[11] at the level of the section. Under the PKD there are 17 sections. However, for this research it is sufficient to mention these sections of industry, which are represented in examined CLAs. They are referred in the figure by their mark in the PKD as follow:

(A)   B Mining and quarrying
(B)   C Manufacturing
(C)   D Electricity, gas, steam and air conditioning supply
(D)   E Water supply, sewerage, waste management and remediation activities
(E)   H Transportation and storage
(F)   L Real estate activities
(G)   Q Human health and social work activities (see Figure 3.2).

CLAs registered at the District Labour Inspectorate in Katowice are of companies belonging to 13 sections. Out of 115 CLAs, 42 are of companies belonging to manufacturing sector, 14 – of real estate activities sector, 12 – of electricity, gas, steam and air conditioning supply sector and 11 – of water supply, sewerage, waste management and remediation activities' sector. Only five CLAs registered in the analysed period represent the mining and quarrying sector. While the CLAs offer important data for our understanding of the regional collective bargaining context, they are limited in that they do not provide data on the number of people in total or by gender. Some of the agreements date back to the 1990s.

The CLAs filed at the District Labour Inspectorate in Katowice in the years 2009–2015 totalled 115, of which only 35 (30%) contained an anti-discriminatory

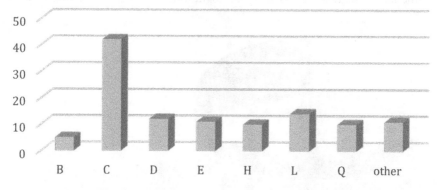

Figure 3.2 Registered CLAs classified in accordance with industry sector

clause (see Figure 3.3). Importantly, these anti-discriminatory provisions constitute merely a repetition of a legally binding regulation of the LC. Only five of them (that is less than 5% of the total) encompass an anti-discriminatory clause whose scope is wider than the wording of it in the LC. These are:

Employer is obliged to use objective and just criteria of employees' and their work performance's evaluation.

Access to employment, training and promotion be on a fair basis; any segregation based on gender of employees is prohibited.

Employer is obliged to respect the equal opportunities' rules; the awarding of any remuneration benefits and treatment in the employment shall be free from any discrimination; any segregation of employees based on gender and leading to diminishing or disregard of equal opportunities and equal treatment in employment or professional activities is prohibited.

Gender may be considered only with respect to technological requirements and the provisions on health and safety at work.

Breast-feeding employees have a right to additional breaks at work; employer is obliged to counteract discrimination and to provide access to the regulations on equal treatment.

As a rule, all the CLAs examined establish that the level of basic remuneration depends on the employee's classification to a particular remuneration tariff (that relates to specific positions or groups of positions), so the criterion seems to be gender-neutral. However, it is possible to indicate that in more than half of the CLAs (53%; 61 of all 115) the remuneration tariffs contain particular female positions (usually of lower categories and in consequence less paid), which may suggest the presence of some GPG-related issue (see Figure 3.4). This does not seem to be the case, however. The most probable explanation of the lack of gender-neutrality in the remuneration tariffs is the usage of the categories (names of positions) established in the Regulation of the Minister of Labour and Social Policy of 7th August 2014 concerning classification of professions and specialisations for use in the labour market and its scope of application.[12] It is worth noting that the

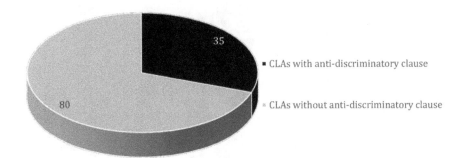

35

■ CLAs with anti-discriminatory clause

80

■ CLAs without anti-discriminatory clause

Figure 3.3 Anti-discriminatory clauses in CLAs

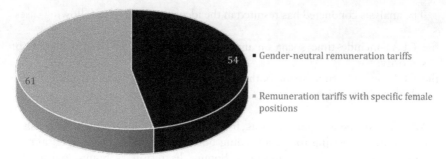

Figure 3.4 Gender in remuneration tariffs

regulation underlines that 'a profession has no sex', and further explains that the fact of using the traditional male and female grammatical names (in the professions dominated by women) shall have no impact on the professional classification of individual persons. There is little doubt that using the language which refers explicitly to only one sex certainly strengthens the stereotypes that certain (and usually lower-paid) professions are dedicated to women.

All the CLAs examined specify what the additional components of remuneration (such as additional pay for overtime work, additional pay for night work, seniority supplement, supplement for particularly arduous working conditions, jubilee award, purposeful bonus, incentive bonus, performance bonus, etc.) are. None of them contain provisions that directly link the assignment of the additional components of pay or their level with the gender of the employee. Further research revealed that most the CLAs (23 out of 30 identified cases with regard to seniority supplement and 35 out of 55 identified cases with regard to jubilee award[13]), while establishing criteria for awarding additional components of remuneration depending on the length of employment (such as seniority supplement, jubilee award, annual bonus, etc.) also refer specifically (although differently) to the time spent on maternity/unpaid parental leave (see Figure 3.5).

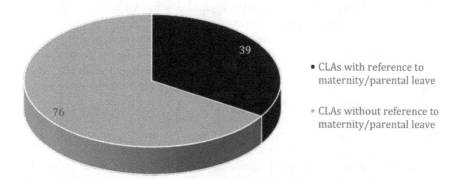

Figure 3.5 Additional elements of pay and establishing the length of employment

The analysis conducted has resulted in the identification of the following cases:

the CLAs include time spent on unpaid parental leave in the calculation of seniority;
the CLAs include time spent both on maternity/unpaid parental leave in the calculation of seniority.

We then deepened our analysis by focusing on CLAs which established certain criteria relating to the awarding bonuses (of diverse character: annual bonus, performance bonus, incentive bonus, discretionary bonus, purposeful bonus, etc.) that indirectly may affect the level of the GPG. Nearly a quarter of the CLAs (20 out of 77) met these criteria and were chosen for further analysis. The criterion used most frequently is work attendance and it appears in two versions: either bonuses are granted for actual working days and pro-portionately reduced by absences or are granted for actual working days and proportionately reduced by absences but maternity/parental leaves are excluded from the calculation of absences. Only in two CLAs different criteria were used – effectiveness and availability – but without any further explanation how there are measured.

As noted above, the majority of CLAs introduce a proportional reduction of bonuses in case of sick leave, not differentiating between the causes of such a leave. However, in one of the CLAs analysed a model solution relating to absenteeism caused by sick leaves was introduced. The CLA in question per-tains to an international shipping company, whose employees are entitled to receive an individual annual bonus depending on the number of actual days of absence at work. The financial basis for calculating an employee's individual bonus includes the employee's year salary, regulatory monthly bonus, compen-sation for night-time work, and bonus for welders. The level of the individual annual bonus depends on the number of actual days of absence at work and is established as a percentage of the annual bonus. If the number of sick leave days is up to 18 days, the individual annual bonus is 0.5% of the financial basis, for sick leave of up to 14 days – 1%, up to 11 days – 1.5%, up to 7 days – 2.0%, up to 3 days – 2.5%, to reach the level of 3% in case of an absolute lack of absences. Particular incapacities to work are excluded from the total number of sick leave days that influence the level of bonus. These are: absences resulting from a work accident or occupational disease and, what is of paramount importance for the question of the GPG, absence caused by illness during pregnancy and sick leave due to illness of a child or another member of the family corroborated by a medical certificate.

The majority of the CLAs involved in the investigation (70%) do not contain any provisions relating to discrimination at work. Moreover, even if the agree-ments contain such norms, they very seldom include regulations that can be considered as more favourable for female employees than the minimum stipulated in the provisions of the Labour Code. In addition, there are clear indications (confirmed by information provided by social partners) that the problem of reducing the GPG is of limited, if any, importance in the process of negotiation of CLAs. In consequence, the majority of agreements do not include provisions that could highlight gender-related issues.

It should be also noted that CLA regulations on additional elements of remuneration implicate possible gender bias deriving from the time gap between women and men at work due to the traditional distribution of family and caring burdens. However, importantly, they also show that certain corrective provisions are introduced. If the CLAs stipulate criteria for awarding additional components of payment based on the length of employment, in most cases they introduce gender-related corrective provisions by including both maternity and unpaid parental leaves or unpaid parental leave in the calculation of seniority. Here, an additional observation must be made: the right to have maternity/ unpaid parental leave included in the calculation of seniority results from the law and in consequence has an impact on the number of seniority-based elements of remuneration. Therefore, inclusion of specific provisions in this respect into CLAs is of no relevance in practice – the employer, irrespective of CLAs, is obliged to include these periods in the calculation of seniority. Nevertheless, if particular solutions are explicitly introduced in the CLAs, in practice it raises overall awareness of the scope of employers' legal obligations.

If the CLAs explicitly indicate criteria for awarding bonuses, in the majority of cases, the level of bonuses is granted for actual working days and pro-portionately reduced by any absences and, in some cases, maternity/unpaid parental leave is excluded from the calculation of absences. It may induce pos-sible indirect discrimination. During pregnancy, women more frequently take sickness absence; in addition, in case of the illness of a child or another member of the family, it is women who usually are absent from work to take care of them. As women earn less, the loss of family income is arguably less significant if the women take time out of work, which results in a vicious circle.

As is proved by this case study, in the Polish context GPG has not been an important element of collective bargaining and is not specifically underlined in CLAs. It should be taken into account, however, that minimum guarantees for employees are provided for in LC, also the principle of equal pay. Probably this is the main reason why GPG is not an issue in the negotiations on terms and conditions of employment.

Case Study 2: the regulation on remuneration in practice – the case of an international shipping company

The anti-discriminatory policies and practices at the level of employer are as important for fighting GPG as legislative provisions. The inclusion of specific solutions (of correctional character) relating to establishing the additional components of remuneration can have an impact on GPG.

The analysis of the second case study was carried out on an interdisciplinary basis, particularly law and economics. It involved an analysis of data provided by representatives of the company and an economic analysis, carried out on the micro-data of the population of employees. However, due to the lack of access to the company agreement, it misses a thorough legal analysis. It must also be underlined that all the information was provided by the company representatives and we were not able to verify its validity. Our findings are indicative rather than reliable as there was a lack of sufficient, specific data on the employees, which limited the degree of economic analysis that we were able to undertake.

Notwithstanding these limitations, we were advised that the company employs approximately 3,000 persons, of whom 42.52% are women and 57.48% are men, and all are contractual workers. Interestingly, more men are part-timers (12.4% of all male employees in comparison to 8.41% of female employees). Characteristically, men prevail on managerial provisions and in decision-making bodies (65.4% of higher posts are occupied by men). It is important to note that 24.94% of employees are members of trade unions (47.5% of them are women).

Normative sources relating to remuneration in the company include:

Labour law (as was underlined by a representative of the company, most of the particular solutions stem from the binding legal provisions).

Regulations on remuneration and specific regulations on bonuses (here, the representative of the company claimed that they, in particular: do not contain any special equality provisions, as the requirement of equality is established by the law; do not contain provisions relating to gender issues; do not differentiate the remuneration based on gender; establish instruments of work–life balance arrangements (e.g. flexible work commencement times, possibility of home-office work in IT Division)).

Additional elements of remuneration in the company include:

Bonuses (paid on a quarterly, monthly or half-yearly basis, depending on a specific workplace). Criteria for granting them are established in the regulations on bonuses. What is important, the company has over a dozen different bonus systems depending on the workplace. The bonus can be between 20 and 60% of basic remuneration. For instance, a storekeeper gets 15% of the performance bonus and 5% of the discretionary bonus while a shipper gets up to 30% of the discretionary bonus and 30% of the performance bonus. It was underlined that bonuses do not depend on the seniority, but, as a rule, are based on the employee's performance. Absences at work reduce bonuses proportionally to working time in the reference period. Generally, all men and women employed at the same positions have a right to the same level of bonus (the actual level depends on the achievement of the assumed targets). Bonuses are proportionally reduced by absences in accordance with the law.

Jubilee awards for all employees.

Annual awards for all employees. The amount of the award to be paid also depends on the number of absences but one should note that maternity and paternity leaves are excluded from the calculation of absences.

Special medical care and life insurance, etc.

As of September 2015, the remuneration of women, in most of the divisions, was lower than that of men. It is especially true for blue-collar workers: in the sorting centre, transport, and operational divisions women tend to earn less than men. Only in the legal division, IT and business administration is the level of the average woman's remuneration higher (see Table 3.1). The data show the average salaries of female and male employees by division. The company did not provide information either on the number of women/men in each division or the total number of employees in the division. Moreover, there is no information on specific positions.

Moving to the economic part of the analysis, the data provided by the company for economic analysis encompass 194 persons and the information on their position, education, work time (full-time or part-time), type of employment contract (for an indefinite period or for a definite period), starting date of employment, and monthly remuneration. 49.5% (96 persons) were male, and 50.5% (98) were female. A majority (75.5%) of the females, as opposed to 42.7% of the males, were full-time employees.

The analysis reveals the existence of a GPG in favour of men. Only in the case of employees with higher education working full-time and among part-time workers (0.5 FTE) the gap is lower than 10%. By contrast, it is especially high (over 20%) in favour of men in the case of employees with secondary education working full-time, part-time (0.75 FTE), or with longer seniority. The average median GPG in the analysed sample is approximately 16%.

This case study confirms the existence of GPG in the private sector. Even though we were provided by the company with some selected data, the results reveal that the differences in the wages do exist and are especially high with regard to blue-collar employees. Interestingly, it also proved that GPG increases with the length of employment (see Table 3.4). It suggests that there are factors that have a negative impact on women's remuneration, which are long-term in character.

Table 3.1 Gender analysis of remuneration by division

Division	Women (PLN)	Men (PLN)
Sorting centre	2,986	3,119
Administration and finance	5,108	6,278
Transport	4,003	4,761
Legal division	8,241	7,814
HR	6,709	7,049
IT	8,832	7,188
Business administration	14,358	7,038
Operational division	3,240	3,633
Sales and market	4,803	5,799

Case Study 3: the regulation on remuneration in practice – the case of a university faculty

This case study involved an analysis of legal provisions, data provided by representatives of the university and, principally, information obtained thanks to the courtesy of our social partner – the Polish Teachers' Union (ZNP). Moreover, it encompassed an economic analysis, carried out on the micro-data of the population of two categories of employees: teaching and research faculty members and technical and engineering staff. The faculty was chosen for our analysis because of its representativeness – it has a similar number of female and male employees. Of relevance was also the access to and availability of data. The first part of the case study concerns teaching and research faculty members working at one of the university's faculties having a similar number of female and male employees. The analysis covered a group of 54 males and 45 females, all of them employed full-time and holding a doctoral degree or a higher qualification.

Salaries of senior lecturers (in Polish: *starszy wykładowca*), and one visiting professor (a woman) were excluded from the analysis because this group (in both categories) is not representative as it numbers only five persons. Also excluded were research/teaching assistants (in Polish: *asystent*), who are usually PhD candidates, the reason for the exclusion being the fact that part-time employment prevails in this group (14 females and one male). With respect to research/teaching assistants, it is worth pointing out that *if* they are given employment contracts at all, it is usually females who are hired part-time under such contracts due to marginal – if any – interest of males in these contracts. It should be remembered that the salaries of this category of researchers are very low but as PhD candidates they may be also granted a scholarship. Absence of males in this group may indicate that they are interested in taking up employment outside the university and embark on doctoral studies without tying themselves to the university at this stage of their careers. Interesting proportions can be observed among junior researchers with a doctoral degree. Full-time employment in this group applies to 26 females and 15 males. The proportions are considerably different in case of the next academic

Table 3.2 Pay structure and gender pay data (full-time workers)

Education level	No. of females	No. of males	Monthly average female salary (PLN)	Monthly average male salary (PLN)	F as % of M salary	GPG (%)
All workers	74	41	2,795	3,239	86.3	**13.7**
Higher education	30	12	2,924	3,088	94.7	**5.3**
Secondary education	37	18	2,760	3,594	76.8	**23.2**

Table 3.2a Average (median) earnings

	No. of females	No. of males	Monthly average female salary (PLN)	Monthly average male salary (PLN)	F as % of M salary	GPG (%)
All full-time workers	74	41	2510	3000	83.7	**16.3**

degree, i.e. habilitation, where there are 16 males and 12 females employed full-time. Among the factors influencing such a change in proportions are, without a doubt, household duties and motherhood, both of which delay or restrict academic career progression. An employee with a doctoral degree who fails to earn his or her habilitation within the statutory time limit is subject to job rotation. It should be noted at this point that maternity/parental leave is not included in the period of time allowed for earning one's habilitation. In specific situations, a doctor who failed to earn his or her habilitation in the required time, may be offered a teaching position as senior lecturer. Due to a significant number of hours of didactic teaching, this position is not attractive for women with family obligations.

Where base salary analysis is concerned, adjuncts with a doctoral degree receive the same base pay. Among adjuncts with habilitation, females have a slightly higher average base salary than males. The same applies to doctors with habilitation (in Polish: *doktor habilitowany*) employed as associate professors (*extraordinarius*), where females out-earn males by 1%. Nevertheless, neither this group (four males and one female) nor titular professors (academics with the professorial title conferred by the President of the Republic of Poland) employed as full professors (*ordinarius*; eight males and one female) can be considered representative due to their size. That notwithstanding, it cannot pass unnoticed that the pay gap between the males and female in this group is 5% in favour of men. More representative is a group of titular professors employed as associate professors. With 11 males and five females, the average pay gap in this group is 3% (see Table 3.5). However, as has been explained by the university's HR department, these

Table 3.3 Pay structure and gender pay data (part-time workers)

	No. of females	No. of males	Monthly average female salary (PLN)	Monthly average male salary (PLN)	F as % of M salary	GPG (%)
0.5 FTE	6	32	1,276	1,393	91.6	**8.4**
0.75 FTE	18	23	1,796	2,401	74.8	**25.2**

Table 3.4 Pay structure and gender pay data (in order of length of service)

	No. of females	No. of males	Monthly average female salary (PLN)	Monthly average male salary (PLN)	F as % of M salary	GPG (%)
Full-time workers (10 years or more)	26	7	3,105	4,095	75.8	**24.2**
Full-time workers (less than 10 years)	48	34	2,628	3,062	85.8	**14.2**

differences in remuneration may in fact be caused by the individual histories of employment of the particular employees in these groups or by the individual decisions of the university's authorities.

A component of the remuneration package is the seniority allowance (maternity leave is included in the job seniority), calculated in percentage terms. An employee may receive up to 20% of his or her base salary. Furthermore, according to the dean's decision, taken with the rector's consent, employees performing various functions are entitled to receive special duty allowance. In the academic year 2015/2016 these were payable to two females and four males. Department heads are also entitled to receive a small allowance, which was payable to 14 males and four females.

Additionally, all employees working at adjunct positions or higher are entitled to receive another allowance, whose payment depends on the financial condition of the faculty, and whose amount is based on employees' publications, work for the faculty, e.g. organisation of conferences, didactic achievements, work in various faculty-level or university-level commissions, etc. Here, the allowance pay gap is 10% among adjuncts and 6.3% among the senior category of researchers, in each case in favour of men (see Table 3.6). The question to be answered is whether this is due to men's availability to work longer hours and the fact that women take on a greater share of household duties.

Yet another element of remuneration is overtime pay. An employee cannot refuse to work 25% of the teaching load (i.e. 52.5 hours in an academic year) as overtime hours. As far as other overtime hours are concerned, it is primarily up to an employee whether they want to work any extra overtime. Among adjuncts, approximately the same number of females and males work at weekends (Friday to Sunday), the difference being marginal (2% in favour of males). Both have the same teaching load. However, when it comes to classes for full-time students (classes held Monday through Thursday), while the proportions are identical as far as the percentage of females and males

Table 3.5 Base salary by academic grades I–V in faculty

Position (group)	Gender	Number of persons	Average base salary, in PLN	Difference in %	Difference in % among senior researchers (groups I–IV)
I. Full professors	M	8	6,222		F 1.7% less
	F	1	5,950	F 5% less	
II. Titular professors employed as associate professors	M	11	6,304		
	F	5	6,126	F 3% less	
III. Doctors with habilitation employed as associate professors	M	4	4,732		
	F	1	4,810	F 1% more	
IV. Doctors with habilitation employed as adjuncts	M	16	4,403	F 0.45% more	
	F	12	4,423		
V. Doctors (adjuncts)	M	15	3,820	____	____
	F	26	3,820		

working overtime is concerned, the number of hours taught by females is 35% lower than that taught by their male colleagues. Among senior researchers, 74% of males and 89% of females work on Saturdays and Sundays, but the number of hours taught by females in the academic year 2014/2015 was 12% lower than that taught by males (average annual figures for females and males are 107 and 122 hours, respectively). The situation is different in case of overtime hours taught for full-time students. Whereas the percentage of female and male senior researchers is the same (73%), females teach 31% more overtime hours than males. It must be emphasised, however, that hourly rates for overtime hours taught Monday through Thursday are lower than for those taught at weekends. And while we cannot speak of any unjustified pay gap in case of overtime hours, it is obvious that differences in earnings (in favour of men) do exist. It is also obvious that these differences are larger among senior researchers.

Our second focus of analysis relates to technical and engineering staff; the data obtained encompass 228 persons employed as technical and engineering staff and the information on their position, education, work time (full-time or part-time), seniority and monthly remuneration. 59.6% (136 persons) were

Table 3.6 Additional components of remuneration for grades I–V

Position (group)	Gender	Number of persons	University allowance (average) PLN	Difference in %
I, II, III, IV Senior researchers	M	39	1,594	F 6.3% less
	F	19	1,495	
V Doctors (adjuncts)	M	15	429	F 10% less
	F	26	388	

females and 40.4% (92 persons) were males. A vast majority – 88.2% (201 persons) – of the workers were employed full-time.

The analysis reveals the existence of a marginal GPG in favour of men. The gap is generally less than 3%, and in case of employees with a doctoral degree is even less than 1%. Moreover, in case of employees with a master's degree and in the case of employees working part-time, the data reveal the existence of a GPG in favour of women. Therefore, a general conclusion may be drawn that a GPG among persons employed in the university as technical and engineering staff does not constitute a significant problem. In this case study, the number of cases examined does not make it possible to determine the GPG, especially since a researcher's salary depends on his or her employment record (e.g. on the date when they earned their degree). On the other hand, it cannot pass unnoticed that where base salary is concerned, the higher the position, the larger the difference. It is nevertheless difficult to determine whether this is a steady trend.

First and foremost, attention should be drawn to the fact that a considerably smaller number of females than males occupy the highest positions. While there is a significantly higher proportion of females earning a doctoral degree and a marginal difference between the number of females and males earning a habilitation degree, only one female – as opposed to eight males – is employed as a

Table 3.7 Pay structure and gender pay data of technical and engineering staff (full-time workers)

Education level	No. of females	No. of males	Monthly average female salary (PLN)	Monthly average male salary (PLN)	F as % of M salary	GPG (%)
All workers	121	80	2,284	2,350	97.2	2.8
Doctor's degree	23	15	2,449	2,463	99.4	0.6
Master's degree	74	38	2,273	2,248	101.1	–1.1
Secondary education	23	21	2,311	2,363	97.8	2.2

Table 3.8 Pay structure and gender pay data of technical and engineering staff (part-time workers)

	No. of females	No. of males	Monthly average female salary (PLN)	Monthly average male salary (PLN)	F as % of M salary	GPG (%)
0.5 FTE	11	9	1,060	1,008	105.2	−5.2

full professor. The largest disparities can be observed in cases where a position depends on the university's authorities, i.e. in case of associate professor and full professor positions. However, what we are dealing with in this case appears to have more to do with 'sticky floor' rather than the GPG (for similar findings see Lisowska, 2013).[14] It should be mentioned that the professorial nomination by the president of the Republic of Poland does not automatically entail promotion to the position of full professor. A candidate should meet requirements stipulated in the statute of the university, in particular he or she should create or develop a school of science or art recognised outside the university. Promotion to the position of full professor is undertaken by the university rector after recommendation of faculty and university commissions. Usually, it takes at least five years until a professor receives the highest post at the university. In practice women have less time than men to obtain such a post before retirement, because women are awarded by the president in their later age.

Finally, the technical and engineering staff was also itemised above. Since there is just one person working as a senior technician at the faculty, in the forensic laboratory, the university HR department provided data relating to all employees of this category. The comparison of their posts, seniority and salaries proved the existence of a marginal GPG. Undoubtedly the main reason for a small, or even the lack of, GPG in this group arises from very low salaries.

Conclusions

The results of the Polish case studies confirmed that there is a great need to raise the awareness on the GPG. Characteristically, both the social partners and representatives of legal entities involved in the research claimed initially that gender has no impact on the creation and existence of the differences in wages. However, the project proved that it is not only possible, but it is a reality. It confirmed that a lower remuneration of women is 'a universally known phenomenon' and a sociological factor in businesses, which is a 'surprise with their universalism' (Domański, 1992). Moreover, the case studies revealed that the GPG is lower in the public sector than in the private sector, which confirms that less discretion in relation to pay[15] results in less differences in remuneration between women and men.

It was also confirmed that there are several factors resulting in the differentiation of wages between women and men: gender pay discrimination arises from stereotypes about the role of women in family and society. Another

reason is the lack of mechanisms, which could balance negative impact of cultural bias, promote partnership in family and control respecting the principle of
equal treatment in the labour market and society (see also Lisowska, 2012). The
difficulties in obtaining the data on remuneration demonstrated that an important
obstacle in analysing the GPG phenomenon is the deficiency in transparency in
pay. It seems to be good practice to introduce legal requirements for employers
to publish reports on gender pay equality as recently introduced for large
organisations in the UK (see Chapters 4 and 5). Unquestionably, the practice of
using secrecy clauses in relation to pay makes it difficult, if not impossible, to
prove the discriminatory practices.

It may be concluded that all the statistics indicating the relatively low GPG in
Poland show only one side of the issue. The problem is much deeper. The low
GPG does not arise from equal remuneration, but rather from low remuneration. It is impossible to earn less, regardless of gender. A lot of people get the
same minimum wage. Another regularity is the fact that the higher the job
position, the greater wage differences are identified. However, this regularity is
related to the relatively low number of women holding top positions. The result
is that gender-induced differences in wages amongst the highest earners do not
significantly increase the gap in general. Finally, the top positions are usually
connected with a greater availability at work and additional obligations, so
women, being aware of their family responsibilities, avoid or resign from
promotion. In fact, the situation resembles a vicious circle.

Notes

1 For further information see Chapter 6.
2 The general principles of equality and non-discrimination are established in the
  Polish Constitution but also specific regulations relating to employment are included
  in Polish labour law. For further information see Chapter 1.
3 Act of 26th June 1974 Labour Code, Journal of Laws of 1998, No. 21, item 94 as
  amended.
4 On the tasks of the labour inspectorates see: Act of 13th April 2007 on National
  Labour Inspectorate, Journal of Laws of 2007, No. 89, item 589 as amended.
5 See: Act of 13th March 2003 on special rules for terminating employment for reasons
  not attributable to employees, Journal of Laws of 2003, No. 90, item 844.
6 Accordingly with the Act of 12th December 1997 on additional annual salary for the
  employees of budgetary sphere, Journal of Laws of 2016, item 2217, consolidated
  text.
7 Act of 26th January 1982, Journal of Laws of 1982, No. 3, item 19.
8 Order of the Council of Ministers of 30th December 1981 respecting the special
  entitlements of underground mineworkers, Journal of Laws of 1982, No. 2, item 13.
9 Order of the Council of Ministers of 7th December 1981, unpublished.
10 Until recently the employment of women, e.g. in the mining industry, was limited
   due to the provision of article 176 of LC, which prohibited their employment in
   certain professions considered to be particularly onerous or harmful for women's
   health. This norm was declared by the European Commission incompatible with the
   principle of equal treatment. Now, the restrictions on particular types of employment exist only with regard to pregnant women or nursing mothers. See Regulation
   of the Council of Ministers of 19 April 2017 enumerating the professions considered

to be particularly onerous or harmful for health of pregnant women or nursing mothers, Journal of Laws of 2017, item 796.

11 PKD is established by the Regulation of the Council of Ministers of 24th December 2007 on the Polish Classification of Activities, Journal of Laws of 2007, No. 251, item 1885.

12 Journal of Laws 2015, item 1145.

13 This term requires a further explanation. The jubilee award is a special long-term employee bonus provided for some professions (such as teachers, academics, miners). It is usually paid for the first time after a certain period of employment (10, 15 or 20 years) and thereafter every five years. The level of the jubilee award depends on the length of employment and is between 75 and 400% of a basic salary.

14 Lisowska noted that 'the hindered access of women to the higher and top managerial positions still poses the problem to be solved – among the general directors and company presidents, women are an exception' (2014, p. 21).

15 Negotiations on remuneration in the public sector are limited. For more information see Chapter 1.

References

Central Statistical Office of Poland, Information of 13 July 2015: 'Trade Unions in Poland in 2014'.

Domański, H. (1992) *Zadowolony niewolnik? Studium o nierównościach między mężczyznami i kobietami w Polsce* [*A Happy Slave? The Study of Inequalities between Men and Women in Poland*]. Warsaw: Institute of Philosophy and Sociology, Polish Academy of Sciences.

Grotkowska, G. and Wincenciak, L. (2014) 'Public Sector Wage Premium in Poland: Can It be Explained by Structural Differences in Employment?' *Ekonomia* 38, pp. 47–72.

Lisowska, E. (2012) 'Wynagrodzenie a płeć' [Remuneration and Gender] in E. Lisowska (ed.), *Polityka różnorodności w administracji centralnej* [*Diversity Policy in Central Administration*]. Warsaw: Warsaw School of Economics, pp. 101–118.

Lisowska, E. (2013) 'Gender Diversity in the Workplace' *SMEE Review*, pp. 19–23.

4 Decentralisation and the gender pay gap in the UK context

Case studies

Hazel Conley, Geraldine Healy, Pedro Martins and Stella Warren

Introduction

This chapter considers the UK case from the perspective of local government, financial services sector and rail (infrastructure) sector. Following the aims of the 'Close the Deal, Fill the Gap' project, this UK-focused chapter considers the interaction and interdependences between different EU policy targets and considers the involvement of the social partners in the reduction of the GPG and the high level of decentralisation in the UK collective bargaining context.

As discussed in Chapter 1, collective agreements in the UK are not of themselves legally binding (**Trade Union and Labour Relations (Consolidation) Act 1992 s.179**). However, the terms of the collective agreement may be inserted into contracts of employment which do have the force of law. Where this happens, the terms of the agreement will be applied to all workers in the bargaining unit covered by the collective agreement and not just trade union members. Collective bargaining may be written, unwritten, formal or informal. Its origins and definitions go back to the Webbs (1897), who used the term to describe the process of agreeing terms and conditions of employment through representatives of employers and their associations and representatives of employees and their unions. Collective bargaining in the UK may be multi-employer (similar to industry-wide bargaining), single employer bargaining, enterprise bargaining or two-tier bargaining. With the collapse of the old union 'heartland', i.e. mining and manufacturing, collective bargaining coverage significantly declined. In 1984, 95% of public sector workers and 52% of private sector workers were covered by collective bargaining (Towers, 1997: 75) and union density was over 50% with 13 million members in 1979. Moreover, the union heartland was predominantly white and male.

The 2016 Trade Union Membership Statistical Bulletin (DBEIS, 2017) revealed a very different picture. Some 6.2 million employees in the UK were trade union members in 2016. The level of overall union members decreased by 275,000 over the year from 2015 (a 4.2% decrease), the largest annual fall recorded since the series began in 1995. Alongside the fall in trade union membership levels, there was an increase in the number of UK employees between 2015 and 2016. As a result, the proportion of employees who were trade union members fell to 23.5% in 2016, from 24.7% in 2015. This is the lowest rate of trade union membership recorded since 1995. Over this period, the proportion of employees who were trade union members in the UK has decreased 8.9 percentage points, from 32.4% in 1995. Female employees are more likely to be a trade union member. The proportion of female employees who were in a trade union was around 25.9% in 2016, compared with 21.1% for male employees. Union membership levels in the private sector were around 2.6 million, a reduction of 66,000 since 2015. The proportion of trade union members amongst private sector employees fell slightly from 13.9% to 13.4%, reflecting overall employment growth and the decline in union membership. The yearly changes were not statistically significant. Trade union density in the public sector fell from 54.9% to 52.7% in 2016. The changes were statistically significant. The statistics for collective bargaining coverage indicate that 14.9% of private sector employees had their terms and conditions determined by collective agreement in contrast to 59.9% in the public sector. Thus the UK has a complex structure of collective bargaining.

With this national context in mind, the first challenge we faced was to determine which cases we should investigate. We were very aware that the GPG context in the UK is hugely heterogeneous, with the GPG very occasionally demonstrating a negative figure at one end of the spectrum and up to 60% at the other end. The mean GPG in the UK has tended to stubbornly sit at around 19% for some years. This effectively means that for every £100 earned by men, women earn only £81. Put another way, compared to men, women effectively worked for nothing from around 10 November 2016 to the start of 2017.

We worked closely with our social partners, the TUC, to decide which sector we should investigate in greater depth and these discussions led the final choice of our case studies. We selected three cases which represented the sector with the highest GPG (financial services), a national collective agreement that led to an unprecedented number of equal pay legal cases (local government) and a single employer/union initiative to address the GPG (rail sector). Our case studies therefore include a mix of private and public sector employers.

Case Study 1: local government

This case study examines a national collective agreement, the Single Status Agreement (SSA) in UK local government that has had the greatest influence on the equal pay legislation and potential impact on the GPG. The SSA resulted in tens of thousands of legal cases and, following a change in EU law, an estimated £3 billion in compensation to women workers in local government. The SSA had a profound impact on the legal processes in the UK, testing the Equal Pay Act 1970 (and its amendments) to its limits, establishing some groundbreaking case law that has important implications for the legal system, employers and trade unions.

Local government in the UK is the second tier of public administration, which is regionally based. There are 353 local authorities in England, 32 in

Scotland, 22 in Wales and 26 in Northern Ireland. Local authority workforces exhibit pronounced gender segregation. Care services and education services dominate local government employment and are largely carried out by women who make up 76% of local government employees, whilst environmental services and town planning are largely carried out by men.

Local government has been the target of government attempts to reduce public spending since the 1980s. Following the global financial crisis there have been large cuts (approximately 40%) to local authority budgets as part of the aus- terity measures, which have resulted in extensive job losses. In September 2015 there were 2.257 million workers employed in UK local government, the lowest number since 1999 when the series reporting these statistics began (ONS, 2015). Despite this, local government still accounts for the largest number of public sector workers in the UK (Bach and Strolney, 2014).

This case study consists of analysis of primary and secondary data sources. The secondary data sources comprise of the collective agreement document (the 'Green Book'), local government employers' reports and guidance, trade union reports, legal case reports and existing research. Data from these sources are used to provide the context to the case study and to build up a chronological analysis of the main events in relation to the development and implementation of the SSA. The primary data sources consist of interviews with the lead employer negotiator and one of the trade union negotiators who reflect on the main issues raised by the SSA.

The Single Status Agreement

The SSA was a ground-breaking national agreement signed in 1997 for England and Wales,[1] having taken two years to negotiate (see Figure 4.1 for a full timeline). It was preceded in 1994 by an agreement between the three main unions (Unison, GMB and then the T&GWU[2]) to multi-union/single table bargaining. The SSA is an 'enabling' or 'framework' agreement and, although it was signed nationally by representatives for the employers and the three trade unions, the actual implementation was carried out voluntarily between indivi- dual local authorities and local 'lay' trade union representatives from each of the unions. The agreement document has been amended/updated six times since 1997 and is 289 pages in length. Like all collective agreements in the UK, it is not itself legally binding, but any changes to terms and conditions made under the agreement will be entered into individual employment contracts, which are legally binding.

The aim of the SSA was to harmonise the terms and conditions of manual and allied professional, technical and clerical (APT&C) workers in local gov- ernment, who were previously employed on a wide array of formal and informal arrangements, and to merge the national negotiating structures to accommodate this. Although the main aim of the SSA was to introduce a single national pay spine for all workers in local government, it is interesting to note that closing the GPG or attaining equal pay is not specifically referred to in the agreement document, although there are extensive provisions for ensuring that all outcomes of local implementation should be 'equality proofed'.

The implementation of the SSA required local authorities to introduce a national pay spine into which all of their current jobs should be assimilated using a job evaluation scheme. Although there is flexibility in the SSA in relation to the choice of job evaluation scheme and how jobs should be assimilated, the scheme has to be free of gender bias, which requires detailed factor based analysis on a number of factors for each job role. Wright (2011) argues that the choice of job evaluation scheme significantly influenced the gendered outcomes of pay assimilation in local government. However, it was quite clear that once a single pay spine, single table collective bargaining and job evaluation was under way, the extent of pay inequality, particularly in relation to bonus schemes, became apparent:

> local authorities ... immediately ran into issues of bonuses and historic arrangements that they'd had and actually, for the first time, had to face some of those questions. Because whereas those arrangements had sat in separate bargaining groups that employers argued didn't really cross to each other – rightly or wrongly, that's what they argued – and now they have no choice but to say: 'Well of course they do really cross and we've got to ensure equality.'
>
> (GMB national lead negotiator)

The most problematic element of the SSA was that it was unfunded by central government and therefore local government employers argued that its implementation should be cost-neutral. In practice this meant that any increases in pay that resulted from job evaluation, largely in relation to GPGs, should be counter-balanced by pay decreases elsewhere. This policy, of course, ran counter to the expectations of the trade unions and instead of the hoped for levelling up of low-paid workers, all three trade unions have been engaged in protracted negotiations around pay protection for down-graded workers:

> both sides agreed to disagree and we sent out conflicting messages. Employers sending out messages saying we've told the unions it's cost-neutral and the unions sending out messages saying it cannot be cost-neutral. So fundamental when you are harmonising sets of terms and conditions, leading into job evaluation, equal pay and so on ... How do you do these things on a cost-neutral basis? You have winners and losers and problems and problems.
>
> (GMB national lead negotiator)

The circumstances surrounding the SSA meant that its implementation in local authorities was extremely slow. In the first years of the SSA very few authorities reached local agreements on its implementation (Oliver *et al.*, 2014; Deakin *et al.*, 2015). The realisation that early attempts at job evaluation were uncovering extensive gendered pay inequality deterred most authorities from even starting the process. Progress was so slow that a second implementation agreement was signed in 2004 which placed a time limit on completion of the SSA for April 2007. Despite this, by 2006 only 30% of local authorities had implemented the agreement (Godwin, 2006) and less than half by 2009 (Oliver et al., 2014).

Two ECJ rulings in 1998 (*Magorrian and Cunningham* v *Eastern Health and Social Services Board and Department of Health and Social Services C-246/96* and *B.S. Levez* v *T.H. Jennings (Harlow Pools) Ltd C-326/96*) (effective 2000 in the UK) meant that compensation in successful equal pay cases could be backdated for six rather than two years. This considerably increased the costs of settling equal pay cases. The possibility that women working in local government might be entitled to substantial sums of compensation, coupled with a relaxation on the regulations in relation to contingent law services in the UK (Deakin et al., 2015) meant that local authorities who were undertaking job evaluation to implement the SSA became a target for 'no win, no fee' lawyers. One such solicitor, Stefan Cross, became particularly active in these cases. Indeed a number of cases taken against Cumbria County Council were taken by Stefan Cross and further cases in English local authorities Leeds, Sheffield, Rotherham, Kirklees and several Scottish local authorities (Godwin, 2006).

In addition to taking cases on behalf of individual women, Cross also began to instigate legal cases challenging negotiated settlements between local authorities and women who were entitled to backdated payments. In a number of local authorities negotiated settlements had involved quicker but reduced amounts of back pay than if the women involved had proceeded with legal cases. Cross launched a series of cases, not against employers but against third parties such as the Advisory, Conciliation and Arbitration Service (ACAS) and the trade unions who had advised women to take reduced compensation amounts. The initial cases failed but one case against the GMB, the Allen case (*Allen and others* v *GMB [2008] EWCA Civ 810*), succeeded.

The success of the *Allen* case had a number of repercussions for the trade unions and the SSA. First, the trade unions feared that the *Allen* case might result in a large number of similar claims that would have severe financial implications for the trade unions. Second, it meant that trade unions were reluctant to enter into any negotiated agreements with local authority employers that involved reductions in back pay.

> That case [*Allen*] caused a lot of problems because it inhibited the ability to resolve some of these things through local collective agreements, because all of a sudden the unions panicked about potentially doing deals that could be unpicked, as they were in that particular case. So that was one, from the time I've been involved in it, that was one that's been particularly problematic.
>
> (LGA, Head of Employment)

Third, when employers would not reach agreement, it meant that the trade unions, faced with competition from non-win-no-fee lawyers, were pushed into taking further and numerous equal pay cases. The number of equal pay cases outstanding at English tribunals peaked in excess of 60,000 in 2008 (Deakin *et al.*, 2015). In a later case, *Nichols* v *Coventry City Council*, the EAT found that employers and not trade unions are liable for equal pay, which reduced the legal pressure on trade unions. Financial pressure was reduced when central government relaxed regulations allowing local authorities to raise extra funds to meet back pay entitlements. Initially the amount that local authorities could capitalise (borrow to raise further funding) to meet back payments was limited to £200 million (LGE, 2006), which was increased to £500 million in 2007.

The impact of the SSA on the GPG in local government

There were different views between the employer and trade union representatives on whether the SSA had resulted in equal pay in local government. The employers' representative felt that, following the SSA, the GPG in local government stood at around 5%, much lower than the UK or European average.

> I think [local government] deserves a huge amount of credit because we've managed to largely deal with equal pay and we've got a much smaller gender pay gap in local government than we have in many of the bits of the public sector in the UK and we did it without any money bailing us out from central government.
>
> (LGA, Head of Employment)

The trade union representative, on the other hand, felt that the SSA had not resulted in ongoing equal pay or reduced the GPG but had simply in the end been about compensation payments for the majority of the women trade union members concerned:

> the net gains for women weren't particularly great. Lots and lots of compensation payments, but not much in the way of better pay. Instead, men's pay was reduced.
>
> (GMB lead national negotiator)

Certainly the cost in terms of compensation alone is estimated to be in the region of £5–6 billion by the employer representative.

The employer representative felt that, although hugely problematic, the use of the Equal Pay Act and case law had eventually acted as a stimulus to the completion of the SSA:

> But I think the thing that's really acted as a stimulus to getting equal pay sorted is two-fold. One is councils seeing what was happening in other

councils and seeing costs potentially spiralling out of control ... The second was, linked to that, was the legal developments.

(LGA, Head of Employment)

And particularly the actions of the 'no win, no fee' lawyers:

So, you know, love him or loathe him, you do have to say that Stefan Cross acted as an impetus to equal pay and getting Single Status sorted out in local government.

(LGA, Head of Employment)

The employers' representative interestingly highlighted how the legislation on its own had failed to ensure equal pay in local government. The combination of the law and collective agreement had been problematic and adversarial but it had moved the debate on:

it's reminded everybody that we do predominantly employ a female part-time workforce, many of whom are not particularly well paid, but all of whom do important work ... I think it's made ... particularly elected members, but also other people who work in councils, realise the value of the work that all of their workforce do.

(LGA, Head of Employment)

There was a shared feeling between the employers' representative and the trade union representative that the SSA had not been treated advantageously as a similar agreement in the NHS had. First, the equal pay outcomes in the NHS agreement had been funded. Second, there had been a more centralised approach to the use of job evaluation and pay and grading. Third, where litigation had arisen, cases were heard by the same Employment Tribunal and the trade union representative felt that this had resulted in more uniform rulings and outcomes. Finally, there was a shared view that the need for vigilance and continued monitoring of pay and grading was essential if pay inequality was not to creep back in.

The LGA analysed the submissions of local authorities to the Gender Pay Gap Reporting Regulations that came into force in April 2017 (LGA, 2018). A total of 319 English authorities reported their GPG with the remainder falling below the 250-employee threshold. Supporting the estimates of the LGA Head of Employment, the average median GPG is 5% (6.8% mean). However, the concerns of the trade union SSA lead negotiator were not unfounded as there was a huge variation between local authorities, with the lowest mean GPG in negative figures at -14.1% (women earning more than men) to a high of 31.7%. Therefore, despite the SSA, women are still, on average, paid less than men in 67% of the local authorities who reported.

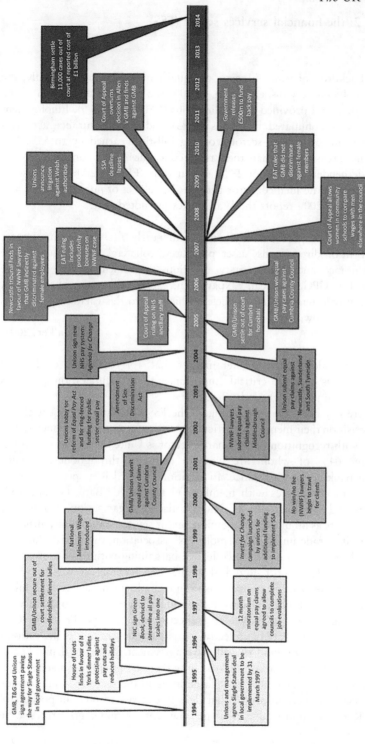

Figure 4.1 Single Status Agreement (SSA) timeline

Case Study 2: the financial services sector (FSS)

FSS context

Against the backdrop of some 40 years of equal pay legislation in the UK, the context for the FSS is very disheartening. In 2008 the sector employed 4% of the British workforce and provided 1.3 million jobs (EHRC, 2009: 9). Employment in the industry is dominated by banks (43%) and other insurance activities (21%). Women in the finance sector working full-time earned up to 55% less annual average gross salary than their male colleagues. This compared to the economy-wide gender pay gap of 28% at that time (EHRC, 2009). Because of the economic crisis, the finance sector became the subject of public scrutiny and concern. In its July 2009 report the Walker Review noted that:

> The taxpayer has provided UK banks with nearly £1.3 trillion in support in the form of direct loans, asset purchases, collateral swaps, guarantees, asset insurance and direct equity injections, equivalent overall to some 90% of UK GPG. Political, taxpayer and social tolerance of practices, including unsafe remuneration policies, which led to this calamitous state, is understandably low.
>
> (Walker, 2009)

The EHRC responded to the Walker Inquiry that, for reasons of equity and public policy, it is also of critical importance that remuneration practices should not discriminate on grounds of sex.

Unions were key actors in responding to the FSS GPG and dealing with the effect of the crisis on their members, particularly with respect to redundancies. The major union with recognition in the finance sector is Unite the Union which has 130,000 (some 64% of whom are women) members throughout all major employers in banking and insurance. In addition, Accord is a specialist union for staff in financial services with members in the Lloyds Bank Group, TSB, Equitable Life and Sainsbury's Bank. There is also an organisation, Alliance for Finance, which acts as an umbrella organisation for several staff unions, although it is not in itself a trade union. The employers' association, the British Bankers' Association, does not participate in collective bargaining within the sector.

A 2011 EurWORK report found that the UK banking sector has been adversely affected by the economic crisis and employment levels had fallen (Prosser, 2011). It noted that collective bargaining is decentralised to the level of the firm and there are no sector-level collective agreements. Prosser (2011) reported that the sector's rate of collective bargaining coverage (i.e. the ratio of employees covered by any kind of collective agreement to the total number of employees in the sector) is, according to Unite the Union, approximately 20%. Trade union density is 25% and most large firms in the sector recognise trade unions, although we were informed that density can rise to 60% in pockets of the sector. Rates of industrial action are low, for example, no strikes were reported from 2006 to 2008. The sector's most important four collective agreements in terms of the number of employees covered are all with large firms and operate at the national level, i.e. Unite and Barclays Bank; Unite and Lloyds Banking Group; Unite and Royal Bank of Scotland; and Unite and HSBC (Prosser, 2011).

The effect of the recession on pay and pay cuts has been variable in the UK context. In the private sector, freezes or cuts were most likely to be experienced by employees in the construction industry (43%) while those in electricity, gas and water and, importantly for this case study, financial services, were less likely to be affected (both 14%). Interestingly, the impact of the presence of a recognised union was twice as large in the private sector as it was in the public sector (an eight-percentage-point reduction in the likelihood of reporting a wage freeze or cut, compared to a four-percentage-point reduction in the public sector) (Wanrooy *et al.*, 2013: 93). The sixth Workplace Employment Relations Survey (WERS6) also considered the use of employee incentive schemes, i.e. payment by results (PBR), merit pay, profit related pay (PRP), and share schemes. Some 40% of workplaces use such schemes (Wanrooy *et al.*, 2013: 96) and their use remained fairly steady between 2004 and 2011 in the private sector, which is more likely to use such incentive schemes than the public sector. The FSS was among those experiencing the greatest decline in the use of share plans (alongside electricity, gas and water). However, with respect to PRP, some 65% of the employees were in receipt of PRP compared to only 4% in education and 7% of public sector employees.

FSS culture

The culture of the FSS is an important explanatory factor of gender segregation and the pay gap of the sector. It has been widely recognised in the press and the academic literature that the culture in the FSS leads to women being treated, not only less favourably, but also with little respect. Özbilgin and Woodward (2004) found in their comparative study of Turkey and the UK that despite local and cross-cultural differences, the cumulative disadvantage suffered by women seeking career development in the industry was remarkably similar (Özbilgin and Woodward, 2004). McDowell followed up her earlier work on the gendered nature of work in the FSS in the immediate post-crisis period and found:

> Exaggerated forms of masculinized language and behaviour are still commonplace. Horseplay, sexualized banter, loud and aggressive talk, as well as forms of sexual harassment are tolerated and women are often forced either into the position of unwilling arbiters of boundaries or less than willing participants in the sexualized banter. Social exchanges are still commonly set in masculinized arenas, including in golf clubs or hospitality suites at major football clubs as well as the lap dancing clubs.
>
> (McDowell, 2010: 653)

The discriminatory culture is further supported in Roy Davies's compilation of articles documenting some of the appalling treatment experienced by women in the FSS (Davies, 2015). The FSS culture therefore is characterised by the interrelationship between jobs, bodies and hierarchies (Acker, 1990) to the detriment of women.

The FSS culture and its GPG led the EHRC to use its unique power to investigate inequality within the FSS by setting up an Inquiry[3] to examine the extent of the GPG, the causes and potential solutions. Thus, early in 2009, the EHRC initiated the Financial Services Inquiry under Section 16 of the Equality Act 2006 into sex discrimination and unequal pay in the FSS.[4] The Inquiry was published in 2009 and, significantly, a follow-up report was published in 2011 (EHRC, 2011). The Inquiry revealed horizontal and vertical segregation with women's high concentration in administrative and secretarial jobs and their substantial underrepresentation in higher-paid managerial jobs, including at the most senior level. Other challenges to increasing the proportion of women in higher-paid occupations identified by the EHRC included: the long working hours, which is a particular feature of City firms; the more general lack of opportunities to work flexibly; a perception that the workplace culture is more amenable to men; and the effects of unwritten assumptions about 'whose face fits' – meaning that women often find themselves assigned to less prestigious roles and business divisions. The EHRC (2011) also reported examples of good practice, but noted that progress was slow.

The wider issue of legislation to enforce transparency of pay in the UK is the subject of Chapter 6. The mantra of transparency became evident in the FSS following the EHRC 2009 Inquiry. It was reinforced in 2010 following the Treasury Select Committee on 'Women in the City', in its examination of sex discrimination in the FSS, which also concluded that transparency and public scrutiny are important ways to ensure that discrimination does not persist (HM Treasury, 2010). It recommended that boards should put in place effective processes to ensure both visibility of the GPG and transparency of pay determination with the aim of closing the GPG.

It is noteworthy that further surveys by Astbury Marsden (2014/2015) and the growth of crowd-sourced data (Emolument, n.d.) also contributed to increasing transparency, although somewhat arbitrarily. Thus awareness of the pay gap is not only created by unions but also by consultants, who may find that representing high paid workers in the FSS is a lucrative business. One consultant, Equal Pay Legal, stated that 'there is clear evidence that equal pay claims in the financial sector can be very valuable' (Equal Pay Legal, n.d.). Equal Pay Legal (EPL) was founded with one goal in mind, 'to put an end to unfair pay based on gender'.[5] Nevertheless, it is only those who are already well paid who are likely to be able to pay lawyers/consultants to access justice although this is mediated by the 'no win, no fee' consultants/lawyers such as EPL (see above for role of 'no win, no fee' lawyers in local government). Unionised workers may rely on their unions (notwithstanding the low union density and the complicated route to access equal pay justice through the courts) but for the less well-off not in unions, justice may remain inaccessible (see Chapter 1).

Data analysis and findings

This section, informed by quantitative analysis, draws data from the Quarterly Labour Force Survey (LFS) for the period 2003Q1 to 2015Q3[6] and interviews with union negotiators provides a brief insight into the nature of the GPG in the FSS. For a more detailed analysis see Healy and Ahamed (2018).

Despite the transparency imposed on the employer and the efforts by unions, it is the case that the GPG in the FSS is resilient, particularly when compared with the GPG across the economy. We find that there continues to be a huge difference between gender pay differences in the whole economy (just £3) and the FSS (see Figure 4.2) where it is almost £10 in finance sector – emphasising the need for a detailed analysis on the factors that contribute to the pay differentials.

Figure 4.3 shows that at the lower pay grades, the GPG is small, in contrast to the top three occupations, namely Associate Professional and Technical, Professional, and Managers and Senior Officials. Thus as women become more successful, they are more likely to suffer an increasing GPG.

Of particular interest to social partners campaigning for a reduction of the GPG is our analysis of the average hourly wage by age in the FSS as shown in Figure 4.4. It is evident that the pay gap begins very early, and well before the years when many women will consider having children. This is particularly important as studies suggest that it is often the arrival of children that cause the GPG (Institute of Fiscal Studies, 2016); our study indicates this may not be the case. Rather the findings suggest that it is the potential of women's

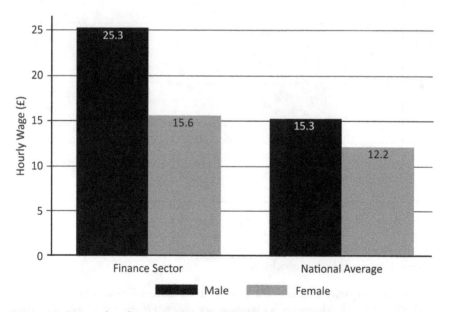

Figure 4.2 Average hourly wage: national v FSS 2015
Source: Quarterly Labour Force Survey (LFS) for the period 2003Q1 to 2015Q3.

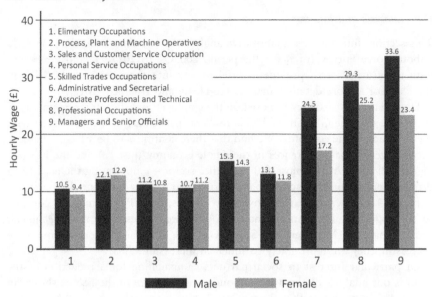

Figure 4.3 Average hourly wage in the finance sector by major occupation 2015

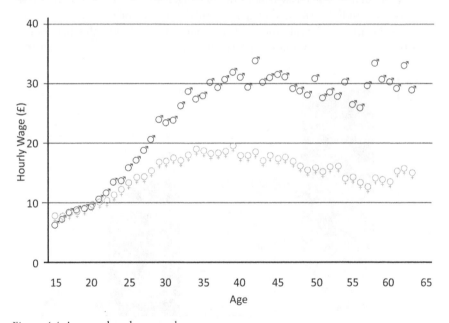

Figure 4.4 Average hourly wages by age

reproductive capacity that is at the heart of their unequal treatment, rather than motherhood itself. Moreover as women get older, Figure 4.4 shows that they tend to get lower wages compared to men of the same age. Women are effectively underpaid throughout their working lives from first job to retirement.

What makes a difference?

In the case of the FSS, the EHRC Inquiry does not seem to have made a huge difference to the GPG although the Inquiry no doubt found itself competing with the fall-out of the financial crisis. However, the Inquiry does seem to have led to greater attention to the GPG, to greater use of gender audits and greater sharing of GPG information with the unions. These are all important steps forward. However, we do not notice a major reduction in the degree of horizontal or vertical segregation with women still more likely to be located at the lower levels of the organisation, where admittedly the GPG is low within these grades. This alerts us to the fact that while the GPG is one important indicator, alone it is not sufficient – it is the level of pay that will make most difference to people's daily lives. Thus both low pay and the GPG (which is greater at the higher pay levels) matter.

Our study does indicate a number of conditions that, when present, may lead to a reduced GPG. Our findings for the period in question indicate that being a union member may reduce the GPG by 2%. Moreover, when pay and conditions are affected by a union agreement through collective bargaining, the GPG may be further reduced by 5%. Interviews with social partners indicated that the GPG had certainly risen in importance with more union–management discussions taking place. These may be the result of the unions' push for equal pay audits, which expose the complex nature of the GPG. Agreement to undertake equal pay audits has been included in some collective agreements:

> Those collective bargaining agreements give us the ability to negotiate on all aspects of pay, terms and conditions, but also it's been our opportunity to push for these organisations to carry out equal pay audits and also the steps that they themselves are obviously now legally required to do which is to address the issue of the gender pay gap.
>
> (Union official)

Importantly, unions have pushed to ensure that the GPG is calculated beyond the base salary to also include incentives and bonuses, i.e. the overall sum paid. However, the significance of horizontal segregation confined the GPG within grades, for example, we were told that some banks now share basic pay plus bonus data with unions, with the result that:

> Women in the lower grades did tend to do slightly better in terms of the bonus that they got and the performance ratings they got than men on average in those grades.
>
> (Union official)

So that:

> [Banks] have now accepted that they need to look at total cash because obviously total cash includes incentives and bonuses and that's really in the

finance industry where you see greatest disparity on gender. Because at the lower levels the bonus structures are fairly well, are fairly regimented and fairly limited. But obviously if you still have at the very high grades in these institutions considerable bonus opportunities and again those are skewed more towards men than they are to women so that compounds the pay gap for them.

(Union official)

The above response points to the importance of ensuring that there is a between-grade analysis in order to fully understand the nature of the GPG in the FSS. Greater movement between grades is one of the key challenges and means to dent the GPG and contest a resilient gender segregation. Our interviews also demonstrate an increasing transparency between some of the social partners. Transparency is, therefore, not new to social partners; what remains key is the ability of the FSS to recruit and retain women to the middle and senior levels of the hierarchy. Moreover, unions have also been involved in negotiating other equality issues; a good example is the close involvement of unions in the negotiating of a better than the statutory minimum parental leave agreement.

The FSS is a particularly interesting case as it captures the tensions, challenges and opportunities facing a highly successful sector with one of largest GPGs in the UK. The case is important as it provides insight into the gendered culture of the FSS, the relevance of unions and collective bargaining, the EHRC Inquiry and more recent approaches that seek to make pay more transparent, whether by formal regulation, collective bargaining or by informal crowd-sourcing.

It is clear that the FSS has a substantial way to go in improving its GPG. The study does reveal the importance of unions in sustaining fair pay so that trade union membership and collective bargaining are shown to reduce the GPG. We conclude that while greater attention has been paid to equality and the GPG in the FSS, there is far to go. The FSS needs to confront its culture which affects how jobs are constructed, rewarded, allocated and opportunities made available, as well as the way that women are treated and mistreated.

In this brief outline, it is evident that there is no one way that is most effective in influencing and closing the gender pay gap. It is the case that a multiplicity of factors may come into play in the challenge to 'close the deal and fill the gap'. These factors include: legislation, social partners, collective bargaining, management strategy, management discretion in a decentralised context, individual negotiation, transparency and even crowd-sourced data, which all have the potential to play a part in the complex web that leads to a resilient GPG.

Under the gender pay gap reporting regulations, the financial services' average GPG was 26.2%; median pay gap 22.2%; and the average bonus gap was 45.9%. These figures concealed vast differences with for example, the Goldman Sachs pay gap is 55.5%, meaning women earn 44p for every £1 that their male colleagues earn. At JP Morgan Securities, women earn 47p for every £1 that men earn. The bonus gap across the sector averages 67% – for every £100,000 in bonuses given to men, women get £33,000.[7] Barclays Bank is acknowledged as having adopted positive gender strategies and yet women's mean bonus pay is 60.1% lower than men's and their mean hourly rate is 26% lower than men's.[8] Thus despite a high level of awareness of women's equality over a number of years, the entrenched nature of women's inequality persists, suggesting that transparency, while important, is not sufficient. The struggle for fairness and equity will continue and may be given a boost with the introduction of the UK 2018 GPG reporting regulations, although without the active engagement of the social partners to respond to the GPG revelations and state enforcement, the intention behind the GPG reporting law will not become a reality.

Case Study 3: the rail sector

This case study offers an example of a company level project to reduce gendered pay inequality, which was prompted by trade union action in relation to equal pay following a membership survey that identified areas of gendered pay inequality in the rail sector. The main employer in the rail sector is Network Rail (NR) which was, at the time of the research, a public corporation with no shareholders and limited by guarantee. In July 2015 NR employed over 35,500 staff (NAO, 2015). NR is responsible for the running, maintenance and development of the rail infrastructure (track, signals, overhead wires, crossings, tunnels and bridges) in the UK. NR also owns 2,500 stations and directly manages 18 of the busiest stations in the UK.

Collective bargaining in the rail sector takes place at the company level. Rail sector employers recognise three main unions: the RMT (largely non-driving train staff and station staff); ASLEF (train drivers) and the TSSA (white-collar and managerial staffs). This case study focuses on a campaign by the TSSA (Transport and Salaried Staff Association) in relation to equal pay followed by a partnership project with NR. The TSSA has approximately 20,000 members, not all of whom work in NR. In NR TSSA members are largely located within the higher pay bands 1–4. As a 'white collar' union the TSSA is less male dominated than the other rail sector unions but women still only make up approximately one-third of the membership.

The case study consists of analysis of primary and secondary data sources. The primary data sources consist of interviews with a national trade union officer, a lay union negotiator and the HR officer with responsibility for the project. The secondary sources include trade union publications, analysis of a trade union survey of members that prompted the union to identify and take 39 legal cases and company level statistics that were produced prior to the Fair and Transparent Pay Project.

The Fair and Transparent Pay Project

The Fair and Transparent Pay Project is the outcome of a pay dispute in 2011. Following the failure to agree on the proposed pay offer in 2011, the TSSA decided to launch a survey of its members to ascertain the strength of feeling in relation to the current pay offer, performance related pay and pay levels more generally. Approximately 1,200 members completed the survey. The analysis of the pay data revealed that, in some grades, there was a clear tendency for women to earn less than men. The union estimated that on average women were paid approximately £4,500 per year less than men for work within the same grade (membership communication, 4 January 2013). The survey also found that:

- Six out of ten female staff are in junior managerial positions in the salary range of £24,000 to £34,000, compared with only one in four male colleagues.
- Only one in three women make it into the £34,000 to £45,000 range, compared with six out of every ten men.
- And while one in six men are in middle managerial positions in the £45,000 to £55,000 range, only one in 40 women make it into the higher tax bracket league (union press release June 2011).

The union balloted for industrial action on equal pay in July 2011, but with a minority female workforce the ballot was unlikely to return in favour of industrial action. The union, therefore, devised a legal strategy. Once the key sites of potential pay inequality had been identified the union undertook a series of more detailed surveys on seven specific job titles, requesting information from male and female members within them. The union received over 200 responses and set about identifying potential equal pay cases and comparators from amongst the respondents. An initial group of 14 women were identified, at which point the union instructed its solicitors to begin the preliminaries for equal pay proceedings, at that time the issuing of statutory equal pay questionnaire and formal grievance procedures. Eventually 35 more cases (including two men as claimants) were identified and in March 2012 the first equal pay claims were submitted to an Employment Tribunal.

The union used the identification of pay cases to encourage NR to the negotiating table in relation to equal pay:

> We were using the pay cases to get the discussion. [The Assistant General Secretary at that time] said: 'We believe you've got an equal pay problem.' And they [NR] said: 'No, no, we haven't got an equal pay problem.'
>
> (TSSA, full-time officer)

As a result of this action, in July 2012 NR agreed to work jointly with the TSSA on a pay and grading review, the Fair and Transparent Pay Project, on the condition that the union did not actively seek further cases (membership communication, 2 July 2013). Interestingly, the Allen case in relation to the SSA in local government (see Case Study 1) influenced the union's behaviour in relation to negotiating equal pay cases with their members:

We committed to not harvesting any more, but we said up front, at the beginning ... because it's out there now, anyone who comes to us and says I want to raise a claim, we have to raise a claim. You can't say no, we've done a deal with the employer because of *Allen* v *GMB*. If they come to us of their own volition, we will respond, and we ended up with 39 claims in there.

(TSSA, full-time officer)

The pay review affected over 9,000 NR staff employed in pay bands 1–4 covering over 4,500 job titles. The joint working group consisted of ten people, five union-side and five employer-side, including the HR manager, the lay union negotiator and the union full-time officer interviewed for the case study. The details of the Fair and Transparent Pay Project were to include an existing job evaluation using the Hay job evaluation scheme coupled to a restructuring of the pay grades that would involve shorter pay and grading ranges and full transparency. The placing of jobs into the new pay structure was completed and agreed by a joint employer and trade union panel. The joint working party also devised a set of 'remuneration rules', which were designed to guide managers with responsibilities for setting and awarding pay levels for new entrants and pay increases for existing staff. One of the major concerns of both the union and HR at NR was that individualised pay setting within the organisation meant that there was no way of justifying pay differences between or within pay grades:

Anecdotally, I've had managers tell me stories of people in their teams who ... five people doing the same job, four of them paid within a similar amount and one paid significantly more for no apparent reason that the manager could determine; he'd inherited that team and I think there were pockets of consistency and pockets of difference all over the organisation, which was why Network Rail agreed to sit down with the TSSA and the *Fair and Transparent Pay Project* initially began from there in May 2012.

(HR manager, NR)

Much of the discrepancy resulted from wide pay bands and senior manager discretion in awarding pay on recruitment:

To a certain extent you could be placed in a role and although there would be benchmark guidelines but if you just shouted a bit louder and the manager really wanted you he could just give you £10,000 more or whatever.

(TSSA, lead negotiator)

The process was completed and agreed by the TSSA in principle in July 2014, but a membership referendum conducted in July 2015 rejected the pay structure (55% against). The main cause for concern came from those who would not benefit from the new system:

> Of course the people who worked above the pay scales and were going to
> have their pay frozen, they were upset, clearly.
>
> (TSSA, full-time officer)

Despite this the new pay structure was implemented in September 2015.
There is an appeals process, which had recently started and was jointly
chaired by the TSSA and NR. At the time of the research 800 appeals were
being heard.

The main areas of disagreement between the union and NR were how far the
new pay structure should be based on 'market forces', with the union favouring
a traditional pay spine structure and NR initially preferring a market-based
approach and a greater use of bonuses. However, it was noted by the HR
officer that the market-based approach had led to the historic anomalies
between pay rates, usually imported during the recruitment process. The HR
manager felt that the development of remuneration rules would help to ensure
consistency on what had previously been a rather ad hoc system:

> But, what we're now seeing is, along with this pay structure, we've actually
> bought in a formalised pay policy for this group, which is something that
> we didn't have previously. So whilst there were pockets of consistency,
> actually there was no way of knowing, for managers, how to appoint
> people, how to pay people on appointment, how to pay people when they
> moved. There was no consistent message saying – this is how you should
> do it.
>
> (HR manager, NR)

One of the areas that concerned the union was that there were still too
many small pay points in the structure, which would mean that it would
take a long time for employees to progress through the pay structure. This
could potentially be a gender-related issue, since women tend to have broken
service for care-related reasons to a greater extent than men. Another area
of potential concern is that the Fair and Transparent Pay Project only considered base pay and not PRP or bonuses, since our knowledge from previous
equal pay research and cases is that variable pay can be a major cause of
pay inequality. The HR manager felt that the pay for performance matrix,
which allocates annual pay awards, was one way in which pay disparities
could be reduced as more generous awards are made to those on the lower
salaries. The TSSA had done its own analysis of PRP payments and found
that patterns were not consistent but, if anything, the PRP system tended to
benefit women:

> It wasn't an absolute pattern, but there was ... you could see that there'd
> been a tendency from managers to award a higher performance pay to
> some women, because they were lower paid.
>
> (TSSA, full-time officer)

The impact of the Fair and Transparent Pay Project on the GPG in Network Rail

There was a feeling that the Fair and Transparent Pay Project had genuinely broken new ground in the industry. Not just in relation to progress on equal pay, but also in relation to joint working and joint problem solving between the union and NR:

> It totally changed the way that the organisation worked. Never, ever had we done that before. So in March 2014, [the union lay negotiator] and I delivered a joint presentation to the national management council, first time ever a joint presentation had been presented and it was great because … what was really good was the way that the questions were coming from both sides and we were both equally answering the questions.
> (HR manager, NR)

There was also the feeling that the project had opened the way for more detailed and nuanced work on what might lead to the GPG such as internal promotion processes and flexible working arrangements.

At the request of the TSSA, NR completed an equal pay audit both before and after the new pay scales in the Fair and Transparent Pay Project to be reviewed by an independent expert. The reviewer was Sue Hastings, the national expert on job evaluation and equal pay structures. The following tables (4.1 and 4.2) show the GPG for each pay band in 2014 before the implementation and then in 2015 following the implementation.

Prior to the implementation of the Fair and Transparent Pay Project there was a GPG larger than 5% in all but the highest pay band (1). Following the project the GPG is only larger than 5% in the bottom four pay bands. However, the overall GPG remains at 10%, a reduction of 1.6% on the previously reported gap. The agreement is that NR will continue to monitor the GPG on an annual basis and will provide the data to the TSSA. The feeling from both the HR manager and the trade union lead negotiator was that the smaller ranges within the pay bands and the remuneration rules for new recruits and promotions would work to stop greater inequality creeping back in. The union felt that greater transparency had also been achieved:

Table 4.1 Pay structure and gender pay data 2014

Band	No. of employees	Average pay (£)	Female average pay (£)	Male average pay (£)	Differential %	GPG %
1	271	101,992	99,825	102,367	97.5	2.5
2	1,123	73,030	69,845	73,674	94.8	5.2
3	3,164	52,272	49,215	53,048	92.8	7.2
4	4,553	39,276	36,148	40,214	89.9	10.1
Total	9,111	49,815	45,147	51,061	88.4	11.6

Table 4.2 Pay structure and gender pay data 2015

Pay range	Number female	Number male	Average salary (£) female	Average salary (£) male	F as % of M salary	GPG %
1C	16	78	117,242	115,121	102	+2
1B	15	94	100,890	99,556	101	+1
1A	12	40	86,818	87,751	99	1
2C	20	126	83,324	83,012	100	0
2B	136	579	71,280	74,776	95	5
2A	41	140	68,063	69,783	98	2
3C	182	1,171	54,989	56,728	97	3
3B	475	1,124	49,789	52,667	95	5
3A	26	60	46,542	50,759	92	8
4C	229	1,334	41,731	44,736	93	7
4B	792	1,782	36,618	39,248	93	7
4A	74	98	34,595	37,662	92	8
Total	2,018	6,626	46,868	52,329	90	10

We have supported it all of the way through because it is transparent and because the managers can't just pick arbitrary amounts to pay people when they come in or when they transfer internally.

(TSSA, lead negotiator)

The good working relationship was going to be continued as the joint working group have agreed to continue to meet quarterly to review the remuneration rules, feedback from managers, HR managers and TSSA representatives and from the joint validation panel.

Network Rail Infrastructure, the NR 'parent' company, reported a median GPG of 11% for the whole company as part of the Gender Pay Gap Reporting Regulations. Their written submission[9] cited the Fair and Transparent Pay Project as the way forward for the rest of the company.

Conclusions

Although the three case studies we have presented above cover very different sectors and occupational groups, it is possible to identify some common themes. First, the presence of variable but substantial GPGs that disadvantage women is evident in each of the cases. Second, the complex nature and resilience of the GPG is highlighted across the case studies. As has been long established in academic literature and research, the GPG stems from multi-faceted and multi-layered factors that are historic, structural, institutional and social. Vertical and horizontal gender segregation, management discretion and the payment of non-negotiated and historic bonus schemes underpinned by gendered social relations were all factors identified in our case studies. The combination of these factors often serves to obfuscate the extent and causality of the GPG, providing the basis of its resilience. Transparency in pay structures has gained popularity as a tool for reducing the GPG and is discussed in detail in Chapter 6. However, our Case Studies 2 and 3 show that superficial attempts at transparency do not result in significant reductions in the GPG. In Case Study 1, more rigorous attempts at transparency using complex systems of job evaluation revealed deep-seated, historic pay inequality that has cost billions of pounds to rectify. Furthermore, in each of the cases, only threats to resort to legal remedies by trade unions and the EHRC led to any action by employers to reduce the GPG. In Case Studies 1 and 2 solicitors, working independently of trade unions, have also sought to capitalise on the litigious nature of equal pay. Lastly, our case studies indicate that, even if immediate measures are taken to close GPGs, without radical structural and institutional transformation coupled with ongoing vigilance, like a stubborn weed, they will re-emerge.

Notes

1 A similar agreement was reached in Scotland in 1999 for implementation by April 2002.
2 The T&GWU merged with Amicus in 2007 to form Unite.
3 The Equality and Human Rights Commission can conduct an Inquiry into any matter which relates to Sections 8 or 9 of the Equality Act, namely equality and diversity or human rights. The Commission conducted its Inquiry into the Financial Sector using powers granted by s16 of the Equality Act 2006. The Terms of Reference of the Inquiry were:
   • To inquire into the gender pay gap and pay trends across the financial services sector.
   • To inquire into the extent and nature of sex discrimination in relation to recruitment, terms and conditions, promotion, career paths, retention and workplace culture across the financial services sector.
   • To examine measures used by employers and other organisations to address sex discrimination and inequalities in pay and status, and to assess the effectiveness of such measures.
   • To assess and analyse the differential impact of job losses in the sector.
   • To consider any other matters as appear to the Commission to be relevant to the above.
4 We have defined the financial services sector as all activities covered by Standard Industrial Classification 1992 Section J: financial intermediation (65), insurance and pensions (66), auxiliary activities (67).
5 www.equalpaylegal.co.uk/index.html (accessed 7 January 2018).
6 LFS is conducted by the Office for National Statistics (ONS), and has a panel design. Almost 138,000 respondents are interviewed for about 59,000 addresses in each quarter, with a response rate of about 79% in the first wave. In this study, we collect information on earnings, employment and socio-economic characteristics such as age, ethnicity and education. To understand gender wage differentials, we first draw information on individual's employment status from LFS. Second, we collect gross hourly pay information for each of the respondents in the main job. We deflate all monetary values to 2015 (2015 = 100) prices using quarterly consumer price index of the UK.

7 www.thetimes.co.uk/article/gender-pay-gap-in-financial-services-companies-bhbzd8mg 9 (accessed 31 May 2018).
8 https://gender-pay-gap.service.gov.uk/viewing/employer-details?e=DnO2Jeq_VILW0Z bEXEfg-g%21%21 (accessed 31 May 2018).
9 https://cdn.networkrail.co.uk/wp-content/uploads/2017/12/Gender-Pay-Gap-report-201 7.pdf (accessed 31 May 2018).

Acknowledgements

Thanks are due to Dr Mostak Ahamed who undertook the quantitative analysis for the FSS case.

References

Acker, J. (1990) 'Hierarchies, Jobs, Bodies: A Theory of Gendered Organizations' *Gender and Society* 4(2), pp. 139–158.
Astbury Marston (2014/2015) *Report 013 Compensation – Life Working Series 2014/5.*
Bach, S. and Strolney, A. (2014) 'Restructuring UK Local Government Employment Relations: Pay Determination and Employee Participation in Tough Times' *Transfer* 20(3), pp. 343–356.
Blinder, A. S. (1973) 'Wage Discrimination: Reduced Form and Structural Estimates' *Journal of Human Resources*, pp. 436–455.
Davies, M. (2015) 'Women on Board: 5 Year Summary'. London: Department of Business, Innovation and Skills, Ref: BIS/15/585.
Davies, R. (n.d.) 'Bankers Behaving Badly: Sex, Harassment, Racism, Embarrassing E-Mails, & Outrageous Extravagance'. Available from: http://projects.exeter.ac.uk/RDa vies/arian/scandals/behaviour.html (accessed 1 September 2017).
DBEIS (2017) *Trade Union Membership 2016: Statistical Bulletin.* Available from: www. gov.uk/government/uploads/system/uploads/attachment_data/file/616966/trade-union-m embership-statistical-bulletin-2016-rev.pdf (accessed 20 October 2017).
Deakin, S., Fraser Butlin, S., McLaughlin, C. and Polanska, A. (2015) 'Are Litigation and Collective Bargaining Complements or Substitutes for Achieving Gender Equality? A Study of the British Equal Pay Act' *Cambridge Journal of Economics* 39(2), pp. 381–403.
EHRC (2009) *Financial Services Inquiry: Sex Discrimination and Gender Pay Gap Report of the Equality and Human Rights Commission.* Manchester: Equality and Human Rights Commission.
EHRC (2011) *Financial Services Inquiry: Follow Up Report.* Manchester: Equality and Human Rights Commission.
Emolument (n.d.) *Gender Equality and Banking: The Pay Gap Continues.* Crowd Sourced Data. Available from: www.emolument.com/career_advice/gender_equality_a nd_banking (accessed 26 March 2018).
Equal Pay Legal (n.d.) *Financial Services.* Available from: www.equalpaylegal.co.uk/ep l-financial-services.html (accessed 26 March 2018).
Firpo, S., Fortin, N. and Lemieux, T. (2009) 'Unconditional Quantile Regressions' *Econometrica* 77(3), pp. 953–973.
Godwin, K. (2006) 'Equal Value Update 2006' *Equal Opportunities Review* 153, pp. 5–16.
Healy, G. and Ahamed, M. (2018) 'Gender Pay Gap, Voluntary Interventions and Recession: The Case of the British Financial Services Sector', unpublished paper.

HM Treasury (2010) *Treasury Committee Report on Women in the City*. CM 7900, July 2010.

Institute of Fiscal Studies (2016) *The Gender Wage Gap*. IFS Briefing Note BN186. Edited by M. Costa Dias, W. Elming and R. Joyce.

LGA (2018) *The Gender Pay Gap in Local Government 2018*. Available from: www.local. gov.uk/sites/default/files/documents/Summary%20Data%20on%20Gender%20Pay%20G ap%20in%20Local%20Government%202018%20for%20publicationv%20%20%20.pdf (accessed 31 May 2018).

LGE (2006) *Unblocking the Route to Equal Pay in Local Government*. Local Government Employers Report, November 2006. London: Local Government Association.

McDowell, L. (2010) 'Capital Culture Revisited: Sex, Testosterone and the City' *International Journal of Urban and Regional Research* 34(3), pp. 652–658.

NAO (2015) *A Short Guide to Network Rail*. London: National Audit Office. Available from: www.nao.org.uk/wp-content/uploads/2015/08/Network-rail-short-guide1.pdf (accessed 26 March 2018).

Oaxaca, R. (1973) 'Male-Female Wage Differentials in Urban Labor Markets' *International Economic Review* 14(3), pp. 693–709.

Oliver, L., Stewart, M. and Tomlinson, J. (2014) 'Equal Pay Bargaining in the UK Local Government Sector' *Journal of Industrial Relations* 56(2), pp. 228–245.

ONS (2015) *Public Sector Employment, UK: September 2015*. Statistical Bulletin Office for National Statistics. Available from: www.ons.gov.uk/employmentandlabourmarke t/peopleinwork/publicsectorpersonnel/bulletins/publicsectoremployment/september2015 (accessed 26 March 2018).

Özbilgin, M. F. and Woodward, D. (2004) 'Belonging and "Otherness": Sex Equality in Banking in Turkey and Britain' *Gender Work and Organization* 11(6), pp. 668–688.

Prosser, T. (2011) 'UK: The Representativeness of Trade Unions and Employer Associations in the Banking Sector' Observatory: EurWORK: Eurofound.

Towers, B. (1997) *The Representation Gap: Change and Reform in the British and American Workplace*. Oxford: Oxford University Press.

Walker, D. (2009) *A Review of Corporate Governance in UK Banks and Other Financial Industry Entities, Final Recommendations*. November 2009, HM Treasury.

Wanrooy, B. van, Bewley, H., Bryson, A., Forth, J., Freeth, S., Stokes, L. and Wood, S. (2013) *Employment Relations in the Shadow of Recession: Findings from the 2011 Workplace Employment Relations Study*. Basingstoke: Palgrave Macmillan.

Wright, A. (2011) '"Modernising" Away Gender Pay Inequality? Some Evidence from the Local Government Sector on Using Job Evaluation' *Employee Relations* 33(2), pp. 159–178.

5 Avoiding gender bias

The role of the social partners

Geraldine Healy, Marco Peruzzi and
Magdalena Półtorak

Introduction

Our project had an ultimate aim to disseminate good practice and in doing so, we elaborated a set of guidelines (see the Appendix) that can usefully support trade unions, employers' associations and companies at whose door the task of combatting the GPG lies. These guidelines were presented to the European Trade Union Confederation (ETUC) in June 2016. The analysis of the case studies and national contexts presented in the previous chapters of the book highlighted seven topics addressed by the guidelines: a lack of awareness and information; a gendered conception of work–life balance targets and arrangements; ambiguity and lack of regulation; gender bias in the setting of pay and in the awarding of performance/productivity-related pay elements; vertical segregation; transparency; and the use of proactive and reflexive forms of legislation.

The aim of this and the next chapter is to focus on these issues, nourishing a proactive approach to build on the lessons learnt from the case studies as well as from the best practices promoted by the institutions and social partners at EU level or developed in EU member states. The analysis will present some guidelines and solutions that can usefully support trade unions, employers' associations and companies in the negotiation of arrangements on GPG-related topics. Moreover, issues raised in our guidelines are closely tied up with the gendered social structure of organisations and specifically of collective bargaining and pay determination. It is evident that collective bargaining and pay determination are shaped by gendered structures and are embedded in what Acker (2006: 443) called 'inequality regimes', i.e. 'systematic disparities between participants in power and control over goals, resources, and outcomes; workplace decisions'. Thus, 'all organizations have inequality regimes, defined as loosely interrelated practices, processes, actions, and meanings that result in and maintain class, gender, and racial inequalities within particular organizations' (2006: 443). It is these inequality regimes that sustain the GPG in the different case studies we examined in Italy, Poland and the UK. A consideration of inequality regimes draws our attention to the interrelated themes of gendered societal structures, organisation practices and regulation that combine to shape the GPG in national contexts. Therefore, gendered societal structures permeate and interrelate with organisations so that they replicate and lead to organisational practices being imbued with gendered biases, segregation and stereotyping. At the same time, it is also the case that actors (such as social partners) can engage and transform negative gendered structures through awareness and transformative action. Such engagement and possible transformative action rests on the gendered decision-making representative structures of social partners, the level of awareness of gendered inequalities, the gender bias in setting of pay and the resilience of vertical segregation and external pressures. It is these themes that are specifically addressed in this chapter.

We begin by discussing women's representation in decision-making and how social partners might raise awareness. Decision-making in different social partner institutions indicates a means of exercising power and control. Gendered awareness is the outcome of a set of different circumstances ranging from engaged key actors in unions and progressive employers at different levels. This in itself is problematic since our communications may be filtered by our own value systems, which in themselves may be gendered (Kirton *et al.*, 2016). Thus for women, inequality may be highly visible through horizontal segregation (men and women undertaking different work) and vertical segregation (men dominating the hierarchies) and that visibility and its associated unfairness may prompt activism to challenge and change the status quo. However, visibility of inequality may also be tolerated by groups who fear that equalisation may lead to lower male pay in the longer term. These fears are important when resources are finite and profit or surplus is the motive. Thus the incentive to challenge the GPG is constrained by interests.

Interests play out in the minutiae of interactions, decisions, formal and informal, the legitimacy and visibility, the degree of control and compliance or indeed resistance to the status quo, which are all part of Acker's (2006) inequality regimes that conspire to sustain the GPG. Moreover, these inequality regimes operate in different ways according to the centralised, decentralised context and the power relations of the social partners, both within and between unions and management. Moreover, strategies and action may differentially affect different classes of worker. This makes easy solutions and strategies perhaps always 'routes to partial failure' (Hyman, 1987). With this caveat in mind, after discussing different patterns of women's representation in different social partner institutions, we raise the issue of awareness of inequalities through actions by women's organisations and through organisational practices. We then expose gender bias drawing on examples from negotiating work–life balance, part-time and flexible work arrangements; combining union and family responsibilities; lifetime social and material effects. We then turn to gender bias in the setting of pay and in the awarding of performance/productivity-related pay elements and finally reflect on the resilience of vertical segregation which is often blamed as a key cause of the GPG.

Gender, decision-making structures and raising awareness

Raising awareness is an immense task and one that can be taken up by trade unions and employers in their different ways. A crucial approach is ensuring

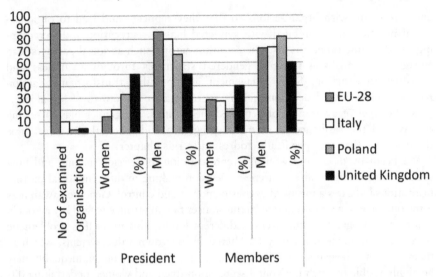

Figure 5.1 Gender breakdown in decision-making bodies of employees' organisations –
national perspective (2016)
Source: http://eige.europa.eu/sites/default/files/documents/wmid_mapping_socpar_1.pdf.

that men and women are involved in decision-making processes. Women's
involvement in decision-making processes in the twenty-first century still
remains a challenge.

European Commission data shows the percentage of women in decision-
making bodies of employee and employer organisations decreases the higher the
rank. Women account for merely 14% and 28% of presidents and members of
the highest decision-making employee organisations (see Figure 5.1).

Figure 5.1 also demonstrates a woefully small number of presidents who are
women and indeed a proportionately small number of women who are on
decision-making bodies in the EU-28, which are only marginally greater than the
EU average for Italy with the UK exceeding that average by about ten points.
Poland has some way to go before it reaches the EU average of members on
decision-making bodies. This gap has important consequences for equality
strategies; as Colling and Dickens (1989) remind us, women need to be *at
the table* for their concerns on substantive and procedural issues to be *on
the table*.

Unions are the main employee body and critical players in challenging
inequality and unfairness. The struggle over time has been to ensure that the
interests of women members are as well represented as male members. The
ETUC Annual Gender Equality Survey 2017 (Fulton *et al.*, 2017) provides
some insight into women's representation within the leadership of the ETUC's
affiliated confederations. The aim is to close the representation gap between
men and women, so that (as the 2011 ETUC resolution on gender balance
proposed) unions have:

- structures that genuinely reflect the diversity of the membership;
- a modern image that is representative of women's interests and needs and that is in touch and relevant with its membership;
- a stronger role in fulfilling and implementing women's economic, social and political objectives; and
- an approach to gender mainstreaming in decision-making and policy-making processes, and in their representative roles in the wider economy and society (Fulton *et al.*, 2017: 19).

The 2017 ETUC survey found that the average proportion of women members in the surveyed union confederations was 43.6%. The proportion of women among union members ranges from three-quarters (75.9%) in STTK (Finland) to one in eight (13%) in TURK-IS (Turkey). Most confederations report an increase in the proportion of women in membership, with 20 confederations reporting an increase in the proportion of their female membership between 2016 and 2017, compared with nine which reported a decrease. However, if the comparison is limited to the 20 confederations replying to the survey every year since 2008, a clear upward trend is evident, with the average proportion of women going up from 46.3% of union members in 2008 to 49.5% in 2017. The TUC (UK) is the confederation with the largest number of women members (see Table 5.1).

It is noteworthy that confederations are the peak national union bodies, therefore leadership of a confederation is a notable achievement for men and women. If we examine union leaders of confederations, we find 11 of the 44 confederations have a woman as the key leader (Fulton *et al.*, 2017: 23). The UK TUC has been led by Frances O'Grady as (the first woman) general secretary since January 2013, in the CGIL (Italy) Susanna Camusso was elected as the first woman to be general secretary in the history of the confederation in November 2010 and the CISL (Italy) is now also headed by a woman, Annamaria Furlan. Following through the critical mass argument, Table 5.1 also shows the proportion of women who are part of the leadership team. The

Table 5.1 Gender of union members and leadership of union confederations (Italy, Poland and UK) 2017

Country	Confederation	% women union members	Leadership team (% women)
Italy	CGIL	47.8	44
Italy	CISL	48.1	50
Italy	UIL	41.1	25
Poland	NSZZ-Solidarność	39.5	14
UK	TUC	50.9	67
ETUC average		44.3	

Source: Fulton *et al.* (2017).

CISL, TUC and CGIL exceed or are in the gender balance zone. This cannot be said of NSZZ-Solidarność which has only 14% of women as members of its leadership team, despite women making up 39.5% of its membership.

Despite the successes outlined above, we should put the Italian and British position in context; most confederations pointed to ongoing obstacles. The most frequently cited was gender stereotyping and men's attitudes, reported by 17 confederations: ABVV/FGTB and ACLVB/CGSLB (both Belgium), CMKOS (Czech Republic), LO-DK (Denmark), CFTC and UNSA (both France), DGB (Germany), GSEE (Greece), CGIL, CISL and UIL (all Italy), UGT-P (Portugal), Nezavisnost (Serbia), ZSSS (Slovenia), UGT and USO (both Spain), LO-S (Sweden), HAK-IS and TURK-IS (both Turkey) and TUC (UK) (ETUC 2017: 28).

Given the data in Table 5.1, it is perhaps unsurprising that the Polish case throws up the following example:

Women's underrepresentation in Polish unions

Poland's largest trade union, representing (a female-dominated profession) teachers (the Polish Teachers' Union; the ZNP) has always been headed by a man, with men also acting as vice-presidents, whereas the Union's Executive Council is composed of 46% women. In the Polish Miners' Union (the ZZG), there are 11% of women in the Union's National Board, but there are no women in the union's leadership.[1]

Another response from four confederations was the lack of a critical mass of women interested in leadership positions, to provide mutual support and be a pool from which leaders could be drawn. The confederations pointing to this difficulty were ABVV/FGTB (Belgium), CFTC (France), FNV (Netherlands), UGT-P (Portugal) and ZSSS (Slovenia), although this is not to say that this is not also a problem in our case study organisations. ABVV/FGTB (Belgium) said: 'women are not sufficiently numerous to create networks or strategies', with the comment from FNV (Netherlands) that 'the first problem is the low number of women applying for leadership positions'. Finally there were three confederations, CMKOS (Czech Republic), CFTC (France) and CGIL (Italy), where women's lack of self-confidence, combined with other factors, was seen as a factor in non-participation. Nevertheless, women's share of union membership is increasing across the EU with the ETUC showing an increase from 43.1% to 45.1% between 2008 and 2017. It is particularly important that union activists are aware of the gradual increase in women's union membership so that they recognise that the bargaining agenda appeals to both women and men and that they do not underestimate the importance of their growing women's membership.

Practice shows that the main group interested in eliminating the gender pay gap is, besides international organisations,[2] women, especially those who have decided to directly oppose the established (and to a large extent stereotypical) remuneration mechanisms. Nevertheless, it is beyond question that fighting the GPG – and, for that matter, working towards parity democracy – should not be perceived as a 'women's only' issue, but as a matter of interest for society generally. This, however, does not change the presumption that as long as the law has not fulfilled its educational role by shaping the fair attitudes and social behaviours against inequalities, lobbying towards including the prevention of the GPG in collective negotiations will mostly be done by women. This is of key importance especially in male-dominated sectors. It should also be stressed that the opposition against the GPG must be audible. This will be more challenging for the UIL and NSZZ-Solidarność confederations (Table 5.1) who are some way from what is argued is a recommended critical mass of 30–35% of a given structure (Dahlerup, 2006; Childs and Krook, 2008).

One of the challenges faced by union social partners is to involve all their members in debating equality issues and to raise awareness amongst employees and more widely in the labour market, regardless of position in the professional hierarchy and their gender. This may lead to improved representative democracy and follow through to the negotiating process. We argue that for the GPG to be articulated at all, merely ensuring the most heterogeneous (best based on gender parity) composition of a committee negotiating a collective agreement will not be sufficient. Instead, it is vital that the women sitting on such a committee have real decision-making power and are willing to use it. Thus power is a hidden component in the inequality regimes sustaining the GPG. Healy and Kirton (2000) drew on Michels' (1911) concept of the 'iron law of oligarchy', and argued that women's slow structural progress in union government was due to an enduring male-gendered oligarchy where women are engaged in a continual struggle to access union power. This holds true today but is challenged by women's high union membership, the presence of strong feminist voices in lobbying or decision-making arenas and gender equality strategies (such as reserved seats; women's committees, conferences and networks; women's courses or other events; national officers dedicated to or responsible for women's issues).

In this section, we have highlighted the democratic progress that women have made in their unions. This progress reflects an international view that women are essential to a union's survival and even revival (Kirton, 2015). Our next case study (drawn from Kirton, 2015) summarises a 25-year chronicle of gender equality strategies in the UK and points to the importance of a wide range of gender equality strategies that work together to bolster women's representation, power and influence.

Union gender equality strategies: UK case

The South-east Region of the TUC (SERTUC) conducted the first survey of all TUC unions (large and small) in 1987 and the most recent in 2012 and provided a representative insight into the position of women in unions. The survey reported on the proportion of women: in membership, attending conferences, present on National Executive Committees (NECs) and paid national officers. Unions also provided information on the existence of specific gender equality (GE) strategies, namely reserved seats, women's conferences, women's committees, women's networks, women's officers, women's courses and ad hoc women's events. The combined surveys offer a 25-year chronicle of the changing patterns of women's representation in UK unions' key structures of democracy and on the changing utilisation of key gender equality strategies (Kirton, 2015). Kirton's analysis of the 25-year period reveals huge progress towards gender proportionality and towards getting women's concerns on the union agenda. The evidence suggests that at least, in part, this progress can be attributed to the wide range of gender equality strategies increasingly adopted over the period. However, the article exposes persistent gaps and warns against regarding the union gender democracy project as finished business (p. 484).

Severe gender barriers in the way of women's full inclusion in union democracy remain. In particular, the gender-segregated nature of the external labour market and women's role as primary care-givers in the family can influence women's union involvement (Bradley and Healy, 2008; Kirton, 2005; Munro, 2001).

In considering union social partner equality strategies, we should not forget that unions operate in often hostile economic environments. It is all the more incumbent on union leaders to ensure that internal environments are supportive to all their members. One way to demonstrate that support is through GE strategies and their contribution to union democracy.

Gender and employer decision-making structures

Turning from unions to management, we see that a similar position of seg-regation and underrepresentation is also present in employer bodies (see fig-ures 5.2 and 5.3). The main difference is that employer bodies are not representative. This is not to suggest that there are not other good reasons for involving women in the management of their companies including fairness and effectiveness.

Developing the point on the significance of women's representation, Erkrut *et al.* (2014), demonstrate that research has shown that when there are only one or two women on a management board, the women feel marginalised, ignored during discussions, excluded from social events and treated as if they somehow auto-matically only represent 'female' interests and become tokens on the board. It is argued that if there are more women on the board, a 'critical mass' appears, and in a way normalises the presence of women. Critical mass theory indicates that in order for a group of people to have real (not just theoretical) opportunity to articulate their needs and postulates, it is estimated that this group should account for a minimum of 30–35% of a given structure (Dahlerup, 2006; Childs and Krook, 2008). The importance of numbers in ensuring effective female participation and

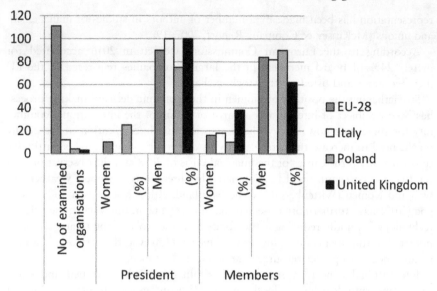

Figure 5.2 Gender breakdown in decision-making bodies of employers: national
   perspective (2016)
Source: http://eige.europa.eu/sites/default/files/documents/wmid_mapping_socpar_2.pdf.

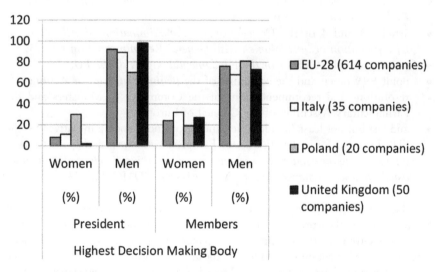

Figure 5.3 Percentage of women in management boards of companies listed on the stock
   exchange: EU and national perspective (2016)
Source: Own elaboration based on: *Database on Women and Men in Decision-Making:
Board Members*, http://ec. europa. eu/justice/gender-equality/gender-decision-making/da
tabase/business-finance/supervisory-board-board-directors/index_en.htm.

representation has been made by a number of authors in studies of management and unions (McKinsey & Company Report, 2007: 19).

According to the European Commission, women in 2016 accounted for merely 24% of board members in the largest companies registered in the EU member states and listed on the stock exchange.

Strengthening the position of women in the economic decision-making process has been a subject of interest and an area of action of the international community for some time now. It is without question that intensification of the debate on the need to increase the heterogeneity of decision-making teams[3] is partly due to discussion on the causes of the financial crisis of 2008 and the observation that the twenty-first century will be dominated by three 'forces', namely weather, the web and women (Wittenberg-Cox and Maitland, 2013). Mierżyńska and Dziewguć (2017) have furthermore observed that a true value in times when the price of technology is rapidly reducing is the ability to gather social capital, and women's potential in this area is much higher than men's. However, the networks with the greatest access to power resources are dominated by men.

International concern concerning discrimination against women and equal rights underpin legislative developments.[4] Encouraging enterprises to adopt 'temporary special measures', recommended in the form of both hard and soft laws, is supposed to offer a remedy to the existing status quo. In this context, the following are of particular importance:

- article 3 of the *International Covenant on Economic, Social and Cultural Rights* with *General Comment No. 16*;
- articles 3 and 4 of the *Convention on the Elimination of All Forms of Discrimination against Women* with *General Recommendation No. 25*;
- article 23 of the *Charter of the Fundamental Rights of the EU*;
- point F (Women and the economy) of the *Beijing Platform for Action*;
- resolutions and recommendations of the Committee of Ministers and the Parliamentary Assembly of the Council of Europe;
- and last but not least (in addition to numerous non-binding initiatives[5]) – the EU's *Proposal for a Directive of the European Parliament and of the Council on improving the gender balance among non-executive directors of companies listed on stock exchanges and related measures*, COM(2012) 614 final.

Achieving gender equality in the economic decision-making process is also one of the priorities of the currently binding *Strategic Engagement to Gender Equality 2016–2019*. Given that the aforementioned 'temporary special measures' are in fact a proposal to implement quota solutions in the area of private law, the majority of the EU member states have (so far) decided to achieve the postulated objectives (usually defined as a 40% representation of women in management boards) by using non-binding mechanisms, as illustrated in our case study countries (see Table 5.2).

The above discussion on decision-making and representation in unions and company boards shows that both sides of the social partner divide have some way to go before women are fully involved in decision-making.

Table 5.2 Women as share of company boards in Italy, Poland and UK 2016

Member state	Share of women on boards(*)	Quotas in place	Other national measures in place
Italy	32%	Yes: 33% by 2015 for listed companies and state-owned companies. Applicable to management boards and supervisory boards (i.e. executives and non-executives).	Yes
Poland	19%	No	The new (2016) *Code of Best Practice for GPW Listed Companies* provides that 'Decisions to elect members of the management board or the supervisory board of a company should ensure that the composition of these bodies is comprehensive and diverse among others in terms of gender, education, age and professional experience'. No sanctions are envisaged.
UK	27%	No	Self-regulation – from 2012 on the basis of principles of the UK Corporate Governance Code (following the Lord Davies' recommendation (Davies, 2011)). 26% reached by 2016. The recommended target for listed companies in FTSE 100 is 33% by 2020 is applicable to all board members. FTSE 350 companies recommended setting their own aspirational targets to be achieved by 2013 and 2015.
EU-28 average	28%		

Source: Author's elaboration based on: 'Gender Balance on Corporate Boards: Europe is Cracking the Glass Ceiling', European Commission, July 2016.

Awareness of inequalities

The issue of awareness and thorough knowledge of the GPG is a *sine qua non* condition for understanding and challenging the GPG at the organisational level (see also Chapter 6). However, it is more likely that the more women who are involved in positions of power, the more likely it is that they will be actors in raising awareness of gender inequality including the GPG. Without the identification and assessment of the scale of the GPG problem and its actual and potential consequences, negotiations are unlikely to be successful. The following case is indicative of the extent of the challenge of what would appear to be a straightforward task of raising awareness:

Lack of awareness in Polish unions

Discussions with an international certification company, carrying out social audits (voluntary audits that enterprises undergo at their own request or at the request of their clients) in the area of prevention of discrimination and respect of the principle of equal treatment indicates that: 'Employers have little knowledge on equal treatment and their respective obligations under the law. Many of them do not even make regulations available to their employees ... Job evaluation is basically non-existent. This is why there are pay gaps not just among employees of different gender, but also among employees on the same position – the system compensates an individual, and not a position ... Employees' knowledge on equal treatment is as limited as that of the employers, and if we take into account the level of trade union membership in Poland, I wouldn't count on the educational role of trade unions.'

The above case demonstrates that lack of awareness in Poland is a problem for both employers and unions. Such lack of awareness is not insurmountable providing there is a will to uncover pay gaps, but in the above case this would seem questionable. However the will to uncover the pay gap was evident in the UK Transport and Salaried Staff Association collaboration with Network Rail, the employers, our next case.

Methods of raising awareness: UK case

In the UK case study 'Transport and Salaried Staff Association/Network Rail', analysed in the project by the UK team, a trade union membership questionnaire that asked members for their pay details indicated specific grades in which the GPG was the greatest. These data led to equal pay cases which persuaded Network Rail to complete a gender pay audit and restructure pay grades accordingly. Also the UK financial services case study identifies the potential of crowd-sourced pay data to highlight GPGs (see Chapter 4 for full details of both cases).

The GPG is interdisciplinary in character and is enriched by analysis drawn from economic, legal, political and socio-cultural perspectives. However, therein lies some of the complexities of the GPG and of course the challenges for those who seek to reduce it. While its interdisciplinary nature enriches our understanding it also ensures that its grasp remains elusive for all but the most dedicated or well-informed. We now turn to different aspects of raising awareness which in many ways contribute to challenging the GPG.

Raising awareness by women's organisations

Women's organisations have been shown to be key actors in the struggle to raise awareness. During the period 2014–2016, the Polish 'Foundation for Women's Issues – I am woman' (in liaison with partners from Austria, the Czech Republic, Slovakia and Slovenia) carried out a project 'Fair Income – Fair Pension'. As a lack of awareness of the problem (among both employers and employees) was identified, one of the priority actions under the project was to draw attention to pay inequalities, which directly translate into significant disproportions in retirement pensions. The Business and Professional Women (BPW) Europe, a women's organisation representing 20,000 business women across Europe, has advocated for Gender Equality and Equal Opportunities worldwide since 1930. BPW Europe is part of the International Federation of Business and Professional Women, which was founded in 1930 in Geneva. This international network has some 30,000 members on five continents in 100 countries. BPW International has consultative status at the ECOSOC/United Nations. In 2011, the European Commission initiated the first European Equal Pay Day. Thus women's organisations remain a powerful source of information and lobbying.

In the UK, the Fawcett Society, a charity sustained by women's membership, has a powerful role in campaigning for gender equality and women's rights. The Fawcett Society currently campaigns to:

- Close the gender pay gap. At current rates of progress, it will take 62 years to close it.
- Secure equal power. Just 30% of Members of Parliament and 33% of councillors are women.
- Challenge attitudes and change minds. 20% of men aged 25–34 say women's equality has 'gone too far'.
- Defend women's rights post-Brexit. There must be no turning the clock back.

As part of its campaigns for equal pay, Fawcett also promotes the ideas of an equal pay day each year, which is the focus of our next case:

Equal Pay Day: UK case

Fawcett marks Equal Pay Day each year as the point in the year when women stop earning relative to men. It varies with the actual gap in each year, and is based on the data available at the beginning of the year. So in 2017 Equal Pay Day was on 10 November, because the most recently available ASHE 2016 data showed that the full-time mean GPG was 13.9% – the same as it was in the year before.[6]

The gap varies across the life course – it is at its lowest for women in their twenties (5.5%) and opens up significantly for women in their fifties (18.6%). Even though today's younger women have a smaller pay gap at the moment as they age, research suggests that their pay gap will widen.[7]

It also differs across industries. For example, it is over 32.8% in finance and insurance (see Chapter 4) and less than 6% for those working in administrative and support services.

Graduate women from ethnic minority backgrounds have been found to have lower pay three years after graduation than their white British peers,[8] and Fawcett research finds that women from Bangladeshi and Pakistani backgrounds have a 26.2% aggregate pay gap with White British men, and Black African women have a 19.6% full-time pay gap with White British men (Breach and Li, 2017).

Thus, NGOs are an important communicator of inequality in pay. The good practice example above focuses on the Equal Pay Day in the UK. It alerts the general public to the overall consequences of the GPG, when men are continuing to earn and women effectively work for nothing on or around 10 November until 31 December. The promotion of Equal Pay Day also draws attention to women's heterogeneity in the labour market including by sector, age and ethnicity. Thus, the GPG is not the only gap of concern to key actors challenging inequalities; as the above case demonstrates, the ethnic pay gap is also of contemporary concern. Social partners can benefit from collaborations with women's organisations, as would other equality organisations, in order to raise awareness and promote equality in their organisations and in society more generally.

Organisational practices to raise awareness

A frequently used form of raising awareness is through the organisation of training and meetings with experts, so as to sensitise participants to the problem of pay gaps. Analysis of collective agreements in Poland and cooperation with the social partners has revealed a real need to include the GPG issue in training programmes organised for trade unions. However, other stakeholders, such as labour inspectorates, company managers and NGOs also benefit from such training. The main goals of training tend to be:

- raising awareness on the GPG and indicating its hidden symptoms;
- convincing stakeholders of the necessity to include the GPG issue into negotiations with employers and into the company policy; and
- indicating methods of reducing the GPG.

Recommended methods of training include interactive seminars and workshops conducted by experts in human rights and human resources or gender-equality-oriented organisations as well as by labour lawyers and social psychologists. Moreover, it is important that any training focuses on the needs of particular sectors and/or organisations, otherwise the value of the training may not be convincing. First, a model training programme should introduce the concept of the GPG and provide its definition as well as relevant statistics and examples. During the workshops, special attention should be paid to the issue of stereotyping and searching for effective remedies to fight it. Other topics included in such a programme are non-discrimination law (international, European as well as internal laws) and human rights in business (taking into account the concept of the responsibility to respect). It is also necessary to discuss systems of job evaluation, provide answers to the questions of why and how to compare/evaluate jobs without sex bias, and examine the concept of work–life balance as a solution for both women and men and, at the same time, an important element of CSR. The training should also have a practical dimension. The participants should work on examples of good and bad practices, assess them as good or bad and be able to disclose the GPG sources. A final outcome of effective training would be working out a model of a 'GPG-free' company and the means to achieve it.

The above would be an ideal outcome and one to be sought. However, we recognise the limitations of training in achieving equality and diversity aims. Studies showed that training alone was not sufficient to moderate management bias (Kalev *et al.*, 2006: 589). Depending on the level, whether sector or company, it is crucial that responsibility is assigned and there is commitment from senior management and trade union negotiators to the values of reducing the GPG. This commitment may be the hardest to achieve without some stick or carrot.

Gender bias and inequality regimes

Gender bias permeates institutional policy and practices. Deep-seated gendered stereotypes are fundamental to the way inequality regimes work and are sustained. In this section we discuss, first, the social, legal and negotiating issues of work–life balance and then turn to the social and material effects of gendered lifetime earnings including pensions. We find in both cases the negative gendered effects of essentialist views attributed to men and women leaving the latter materially worse off and the former excluded from aspects of family life.

Gender bias and work–life balance

In our guidelines, we recognised that the pay negotiating process is fraught with potential gendered pitfalls and acknowledges from the outset the need to identify and eliminate those regulating mechanisms that are based on stereotypes and thus lead to indirect discrimination. Let us take the example of Work Life

Balance (WLB). It should be recognised that collective agreements often automatically cement gender-determined visions of solutions intended to ensure work–life balance. This happens especially when parental leave is referred to as 'optional maternity leave'. Not only is it incorrect from the point of view of the law, but it also unconsciously leads to an *a priori* assumption that work–life balance measures are gendered and are intended to help women to reconcile their professional and family life. While this is partly the case, in reality it has always been (and still is[9]), the EU legislature's intention to promote equality and sharing of childcare duties between both parents. Yet, despite numerous political actions, programmes and measures towards real gender equality, promoted and implemented in the EU member states for decades now, it is still women who usually carry the main responsibility for caring for children and seniors and doing household chores. The European Institute for Gender Equality (EIGE) report (2015: 47–49) reveals that when it comes to childcare, the average gap between women and men is 17%, which means that 45% of working women and (only) 27% of working men devote a minimum of one hour per day to caring for their children. The situation is even worse when it comes to broadly understood household management duties, where the gap is as much as 53.1%, resulting from the fact that as many as 77.1% of working women and as few as 24% of working men spend at least an hour per day on household chores (EIGE, 2015). While the European Union has recently made considerable progress in improving the framework for ensuring balance between professional and private life,[10] the *Strategic Engagement to Gender Equality 2016–2019* and the EC Roadmap: *New Start to Address the Challenges of Work–Life Balance Faced by Working Families* indicate that WLB continues to be a prerequisite for increasing women's activity in the labour market and balancing the economic position of women and men.

Furthermore, as is widely recognised women, much more often than men, are likely to be employed part-time and/or on flexible work arrangements. Moreover, women are more likely to take maternity and parental leaves. Thus there is a strong link between childcare and employment ratios for women and men, with potentially negative outcomes for women. In other words, in the majority of member states the higher the number of children, the lower the employment ratio of women. Fair application of WLB is an important contribution to gender equality and is also important from the perspective of corporate social responsibility. A socially responsible employer is one who, for example, respects employees' time and family values, regardless of the gender of the employees (Mazur-Wierzbicka, 2015: 109–110). The research by European Commission (2014), conducted in the EU member states, has concluded that countries with the largest use of instruments facilitating work–life balance are the Netherlands, Austria and Great Britain, where over 60% of employees can request work under flexible working hours in view of their family obligations or request (for the same reason) a day off. At the other extreme are Romania, Lithuania and Bulgaria, where a little over 10% of employees can use such solutions. What particularly stands out is the observation that employers are more likely to offer flexible opportunities to those working in higher positions, that is, those positions which are disproportionately male-dominated. Nevertheless, BusinessEurope in its *2015–2017 Work Programme* has identified 'the promotion of better reconciliation of work, private and family life and gender equality to reduce the gender gap' (p. 6) as one of the priority areas of action. As Goldin (2014: 1091) optimistically states 'the gender gap in pay would be considerably reduced and might vanish altogether if firms did not have an incentive to disproportionately reward individuals who labored long hours and worked particular hours. Such change has taken off in various sectors, such as technology, science, and health, but is less apparent in the corporate, financial, and legal worlds'. Hence the conclusion that efforts must be put into efficient implementation of EU measures, including by social partners at the negotiating table. A crucial role in this respect may be played by good will, including political will. Politics are fundamental to women's rights and this is well illustrated by the following case:

Polish case: action plan for equal treatment

The *Human Capital Development Strategy 2020* reads that 'utilising the professional potential of women may be one of the key impulses for the development of the society. However, it requires a coherent and horizontal approach in the various aspects of professional and family life'. On the other hand, the *National Action Plan for Equal Treatment for the Years 2013–2016* contains the following specific objective (Objective 1.7): *Promoting equal treatment of both parents with respect to engagement in childcare and child raising and promoting a family model based on partnership.* Promoting the idea of equal opportunities for women and men and promoting mechanisms allowing reconciliation between work and family life was considered an action of key importance, and the Ministry of Labour and Social Policy was appointed responsible for it. To achieve the objective, the Ministry was to engage in cooperation with the Government Plenipotentiary for Equal Treatment. However, the presidential and parliamentary elections of 2015 brought about a radical change on the domestic political scene. As a result, the radical conservative party, Law and Justice, abbreviated as PiS, monopolised power, taking over both the legislative and executive power. For the ruling party, gender equality appears to be an entirely abstract concept. PiS has, for example, effected a symbolic change of the name of the Ministry of Labour and Social Policy into 'Ministry of Family, Labour and Social Policy'. The Ministry is carrying out a flagship government project named 'Family 500+', under which an untaxed benefit of 500 PLN (approximately 120 euro) is granted for every second and next child, without any additional conditions attached, and for the first or only child if the family income is low. The programme is meant to address the problem of a low birth rate, and contribute to erasing the largest economic differences between Polish families. As a result, while the birth rate has indeed gone up, the programme is in fact a recipe for a decline in professional activity of women, who have calculated that it is 'more profitable' for them to have more children than to work.[11] In other words, instead of supporting measures intended to facilitate reconciliation between work and family life, the government has decided to keep women at home. As a side note, it is worth adding that while the office of the Government Plenipotentiary for Equal Treatment (and Civil Society) has not been abolished as a result of the aforementioned political change, it is currently a facade without real substance.[12]

There is also a case for greater attention to the rights of working fathers, especially their right to paternity leave or other rights. It is not sufficient for the rights to be available, there is an imperative that these rights are taken in a context of social acceptability. When inequality regimes prevail, men may fear negative career consequences if they take advantage of their rights. Thus, when negative conditions prevail, the outcome will be the re-cementing of the traditional model of the male breadwinner, where men work long hours and women work part-time, may refuse to work overtime, or avoid doing jobs or accepting promotions which require longer working hours.

The Italian, Polish and British confederation respondents to the ETUC 2017 survey also referred to difficulty of combining union activity and family responsibilities. In total, 12 confederations pointed to this: ACLVB/CGSLB (Belgium), CMKOS (Czech Republic), CFTC (France), DGB (Germany), ICTU (Ireland), NSZZ-Solidarność (Poland), ZSSS (Slovenia), CCOO, UGT and USO (all Spain), Travail Suisse (Switzerland), HAK-IS (Turkey) and TUC (UK). NSZZ-Solidarność (Poland) pointed to a 'lack of time for additional duties', and the TUC (UK) referred to 'difficulties combining childcare/periods of maternity leave with high profile job roles and heavy workloads' (Fulton *et al.*, 2017: 29).

In contrast, the Italian unions were more likely to point to gendered structures of power, for example, they pointed to women's exclusion, the promoting of gendered meritocracy and outright prejudices towards women in top positions. In the ETUI 2017 Survey, CGIL (Italy) stated: 'there continues to be a culture and system of power, which attributes to men the prerogative of "promoting" the meritocracy and deciding careers and leadership'; and that 'men need to be made more aware of the valued added by women in enriching CISL's actions and its political and organisational strategy', whereas UIL (Italy) noted the prejudices towards women in top positions. In contrast, the TUC (UK) was more circumspect suggesting that 'within some affiliated unions, although not within the TUC, there is often a perception that sexism and a macho culture still keeps women out of leadership positions'. We know from the literature that this is a view held by British women and that women often testify that they have to work harder in order to succeed in their workplaces and in their unions (Bradley and Healy, 2008; Healy *et al.*, 2011; Kirton and Healy, 2013).

Gender bias and lifetime social and material costs

The consequence of the GPG and the associated inequality regimes has lifetime social and material effects. The level of salary translates into current and future income, and thus into individuals' prosperity over the life course. In this section we focus on the lifetime material effects. The gendered organisation of work, its associated horizontal and vertical segregation and the consequence of inter-rupted work directly translates into pay and pension gaps, which negatively impact on women with the consequence that more women than men are likely to spend their retirement in poverty. According to Lisowska (2016), this qua-lifies as 'motherhood penalty', as a break of up to two years in professional career means in Poland an 18–28% loss of income, whereas a three-year break means losing as much as 37% of income. The full scale of the problem, how-ever, only becomes visible when one looks at lifetime earnings of women and men. In the UK for example, women are likely to earn £300,000 less than men over their working lives, according to a new analysis that has sparked fresh calls for more shared parental leave to close the UK's stubborn GPG.[13] The GPG becomes a significant lifetime pay penalty with the gap widening for older women and becoming a significant pensions gap in retirement.

It is, therefore, hardly a surprise that 'Raising awareness of the link between pay, earnings and pension entitlements in old age' is one of the priorities and key areas of action of the European Union, as formulated in the *Strategic Engagement to Gender Equality 2016–2019* (EC, 2015: 12). As Eurostat data and European Commission Reports (2013 and 2016) show, the average GPG is 39.8% for overall annual earnings and 39% for retirement pensions. The ETUC survey tackled the gendered pension gap as women generally bear a much hea-vier burden than men in terms of caring for children and dependent relatives, by asking whether these periods of care were credited; this was the case in almost all the 29 countries, for which information was available (Fulton *et al.*, 2017: 43). They show that methods of accreditation varied by country; Italy for example credited periods of maternity, parental leave and less usually victims of domestic violence, study and care for disabled, whereas the UK credits for periods of maternity leave or if caring for dependents but they must be applied for. In the UK, for example, in 2018 Statutory Maternity Pay (SMP) is paid for up to 39 weeks giving 90% of average weekly earnings (before tax) for the first six weeks and £145.18 or 90% of your average weekly earnings (whichever is lower) for the next 33 weeks. Shared Parental Leave was introduced in 2015 to encourage more fathers to participate in childcare and provides Statutory Shared Parental Pay (ShPP) at £145.18 a week or 90% of average weekly earn-ings, whichever is lower. These are statutory minimums and may be improved through collective bargaining or locally with the employer. However, in com-pany/occupational schemes, these periods of absence were credited in only eight countries.

In Europe generally, the pension pay gap is 38.6% whereas in Poland it is 22.5%, Italy 37.1% and the greatest pensions gap of our three countries is in the UK at 39%. The relationship between low pay and the GPG remains of huge significance to the proportionately greater pensions gap. Moreover, we should not forget that just as fairness and equality remain important, the bottom line is the need for pay and pensions to 'put bread on the table' and as we know, the greatest poverty is experienced by older women and particularly women on a low pension.

Gender bias in the setting of pay and in the awarding of performance/productivity-related pay elements

We turn now to the organising processes around the setting of pay, one of the key aspects leading to inequality regimes and the GPG. The case studies examined in the previous chapters highlighted that the majority of company agreements regulating performance-related pay elements use work attendance as the sole or one of the criteria for the awarding of productivity bonuses. However, and in addition, discretionary bonuses determined by line managers are also common, particularly in decentralised contexts, and are often outside a collective agreement.

The prevalence of work attendance as a performance element occurs independently of sector or of whether it is a male-dominated sector or not, and it is explained by the social partners in our research as a choice that meets both the request of the employees to have a criterion (they reckon to be) capable of measuring their performance impartially and objectively, and the need of trade unions to ensure employers' accountability.

However, the choice of work attendance as a criterion for measuring employees' productivity is not just indirectly discriminatory on grounds of gender, but for the disparate impact it has on women as a result of the gender time gap deriving from the uneven distribution of family burdens. Such choice is also anachronistic: the development of new forms of work organisation makes it less possible to measure workers' performance and productivity by merely referring to the length of time worked and to the amount of hours or days actually worked in the employer's premises. The spread of off-line and/or mobile teleworking enabled by the digitalisation of work and new technologies requires reflecting on and selecting other criteria of measurement, such as workloads, performance standards, and individual or team productivity targets.

There is also a further aspect that needs to be taken into account: if the awarding of bonuses is based on criteria that imply gender bias, the resulting discriminatory impact is exponentially increased if the legislation fosters the linkage of pay to productivity by applying reductions of tax rates and/or of social security contributions to these pay elements. As shown in Chapter 2, this is the case of the Italian context.

A first solution that the social partners can adopt is to reduce the indirect discriminatory effect connected to the use of the criterion of work attendance. As such effect is a consequence of the gender time gap resulting from the uneven distribution of family burdens and therefore from a higher likeliness of women to take care leave, a possible corrective measure could be to include some types of leave, such as maternity leave, parental leave or childcare leave, in the measurement of work attendance. In the meantime, as the indirect discriminatory impact derives from the actual uneven distribution of family burdens between men and women, in order to overcome such unbalance, corrective measures should be arranged by the social partners with specific attention to paternity-related leave. Finally, when taking this corrective action, social partners can reflect on the extent to which sick leave should be included in work attendance. In fact, this depends on the specific characteristics of the national regulatory framework, on whether women are granted an anticipated/extended maternity leave in the case of risks in pregnancy, or parents are granted leave connected with childcare in the case of a child's sickness and on whether such leave is paid or unpaid. Depending on these variables, one can assess whether the use of sick leave can be connected to parental care and whether a related reduction of productivity bonuses can imply indirect gender discrimination.

As shown in the previous chapters, besides gender bias resulting from the awarding of productivity bonuses negotiated by company agreements, the economic analysis of the case studies demonstrated that the GPG also derives from the individual negotiation or awarding of bonuses, given by the company on a discretionary basis, with a lack of transparency and no room for the social partners to control and take action on them. This was particularly evident as widespread practice in, but not exclusively, the UK financial services sector (see Chapter 4). The analysis of the case studies also revealed that even when the company agreement regulates productivity bonuses, companies may use separate – and not negotiated – systems of productivity remuneration for the highest positions in the company hierarchy, based on a subjective assessment of the employee's expertise development and capability of achieving specific targets.

Confronting the secrecy around discretionary payment is a challenge for the social partners, especially if one considers that discretionary pay accounts for a significant proportion of the pay gap in certain sectors, and is intensified at higher levels of the hierarchy. It becomes all the more important for collective agreements to include transparent criteria on which individual productivity will be evaluated and bonuses will be paid, and push for equality audits with respect to bonuses (see Chapter 6).

To these purposes, a gender-neutral skills evaluation procedure, validated or negotiated by the social partners, could provide a solution. Such procedure would be aimed at assessing and measuring the active and creative contribution of the individual employee to the company's functioning and innovation, his/her 'know-how' acquired and developed through their working activity. These systems are fostered at EU level from the perspective of skills development, reinforcement of workers' capabilities[14] and mobility in the international labour market (see for example, the European Employment Strategies, the European Social Fund, the Qualification framework for life-long learning). As regards the awarding of individual bonuses, such systems could ensure that performance and productivity criteria are spelt out clearly and favouritism and/or

unconscious bias are removed from bonus/productivity decisions. If such clar-
ification is determined by the social partners, discretion at the level of the
individual manager is reduced. Transparency and joint determination of bonus/
productivity criteria would lead to greater sense of fairness in the allocation of
reward as arbitrary discretion would be reduced. A joint determination of productivity criteria could also imply a collectively negotiated process and the
establishment of a bilateral gender-balanced committee responsible for monitoring
the agreement's implementation.

This could lead to three main positive outcomes. First of all, the company if
covered by joint regulation would be accountable, for example, to a joint
union–management bilateral committee (see the Appendix), for the awarding of
any productivity/performance-related bonus. Second, such awarding would not
be exclusively based on a measurement of work attendance but would
nevertheless be transparent and impartial. When the type of work organisation
allows it, performance and productivity targets could be set at team/group level.
Finally, greater transparency and fairness may result in better employee morale
and productivity.

It is noteworthy that the determination of the criteria useful for evaluating
workers' performance and productivity on a more transparent and objective
basis could be helped by a previous evaluation of job requirements. This draws
attention to the key importance of analytical job evaluation[15] carried out on a
gender-neutral basis. Job evaluation is a method of determining on a systematic
basis the relative importance of a number of different jobs while avoiding pre-
judice or discrimination. It enables 'like work' and jobs of equal value to be
systematically compared. Job evaluation is not a method of allocating pay rates
nor is it a way of judging a job holder's performance; however it is a good basis
for a fair pay system and a way of getting a hierarchy of jobs on which to base
a grading system.[16]

As shown by the British system, job evaluation is a key instrument for
implementing the principle of pay equality (as regulated by art. 157 TFEU and
by 'Equal Treatment Directive' 2006/54/CE) when men and women involved in
the comparison perform different jobs. Specifically, when different jobs are
evaluated as having 'equal value' despite their difference, these job should be on
the same pay scale and therefore be equally remunerated. The value of such a
job evaluation exercise will only be justified for equal value or equal pay comparison if conducted on a gender-neutral basis. It therefore provides a key instrument
for putting gender pay equality into effect in a context of intra-occupational
gender-based segregation.

Key questions arise when identifying which level of collective bargaining
should take action in this field of regulation, either in the case of a job evaluation or a skill evaluation procedure. In fact, if both kinds of procedures have
their elective field of development in the company dimension, one might wonder
whether the sectoral level could take on any regulatory role establishing guidelines or a general normative framework for companies to apply and integrate
with adjustments to their specific organisational context. This could be

particularly significant in nationally centred systems of collective bargaining such as Italy, but less relevant in a decentralised system with low collective bargaining coverage.

The analysis of the case studies and of the best practices promoted by the European Commission in its documents highlights that while the UK model provides a good example for job evaluation in company-level decentralised systems,[17] the Belgian model can represent a good practice for member states characterised by a nationally centred system, especially considering Belgium's resistance to the decentralisation process that interested the vast majority of member states during the crisis.

In Belgium, gender-neutral job evaluation is fostered by advisory guidelines, such as those published by the Institut pour l'égalité des femmes et des hommes[18] in 2007, as well as by legislative interventions aimed at supporting the social partners' action in this field as well as monitoring systems at both sectoral and company level (see Loi 22 April 2012, '*Loi visant à lutter contre l'écart salarial entre hommes et femmes*'). In this perspective, some social partners have adopted classification frameworks at sectoral level, providing solutions for the coordination between the sectoral and company level, in the case of non-correspondence of job roles or need for specific integrations/adjustments (see for example *Classification sectorielle des fonctions – Manuel pour les entreprises du secteur de l'assurance*, of 2010). However, it is worth highlighting that the evaluation system taken by the social partners as a reference in a specific national Protocol signed with the company Hudson is the *Job evaluation model 5+1 Compas®*. Despite being intended for setting basic-pay rates, this system, which is not by chance alternatively named as *5+1 Competency Model®*, is strongly shaped in terms of competences required by job positions (technical competences, capacity of managing information, responsibilities, people and interpersonal relationships), while it does not take in due consideration the objective dimension of work, namely working conditions, physical environment, psychological conditions, related mental/physical/emotional efforts.

Despite this remark, the Belgian model is particularly interesting for a development of negotiated rules on job evaluation, but also on a following skills evaluation, in a multi-level system of collective bargaining, as it couples a sectoral regulatory framework with company-based integrations and adjustments.

In conclusion, the social partners are called to reflect on the reform of non-analytical job classification systems in collective bargaining and more generally, so that both the impact of new forms of work organisation on the evaluation of work conditions and workers' productivity, and the need to adopt a gender-neutral approach are taken in due account.

Reflections on vertical segregation and discrimination

Whilst job evaluation addresses issues of horizontal segregation and pay discrimination, vertical segregation has also been a key explanatory factor linking women's representation to their pay. Thus horizontal segregation tends to be associated with relatively low pay and vertical segregation with a greater pay gap (Dex *et al.*, 2008). Blackburn *et al.* argued that the greatest inequality lies in vertical segregation and that pay is only one measure of vertical segregation explaining gender segregation (2002: 516). Dex *et al.* (2008) showed that women's wages grew more slowly than men's wages because they were located disproportionately in lower growth and feminised jobs, that is they were horizontally segregated from men and work of higher value. Much of what has been discussed above has been the consequence of horizontal and vertical segregation, with women and men's work segregated horizontally by doing different work and vertically by one sex (male) dominating the hierarchies with researchers suggesting that wage disparities across male and female occupations are due to gender devaluation (Murphy and Oesch, 2016). As our cases have shown, workplace practices and pay systems shape gender pay inequality (Smithson *et al.*, 2004; Rubery *et al.*, 2005). Our comparative case studies provide some unique insight into the diversity of workplace practices that influence pay and contribute to gender pay inequality. Dex *et al.* (2008) concluded that factors within the workplace rather than home, occupational choice and gender occupational segregation were generating the gender bias to wage growth. From a domestic ties perspective, motherhood as opposed to parenthood, again would indicated a higher GPG. Hence the concerns reflected in our discussion above with respect to WLB. Moreover we cannot shy away from the fact that part of the GPG is the result of discrimination in the workplace. Drolet and Mumford (2012) found that a substantial portion of the GPG in their private sector study in Britain and Canada remains unexplained by the individual characteristics or workplace.

The economic analysis of the case studies highlighted a reverse/negative GPG in some low-pay job positions and an exponential increase of the GPG in high-pay positions, thereby reflecting studies by Dex *et al.* (2008) and Blackburn *et al.* (2002) above. A closer investigation explained such GPG patterns as deriving from the fact that in some low-pay positions women had almost twice as much length of service as men, with consequent twice as much length-of-service compensation as men. However that would only apply where length of service compensation applied. This is not always the case, however the GPG is likely to be lower if pay was determined by collective bargaining (see Elvira and Saporta, 2001).[19] Whereas, this was less the case for women working in medium- and high-level work where formal systems were less likely and gender bias more likely to come in to play and result in an increase of the GPG, particularly prevalent at the top of the company hierarchy.

Contrasting GPG cases

It is recognised that as in the Italian case, manual/repetitive job positions are more likely to be covered by basic pay rates set by national collective agreements and less affected by differences in bonuses and therefore the GPG will be small or even negative. Women who have reached senior levels of organisations may be perceived to have broken the glass ceiling and with it reduced the GPG. On the contrary, as in the case of the UK financial services sector (which has one of the highest GPGs in the UK), discretionary payments increase proportionately in relation to the position in the hierarchy, where women are increasingly underrepresented, and with the increase in bonuses (where men receive proportionately higher bonuses than women) and with seniority comes an increased GPG. This is also the case in Poland where, as a general rule, the higher the position, the higher the GPG, although at the executive level among export/import managers the GPG was less than 10%. Reverse GPG was also observed in case of selected specialist positions, such as a sales representative in the medical/pharmaceutical sector, market analyst or medical representative. The pay gap is generated mainly by the private sector, including microenterprises.

Thus our research in different national and sectoral contexts indicates that an increase in the GPG is usually positively correlated with an increase in hierarchical level. Therefore, it may be said that women experience multiple discrimination as not only do they – statistically – occupy fewer executive positions, but – when they do – they are usually compensated less than men would be for doing the same job. Moreover, Ryan *et al.*'s (2014) research shows that different rules are applied to women who have broken the glass ceiling than men. The analysis of the situation in British companies in 2008 reveals that not only did women sitting on management boards receive smaller base salary than men, but their variable pay was a smaller proportion of their lower salaries (Ryan *et al.*, 2014: 175). Interestingly, Ryan *et al.* (2014) show that when the company's situation was good, men received significantly higher bonuses (classic GPG), whereas when there was a downturn in the company's results, they received less than women on the same positions (reversed GPG). In other words, men's salaries were closely connected with the company's financial standing: good results were highly rewarded, while poor ones were 'penalised' by a significant reduction in bonuses. In the case of women, no such dependencies were observed, and the amount of additional elements of remuneration were stable to an extent. This phenomenon may prima facie indicate a greater financial stability of women. On the other hand, the fact that the bonuses awarded to females were less sensitive to the company's financial standing automatically raises the question as to the existence of gender-based stereotypes and the different evaluation of women's leadership in male-dominated environments or 'typically masculine' role (Ryan *et al.*, 2014: 177). Ryan *et al.* (2014) suggest that female executives may be subjected to greater scrutiny than men, because they occupy roles that are prototypically male and thereby contradict stereotypic expectations. Thus women experience gendered evaluations, i.e. not according to the masculine norm, whereas men are judged by their male gendered performance.

Compensating women without taking into account the actual performance of the company entails a number of consequences, one of them being the strengthening of existing stereotypes. Research has shown that higher compensated people are perceived as more competent, and the lower compensated ones are attributed stereotypically female qualities (Johannensen and Eagly, 2002). What follows is that this mechanism entails the risk of devaluation of both women's leadership skills and actions they undertake. Lower salary strengthens the conviction that women are less reliable and have a smaller decision-making power, which in turn increases underrepresentation in executive structures (a classic case of a vicious circle). On the other hand, inadequate and unequal compensation has serious consequences for an organisation; it may lead to women to quit their jobs (Townsend, 1996) or decide to start their own business.[20] In other words, an underappreciated contribution and absence of possibilities to change the situation may be the direct reason why women may resign from their positions. Known as the leaky pipeline (Wittenberg-Cox and Maitland, 2013), this phenomenon is the direct cause for the existence of another gap, namely the so-called talent gap which cannot be divorced from undervaluation and the associated GPG.

On the one hand, the problem of vertical segregation may be tackled by ensuring that gender-neutral solutions concerning career advancement are introduced into the collective agreement/remuneration rules. A joint management/union bilateral commission/committee, which is thoroughly versed in the multiple ways that pay inequality can arise, may be one solution to reducing the GPG with an accompanying role of supervising the implementation of emerging strategies so that strategy is implemented in practice. Moreover its composition should be based on gender parity, or, alternatively, at least 30–35% of its members should be women (in accordance with the critical mass theory). This might work well in a centralised context, but would be more difficult to achieve in a decentralised setting without collective bargaining. Moreover, the introduction of equality audits on which to base local considerations are important and not sufficiently widely used (see Chapter 6).

Conclusions

In all member states, there is a duty to ensure that men and women are paid equally for the same or equally valued work. Despite the legal framework, this still does not happen, as the resilience of the GPG testifies. This points to the role of the national state and the weakness of its legal enforcement mechanisms. While we may point to the tasks before trade unions and employers, it is also the role of the state to provide some underpinning enforcement which will provide a self-interested incentive for organisations to take the GPG more seriously and comply with equal pay legislation. In this chapter we have sought organisational solutions and emphasised the importance of raising awareness and the impact of gender bias on work–life balance, lifetime social and material effects and wage-setting. Shining a light on the underrepresentation of women in employee and employer institutions has indicated major gaps where women are not represented in decision-making. This representation gap is important as women are more likely to be attuned and sympathetic to challenging inequality regimes and be aware often because of their own experience of gendered inequality. The role of the state is also important in introducing special measures so that gaps in areas where they are the widest can be quickly bridged (for instance by determining *a priori* what percentage of women should sit on management boards as employee representatives). The chapter has identified a low level of awareness that needs to be tackled in multiple ways.

Measures which will make it more likely that the existing professional segregation will be eliminated are primarily work arrangements designed to ensure balancing professional and family life, using flexible working hours and conditions putting more emphasis on task accomplishment rather than on mere presence at work. Furthermore, access to training and professional development opportunities, mentoring and building female support networks, different conditions for women returning from maternity leave, promoting female representation ratios at higher positions within the organisation, and carrying out equality audits. Such work arrangements may make it easier for women to advance in their careers and move to better paid positions. However, we should not expect that such solutions will deliver a reduced GPG in organisations free from stereotypes that stigmatise women and pigeon-hole men. Organisations that offer training, professional development and carry out equality audits are also found in those with gendered cultures and with high GPGs (for examples, the UK financial services sector). Our knowledge of inequality regimes and power imbalances therefore indicates that such measures are difficult to demonstrate progress, other than that organisations are seen to be doing something.

In discussing gender bias with respect to work–life balance, lifetime pay gaps and biases in wage setting, we are uncovering the fundamental deep-seated effects of inequality regimes in organisations and the disproportionately negative effect on women and their life chances including their lifetime pay. Moreover, we also recognise the power of the state and impact that legislation can have, although we acknowledge the inevitable difficulties of enforcing change. We have only to recall some 50-plus years of equal pay legislation to understand that legislation is important but not sufficient. Key social partners are crucial to enforcing change as are women's organisations who need to continue to hold unions and employers to account to ensure equality and fairness in pay at all levels of an organisation.

Notes

1 According to the data of the Central Statistical Office of Poland (GUS), in 2015 there were 950,000 women and 222,000 men employed in the education sector; for the mining industry, the figures were as follows: 20,000 women and 209,0000 men. As cited in: *Aktywność ekonomiczna ludności Polski w latach 2013–2015*, http://stat.gov.pl/obszary-tematyczne/rynek-pracy/pracujacy-bezrobotni-bierni-zawodo wo-wg-bael/aktywnosc-ekonomiczna-ludnosci-polski-w-latach-2013-2015,5,4.html (accessed 28 February 2017).

2 Given the nature of this analysis, it must be stressed that the EU has guaranteed the right to equal pay for women and men since the establishment of the EEC (see Art. 119 of the Treaty establishing the EEC). While the motivating factors have changed to some extent over the course of decades (the first regulations were mostly based on economic factors and were intended to ensure free competition policy), elimination of the GPG is currently a permanent part of programmes and actions of organisations, also under the *Strategic Engagement for Gender Equality 2016–2019*, http://ec. europa.eu/anti-trafficking/sites/antitrafficking/files/strategic_engagement_for_gender_ equality_en.pdf (accessed 28 February 2017).

3 The presence of women in management boards of companies can be an incentive for others and an example to follow, thus leading to an increase in the proportion of females in other executive bodies within a company ('moral' argument). On the other hand, arguments of economic nature are referred to as the so-called 'business case', according to which gender diversity directly translates into a boost in productivity and better results, which in turn improves the company's profitability and shareholder value (Gómez Ansón, 2012). Teams composed of both women and men offer multidimensionality of opinions, heterogeneity of views and assessments, and thus a diversity of solutions. In other words, the greater the diversity of human resources, the more economically efficient the company is.

4 See *Convention on the Elimination of All Forms of Discrimination against Women*, adopted in 1979 by the UN General Assembly and General recommendation No. 25, on article 4, paragraph 1, of the Convention on the Elimination of All Forms of Discrimination against Women, on temporary special measures, adopted by COMMITTEE ON THE ELIMINATION OF ALL FORMS DISCRIMINATION AGAINST WOMEN in 2004. Also, *General comment No. 16 (2005) The equal right of men and women to the enjoyment of all economic, social and cultural rights (art. 3 of the International Covenant on Economic, Social and Cultural Rights)*, adopted by COMMITTEE ON ECONOMIC, SOCIAL AND CULTURAL RIGHTS in 2005.

5 More on the EU measures intended to ensure gender equality in the decision-making process: http://ec.europa.eu/justice/gender-equality/gender-decision-making/index_en. htm (accessed 28 February 2017).

6 ONS (2016), *Annual Survey of Hours and Earnings: All Data Related to Annual Survey of Hours and Earnings: 2016 Provisional Results*. The gap was revised up from 13.9% to 14.1% in both 2015 and 2016.

7 Resolution Foundation (2017), Press release: 'Gender pay gap falls to 5 per cent for Millennials in their 20s – but they are still set to face a huge lifetime earnings penalty', accessed at: www.resolutionfoundation.org/media/press-releases/gender-pay-ga p-falls-to-5-per-cent-for-millennials-in-their-20s-but-they-are-still-set-to-face-a-huge-li fetime-earnings-penalty/ (accessed 5 January 2018).

8 Zwysen and Longhi (2016).

9 The Proposal for a Directive of the European Parliament and of the Council on work–life balance for parents and carers and repealing Council Directive 2010/18/EU, COM/ 2017/0253 final-2017/085 (COD) – among legislative measures – includes: the introduction of paternity leave, strengthening of parental leave, the right to request to take leave in a flexible way, introduction of carers' leave for workers caring for seriously ill or dependent relatives and extension of the right to request flexible working arrangements. It is worth to stress that the initiative contains also a set of non-legislative measures as: ensuring protection against discrimination and dismissal for parents, encouraging a gender-balanced use of family-related leaves and flexible working arrangements, making better use of European funds to improve long-term and child-care services and removing economic disincentives for second earners which prevent women from accessing the labour market or working full-time.

10 Adopting: COM(2008) 635, Council Directive 2010/18/EU implementing the revised Framework Agreement on parental leave (OJEU L 68 of 18.3.2010, p. 13) and

Directive 2010/41/EU of the European Parliament and of the Council of 7 July 2010 on the application of the principle of equal treatment between men and women engaged in an activity in a self-employed capacity and repealing Council Directive 86/613/EEC (OJEU L 180 of 15.7.2010).

11 As the Research on Economic Activity of the Population (BAEL), by the Central Statistical Office of Poland (GUS) show, during the period from March to September 2016 the number of inactive people has increased by 150,000. The people in question quoted 'family obligations connected with household management' as the reason for not taking up employment. An increase in the number of inactive people has also been observed among the 22–44 age group, with women being the only group where professional activity has dropped.

12 *Act of 3 December 2010 on the implementation of some regulations of the European Union regarding equal treatment* (Journal of Laws 2010, No. 254, item 1700), implementing e.g. Directive 2006/54/EC, defined the Polish model of antidiscrimination policy, an important element of which was the office of the Government Plenipotentiary for Equal Treatment. The abolishment of the office would therefore be a clear signal that the Directive's objective is not fully realised in Poland.

13 www.theguardian.com/money/2016/mar/07/gender-pay-gap-uk-women-earn-300000.less-men-lifetime (accessed 5 January 2018).

14 Capabilities are defined by Amartya Sen as 'substantial freedoms' that enable to 'lead lives that people have reason to value' (Sen, 2000: 109); on the topic of capabilities, see also Supiot (2001) and Deakin and Supiot (2009).

15 Job evaluation is promoted at European level by the European Commission, *Report on the Implementation of Directive 2006/54/EC*, Annex I, by the European Parliament in the Resolution of 24 May 2012 on gender pay equality (2011/2285(INI)) and by the ETUC (Pillinger, 2014) it is also fostered at the international level by the Oil (see Pillinger *et al.*, 2016; Chicha, 2008).

16 hwww.acas.org.uk/media/pdf/3/d/Job-evaluation-considerations-and-risks-advisory-booklet.pdf (accessed 22 December 2017).

17 See Lissenburgh (1995), Conley (2014) and Wright and Conley (2016). See Court of Justice, 6 July 1982, *Commission of the European Communities* v *United Kingdom of Great Britain and Northern Ireland. Equal pay for men and women*, C-61/81, Reports of Cases 1982–02601, where the Court clarifies that the previous introduction of a job evaluation system cannot be considered by national law as a mandatory condition for employees to obtain the implementation of gender pay equality for work of equal value.

18 *Institut pour l'égalité des femmes et des hommes, La classification de fonctions analytique: une base pour une politique salariale sexuellement neutre - Guide pratique*, 2007, http://igvm-iefh.belgium.be/fr/publications/analytische_functieclassificatie_-_praktische_gids.

19 https://nwlc.org/wp-content/uploads/2015/02/Union-Membership-is-Critical-for-Equal-Pay.pdf (accessed 25 October 2017).

20 Female entrepreneurs currently account for 29% of all entrepreneurs in Europe, and since 2008 the figure has gone up by 3%. Women dominate in the segment of sole traders (making up 78% of all sole traders), their dominance being particularly prominent in sectors connected with health care, services, education or social work.

References

Acker, J. (2006) 'Inequality Regimes: Gender, Class, and Race in Organizations' *Gender and Society* 20(4), pp. 441–464.

Blackburn, R. M., Browne, J., Brooks, B. and Jarman, J. (2002) 'Explaining Gender Segregation' *The British Journal of Sociology* 53, pp. 513–536.

Bradley, H. and Healy, G. (2008) *Ethnicity and Gender at Work: Inequalities, Careers and Employment Relations*, ed. Peter Nolan (ESRC Future of Work Series). London and New York: Palgrave Macmillan.

Breach, A. and Li, Y. (2017) *Gender Pay Gap by Ethnicity in Britain – Briefing.* Fawcett Society.

Chicha, M.-T. (2008) *Promoting Equity: Gender-Neutral Job Evaluation for Equal Pay. A Step-by-Step Guide.* Geneva: International Labour Office.

Childs, S. and Krook, M. (2008) 'Critical Mass Theory and Women's Political Representation' *Political Studies* 56, pp. 725–736.

Colling, T. and Dickens, L. (1989) *Equality Bargaining: Why Not?* Manchester: Equal Opportunities Commission.

Conley, H. (2014) 'Trade Unions, Equal Pay and the Law in the UK' *Economic and Industrial Democracy* 35(2), pp. 309–323.

Dahlerup, D. (2006) 'The Story of the Theory of Critical Mass' *Politics & Gender* 2(4), pp. 511–522.

Deakin, S. and Supiot, A. (eds) (2009) *Capacitas: Contract Law and the Institutional Preconditions of a Market Economy.* Oxford: Hart Publishing.

Dex, S., Ward, K. and Joshi, H. (2008) 'Gender Differences in Occupational Wage Mobility in the 1958 Cohort' *Work, Employment & Society* 22(2), pp. 263–280.

Drolet, M. and Mumford, K. (2012) 'The Gender Pay Gap for Private-Sector Employees in Canada and Britain' *British Journal of Industrial Relations* 50(3), pp. 529–553.

Elvira, M. M. and Saporta, I. (2001) 'How Does Collective Bargaining Affect the Gender Pay Gap?' *Work and Occupations* 28(4), pp. 469–490.

Erkrut, S., Kramer, Vicky W. and Konrad, A. (2014) 'Critical Mass: Does the Number on a Corporate Board Make a Difference?' in S. Vinnicombe, V. Singh, R. J. Burke, D. Bilimoria and M. Huse (eds), *Women on Corporate Boards of Directors: International Research and Practice.* Cheltenham and Northampton: Edward Elgar, pp. 222–240.

European Commission (2013) 'The Gender Gap in Pensions in the EU'. Available from: http://ec.europa.eu/justice/gender-equality/files/documents/130530_pensions_en.pdf (accessed 28 February 2017).

European Commission (2015) 'Strategic Engagement for Gender Equality 2016–2019'. Available from: http://ec.europa.eu/justice/genderequality/files/documents/151203_strategic_engagement_en.pdf (accessed 28 February 2017).

European Commission (2016) 'The Gender Pay Gap in the European Union'. Available from: http://ec.europa.eu/justice/genderequality/files/gender_pay_gap/2016/gpg_eu_factsheet_2016_en.pdf (accessed 28 February 2017).

European Institute for Gender Equality (2015) *Gender Equality Index 2015: Measuring Gender Equality in the European Union 2005–2012.* EIGE Report, pp. 47–49.

European Social Partners (2015) *The 2015–2017 Work Programme of the European Social Partners: 'Partnership for Inclusive Growth and Employment'.*

Fulton, L., Sechi, C. and Helfferichet, B. (2017) ETUC Annual Gender Equality Survey 2017. Brussels, *European Trade Union Institute (ETUI).* 10: 1–61.

Goldin, C. (2014) 'A Grand Gender Convergence: Its Last Chapter' *American Economic Review* 104(4), pp. 1091–1119.

Gómez Ansón, S. (2012) 'Women on Boards in Europe: Past, Present and Future' in C. Fagan, M. C. González Mendéz and S. Gómez Ansón (eds), *Women on Corporate Boards and in Top Management.* New York: Palgrave Macmillan, p. 25.

Government Plenipotentiary on Equal Treatment (2013) *National Action Plan for Equal Treatment (2013–2016).* Warsaw.

Healy, G. and Kirton, G. (2000) 'Women, Power and Trade Union Government in the UK' *British Journal of Industrial Relations* 38(3), pp. 343–360.

Healy, G., Bradley, H. and Forson, C. (2011) 'Intersectional Sensibilities in Analysing Inequality Regimes in Public Sector Organizations' *Gender, Work & Organization* 18 (5), pp. 467–487.

Hyman, R. (1987) 'Strategy or Structure? Capital, Labour and Control' *Work Employment & Society* 1(1), pp. 25–55.

Johannensen, M. and Eagly, A. (2002) 'Diminishing Returns: The Effects of Income on the Content of Stereotypes of Wage Earners' *Personality and Social Psychology Bulletin* 28, pp. 1538–1545.

Kalev, A., Dobbin, F. and Kelly, E. (2006) 'Best Practices or Best Guesses? Assessing the Efficacy of Corporate Affirmative Action and Diversity Policies' *American Sociological Review* 71(4), pp. 589–617.

Kirton, G. (2005) 'The Influences on Women Joining and Participating in Unions' *Industrial Relations Journal* 36(5), pp. 386–401.

Kirton, G. (2015) 'Progress towards Gender Democracy in UK Unions 1987–1201' *British Journal of Industrial Relations* 53(3), pp. 484–507.

Kirton, G. and Healy, G. (2013) *Gender and Leadership in Unions*. Routledge.

Kirton, G., Robertson, M. and Avdelidou-Fischer, N. (2016) 'Valuing and Value in Diversity: The Policy-Implementation Gap in an IT Firm' *Human Resource Management Journal* 26(3), pp. 321–336.

Lisowska, E. (2016) 'Ekonomiczne korzyści wyrównania płac kobiet i mężczyz', paper delivered at a conference closing the international research project 'Close the Deal, Fill the Gap', Faculty of Law and Administration, University of Silesia, Katowice, November 2016.

Lissenburgh, S. (1995) 'Implementing "Equal Value" through Collective Bargaining and Job Evaluation' *Policy Studies* 16(4), pp. 49–64.

Mazur-Wierzbicka, E. (2015) 'Implementing the Work–Life Balance as a CSR Tool in Polish Companies' *Research Papers of Wrocław University of Economics* 387, pp. 109–121.

McKinsey & Company Report (2007) *A Wake-up Call for Female Leadership in Europe.*

Michels, R. (1911) *Political Parties: A Sociological Study of the Oligarchical Tendencies of Modern Democracy*. New York: Free Press.

Mierżyńska, M. and Dziewguć, M. (2017) 'Musimy obudzić w dziewczynkach łobuza' *Newsweek Psychologia* 1, pp. 82–86.

The Ministry of Labour and Social Policy (2013) *Human Capital Development Strategy 2020.* Warsaw.

Munro, A. (2001) 'A Feminist Trade Union Agenda? The Continued Significance of Class, Gender and Race' *Gender, Work & Organization* 8(4), pp. 454–471.

Murphy, E. and Oesch, D. (2016) 'The Feminization of Occupations and Change in Wages: A Panel Analysis of Britain, Germany, and Switzerland' *Social Forces* 94(3), pp. 1221–1255.

Pillinger, J. (2014) *Bargaining for Equality*. Brussels: European Trade Union Confederation.

Pillinger, J., Schmidt, V. and Wintour, N. (2016) 'Negotiating for Gender Equality' Issue Brief, No. 4, Geneva: International Labour Office.

Rubery, J., Grimshaw, D. and Figueiredo, H. (2005) 'How to Close the Gender Pay Gap in Europe: Towards the Gender Mainstreaming of Pay Policy' *Industrial Relations Journal* 36, pp. 184–213.

Ryan, M., Kulich, C., Haslam S., Alexander, M., Hersby, D., Mette, D. and Atkins, C. (2014) 'Examining Gendered Experiences beyond the Glass Ceiling: The Precariousness of the Glass Cliff and Absence of Rewards' in S. Vinnicombe, V. Singh, R. J. Burke, D. Bilimoria and M. Huse (eds), *Women on Corporate Boards of Directors: International Research and Practice*. Cheltenham and Northampton: Edward Elgar, pp. 165–183.

Sen, A. (2000) *Development as Freedom*. New York: Anchor Books.

Smithson, J., Lewis, S., Cooper, C. and Dyer, J. (2004) 'Flexible Working and the Gender Pay Gap in the Accountancy Profession' *Work, Employment and Society* 18 (1), pp. 115–135.

Supiot, A. (2001) *Beyond Employment: Changes in Work and the Future of Labour Law in Europe*. Oxford: Oxford University Press.

Townsend, B. (1996) 'Room at the Top for Women' *American Demographics* 18, pp. 28–37.

Wittenberg-Cox, A. and Maitland, A. (2013) *Kobiety i ich wpływ na biznes. Nowa rewolucja gospodarcza*. Warsaw: Wolters Kluwer Business.

Wright, T. and Conley, H. (eds) (2016) *Gower Handbook of Discrimination at Work*. Farnham: Routledge.

Zwysen, W. and Longhi, S. (2016) 'Labour Market Disadvantage of Ethnic Minority British Graduates: University Choice, Parental Background or Neighborhood?' University of Essex ISER Working Paper 2016-02. Available from: www.iser.essex.ac.uk/research/publications/working-papers/iser/2016-02 (accessed 27 March 2018).

6   Transparency and the gender pay gap

Hazel Conley and Urszula Torbus

Introduction

Transparency is central to the concept of equal pay since, without it, equality or the lack of it cannot be established. Despite this seemingly obvious logic there remains a failure in social, economic and legal systems to deliver transparent pay systems. The implementation of the equal pay principle in Europe is hindered by a lack of transparency in pay systems (European Commission, 2014), an issue that was identified in early European case law on pay equality (McCrudden, 1993). Without transparency, there is a lack of information and awareness among employers and employees about the existence of possible pay gaps within their company (European Parliament, 2012: 2.1). Transparency is, therefore, the precursor to a consciousness of differences between male and female pay, which is the first step required to close the GPG. Only the awareness of the existence of pay differences between men and women can result in actions undertaken by employees and by social partners to this end (Guidelines, 2016: 1).

Transparency, or the lack of it in pay systems, is a concept that has arisen in all three of our national studies of the GPG. Although common to each of the countries, the lack of transparency in relation to the GPG occurs at different junctures within each, influenced by the distinct features of the national pay setting systems. In Italy, with a relatively centralised system of pay setting, the lack of transparency seeps into pay between men and women where elements of pay and benefits, such as performance related pay, fall outside of tightly regulated sectoral pay setting machinery. In the UK, decentralised pay setting means that the lack of transparency is greatest where pay is individually negotiated, for example, in more senior levels or, like Italy, where elements of the pay package are subject to individualised performance or bonus criteria. Poland, which has the lowest GPG of our three national studies, is characterised by the most gender segregated organisation of work and a culture of secrecy in relation to pay, which has led to a lack of transparency in relation to equal value between the work that men and women undertake and a resulting difficulty in gathering research data.

Surprisingly, there is very little European academic research that focuses on the concept of pay transparency, although there has been some attempt to explore this topic in US legal research (for example, Mas, 2016; Risher, 2014; Ramachandran, 2012; Eisenberg, 2012, 2011; Estlund, 2014, 2009; O'Neill, 2010; Colella *et al.*, 2007). In this chapter we explore the US literature to build a conceptual analysis of pay transparency before drawing on our empirical findings. Our research in three European studies illustrates that, whilst on the surface pay systems might appear to be non-discriminatory, pay inequality is embedded in gendered assumptions of worth, skill and gendered practices of exclusion and segregation that are not easily exposed by simple models of pay transparency. The chapter further considers current regulatory attempts in our case studies, based on legal theories of reflexive and responsive legislation, to change employer behaviour in relation to transparency as a tool for closing the GPG.

Conceptualising pay transparency

The majority of the US literature on pay transparency does not relate specifically to the GPG but originated in relation to executive pay and the gaps between high and low earners in organisations (for example, Mas, 2016; Ramachandran, 2012; Estlund, 2009; Colella *et al.*, 2007). Much of this literature harks back to the **National Labor Relations Act** (NLRA) passed in 1935 as part of the 'New Deal' to protect employees' rights to collective organisation, in which pay transparency is considered to be a precursor to collective bargaining. Others have extended these debates to specifically address pay transparency as an element of discrimination (Cherradi, 2016; Estlund, 2014; DelPo Kulow, 2013; Eisenberg, 2012, 2011; O'Neill, 2010). Implicit in these arguments is that pay transparency for collective bargaining purposes does not automatically result in pay equality. Most of these researchers were prompted to enter the debate on pay transparency following *Ledbetter* v *Goodyear Tire and Rubber Company [2007]* in which Lilly Ledbetter established that for 20 years she had been paid less than a male comparator. The controversial majority decision of the Supreme Court was that Ms Ledbetter could not claim compensation because her claim fell outside of the time limits in the legislation. However, Lilly had not been aware that her pay was discriminatory until after she retired because of the pay secrecy and confidentiality rules operated by her employer, meaning that pay equality could be easily subverted by a lack of transparency (DelPo Kulow, 2013; O'Neill, 2010). A lack of transparency is particularly incongruent when legal remedies for pay discrimination require claimants/plaintiffs to find an actual comparator.

The *Ledbetter* case prompted a change in the Federal statute and the passing of the *Lilly Ledbetter Fair Pay Restoration Act* in 2009, spearheaded by the Obama presidency. The legislation dealt only with the problem of time limitations and did not address the issue of transparency (DelPo Kulow, 2013; O'Neill, 2010). Most authors therefore called for a legislative approach to pay transparency to accompany existing pay equality legislation. There have been several attempts since 2009 to pass a *Paycheck Fairness Act* which, amongst a raft of measures strengthen the **Equal Pay Act** (DelPo Kulow, 2013), would make it unlawful for employers to punish employees who discuss their pay. Even this modest attempt to outlaw pay secrecy has been blocked by Republican senators at each attempt to pass the bill (Rosenfeld, 2017), although wage disclosure has been adopted in some states (DelPo Kulow, 2013: 423).

The US literature highlights that pay transparency needs to be conceptualised from several dimensions. Cherradi (2016) distinguishes between three types of legislative approach to pay transparency. The first, which she calls 'anti-chilling pay transparency laws' (p. 8), refer to laws such as the proposed *Paycheck Fairness Act* that limit pay secrecy. The second, 'anti-retaliation and anti-discrimination pay transparency laws' (p. 9), provide remedies for employees who have suffered pay discrimination and/or victimisation for revealing their pay. The third, 'public reporting or disclosing of pay transparency laws … creates an affirmative obligation on the employers to report and disclose pay information' (p. 9). All three approaches are required and Ramachandran (2012) considers pay transparency laws essential to support traditional anti-discrimination approaches to pay equality. Estlund (2014) and Eisenberg (2011) adopt a business case to justify the development of transparency legislation by arguing that it would ensure the smoother operation of labour markets generally since a basic principle for market clearing is the availability of information to both buyers and sellers of labour. They do, however, acknowledge that outside of abstract models of market equilibrium, individual employers are likely to have serious reservations about the impact of pay transparency on employee morale and consequently loyalty.

Some of the wider US literature on transparency offers useful conceptual direction. Writing on transparency in public policy generally, Fung *et al.* (2004) argue that transparency systems do not usually directly change the behaviour of organisations, but rely on new information to provoke a desired change. They further note:

> that simply placing information in the public domain does not mean that it will be used, or used wisely. In practice, information cannot be separated from its social context. Individuals and organizations simply ignore information that is costly to acquire or that lacks salience for decisions.
>
> (Fung *et al.*, 2004: 8)

As such, devising transparency systems that result in change requires a 'complex chain of events' (p. 4) with an outcome that can be 'unpredictable and ambiguous' (p. 6).

Fung *et al.* (2004: 8) argue the transparency policies that work are usually those that lead organisations to build the information acquired under transparency systems into their decision-making processes. In some respects, this argument is resonant with the concept of equality mainstreaming, which similarly rests on the integration of equality considerations into organisational decision-making. Fung *et al.* identify three factors that they consider are associated with transparency systems that lead to positive decision-making: 'the information's perceived value in achieving users' goals; its compatibility with decision-making routines; and its comprehensibility' (pp. 10–11). Relevant to the issue of pay transparency, Fung *et al.* make the point that, whilst disclosers will usually voluntarily reveal favourable information, 'Government-mandated disclosure generally forces them to reveal unfavorable news about public risks or faulty performance that would not otherwise be made public ... Thus, while many disclosers act in good faith, some under-report or hide risks or performance problems' (2004: 16). Fung *et al.* further warn that legislation is likely to be less effective when the goals of the organisation differ from those of the lawmakers. Since closing the GPG is potentially a costly exercise for organisations and may represent at least a short-term drain in profits, pay transparency legislation clearly falls within this warning. Fung *et al.* (2004) therefore provide a useful pointer to potential hurdles for the implementation of pay transparency legislation. They also provide some useful suggestions on how these hurdles may be overcome. First, they argue that having the legislation in place provides a useful lever for those within the organisation who may be sympathetic to the purposes of the legislation and willing to champion it from within. Second, they consider that transparency legislation that is designed to work 'in tandem with other government actions' (p. 30) is likely to have a better chance of succeeding. This again has resonance with pay transparency legislation, which is likely to sit alongside equal pay laws and other anti-discrimination legislation.

In the United States, literature on transparency is mostly connected with the disclosure of information. In relation to pay transparency it can be perceived to have two aspects; the first concerns information on the remuneration of individual employees and the second the collective disclosure of pay information for certain categories of employees. Measures that provide individual disclosure of pay differences have a retrospective effect, as they can help to build individual cases, while collective disclosure may be the basis for more general measures to reduce the GPG (European Commission 2013: 4.2). The US experience indicates that pay transparency for general collective bargaining purposes is unlikely, without a specific focus on pay equality, to lead to a closing of the GPG. One explanation is that the idea of transparency goes further than simply information on pay. Gender differences in pay are deeply rooted in the social, economic, political and institutional context in which pay systems are embedded. For example, in EU legislation pay equality is closely linked to the concept of work of equal value and gender-neutral job evaluation. Implementation of the principle of equal pay for the same work and for work of equal value is crucial to achieving gender equality (European Parliament, 2012: E). In the United States, the concept of comparable worth addresses this dimension, but it is not embedded in the **Equal Pay Act** and is therefore less influential.

In Europe the issue of pay transparency and its links with pay inequality was highlighted in the Commission's Report to the European Parliament and the Council COM (2013) 861 final. The report stated that a lack of pay transparency and a lack of clarity on equal value reduced the effectiveness of equal pay legislation in member states. The report gave rise to a set of recommendations C(2014) 1405 final. Sub-section 15 of the recommendations state:

> This Recommendation should focus on transparency of wage categories, which is essential for the effective application of the equal pay principle. Increased transparency can reveal a gender bias and discrimination in the pay structures of an undertaking or organisation. It enables employees, employers and social partners to take appropriate action to ensure implementation of the equal pay principle. This Recommendation should present a tool box of measures designed to assist Member States in taking a tailor-made approach to improving wage transparency. Member States should be encouraged to implement the most appropriate measures for their specific circumstances and to implement at least one of the core measures enhancing transparency set out in this Recommendation (entitlement to request pay information, company reporting, pay audits, equal pay collective bargaining).
>
> (European Commission, 2013)

There are 19 recommendations, which include greater clarity on the concept of equal value and the use of gender-neutral job evaluation.

In April 2017 the Commission published a legal analysis of pay transparency measures adopted by member states plus Norway, Liechtenstein and Iceland. The analysis found wide variation in the practices amongst member states, but that only 10 of the 31 countries included had adopted one or more of the recommendations on pay transparency in a way that could be used to decrease the GPG, although two others (UK and Germany) were in the process of doing so. The analysis concludes that the main obstacles to implementing pay transparency measures were 'sensitivity and confidentiality issues around revealing wages; administrative and financial burdens; a lack of collective bargaining structures; no problem awareness or priority of equal pay among the trade unions; and the fear of levelling down' (European Commission, 2017: 9). The report further notes that, even in countries with developed pay structures in place, gender pay information on same work or work of equal value was most difficult for employees to establish (p. 10). Rather surprisingly, there is no mention in the report of the case law generated in the UK in relation to job evaluation and equal pay.

Our research indicates that, for the GPG to become fully transparent, equal value must be taken into consideration. Therefore, job evaluation, although itself imperfect (for example, Gilbert, 2012, 2005; Wright, 2011; Figgart, 2001), is a key instrument to implement a wider concept of pay transparency. It enables a comparison between different jobs, especially in the context of intra-occupational gender-based horizontal segregation (Guidelines, 2016: 2.4). The comparison, possible through gender-neutral job evaluation and classification criteria, constitutes an important factor in bringing equal pay claims before the court and fighting pay discrimination. Therefore, obscure pay schemes and a lack of, or difficult access to, information about levels of pays in a company for employees performing the same work or work of equal value constitutes major difficulties in enforcement of the principle of equal pay. Gender-neutral job evaluation and classification systems are considered effective in establishing a transparent pay system because they detect indirect pay discrimination related to the undervaluation of jobs typically done by women (European Commission, 2014: 22), which in turn helps to tackle the horizontal segregation of women.

Transparency regarded from the perspective of employees is connected to their rights to pay equality. To be able to claim their rights employees should be able to understand payments schemes, compensation strategies and practices. They should be able to compare their salaries and to understand where the possible differences may come from (Guidelines, 2016: 2.6). Transparency from employers' perspectives can provide a legal defence to equal pay claims. To do so it requires the introduction of clear payment schemes, based on equal value criteria, free from gender bias and limits to discretionary power, particularly with reference to extra pay, bonuses and other advantages forming part of remuneration. It requires undertaking job evaluation schemes and implementing job classification systems. It also requires carrying out compulsory pay audits and publishing their results and providing employees' representatives with wages statistics, broken down by gender, ensuring data protection (European Parliament, 2012: 2).

Clearly, ensuring transparency is a crucial factor in the fight against the GPG but it constitutes a major challenge for employers, public authorities, employee representatives and the employees themselves. Not all employers and employees are willing to disclose the amount of remuneration or to introduce objective – often laboriously determined – rules for classifying employees' work related to their remuneration. The development of a method of assessing the GPG is also an important factor, as it is often difficult to identify for both employees and employers. As Fung *et al.* (2004) and Rama-chandran (2012) note, pay transparency requires encouragement from public policies, which can incentivise and support employers' virtuous practices by granting specific benefits (such as tax reductions, or additional points in public procurements procedures) for companies that meet certain targets in the assessment of the GPG (Guidelines, 2016: 2.6).

Furthermore, reducing the GPG cannot be left to retrospective and reactive remedies for pay discrimination. As our case studies in Chapter 4 evidence, such approach is individualistic, adversarial, lengthy and costly for all parties. Greater emphasis should be placed on using the law as a proactive lever to further negotiation (Guidelines, 2016: 2.7) and to achieve what Cherradi (2016) describes as an affirmative obligation to publicly disclose GPG information. Having reached pay transparency in their own organisations, employers (sup-ported by trade unions) have another important role to play – they can spread transparency along the supply-chain of the company by negotiating 'social clauses' in company agreements, making the respect of certain transparency standards (or of certain low GPG rates) a condition of sub-contracting

(Guidelines, 2016: 10). Together these pay transparency measures offer greater potential for reducing the GPG. The following sections assess how far these measures have been developed in Italy, the UK and Poland.

Pay transparency in Poland

In Poland, although the GPG index is one of the lowest in Europe, the situation as far as wage transparency is concerned leaves much to be desired. Whilst a survey conducted in 2016 showed that 73% of employers estimate that their employees are justly paid, only 36% of employees share this opinion. Similarly, only 40% of enterprises surveyed by the PayScale declare transparency in pay (the figure goes up to 47% in leader companies). This indicator does not coincide with assessments of employees, of whom only 21% are of the opinion that their employers provide clear principles for remuneration (Jaszcz, 2016). Interestingly, in an analysis of the GPG in post-communist European countries, Newell and Reilly (2001: 10) suggest that women have slightly higher educational qualifications than men in Poland and, once this is adjusted for, the GPG increases.

With a few exceptions in the public sector discussed below, in Poland there are no legal solutions that introduce transparency in pay. The Polish legislature seems to be blind to the issue of the GPG, despite it being regularly reported by other public authorities, such as the Central Statistical Office (GUS), for example. There are no legislative and consistent policy instruments, nor any special strategies, which oblige or otherwise induce employers to tackle the GPG problem. There are also no legislative provisions which may induce social partners to include the issue of equal pay into collective agreements (Zielinska, 2010) nor is there any non-legislative practice. Out of 117 investigated collective agreements only a few provide pay reviews for inflation, but none of them introduced any measures to inspect wages from a gender perspective. Polish law, contrary to some European countries, does not require employers to asses pay practices, pay differences or to draw any plans for equal pay. There are no obligations to draw up pay surveys or to gather employment-related statistical data based on gender or to provide employee representatives' reports on gender pay equality (European Commission, 2013: 4.2).

One of the main obstacles to tackling the GPG is the secrecy surrounding wages, which is institutionally and culturally embedded in Polish society. Information regarding individual pay is often considered as confidential information under national data protection and privacy legislation. It is can also be treated as the breach of secrecy of trade, based on the Law of 16 April 1993 regarding unfair competition (Zielinska, 2010). Therefore, most employers regard wages as confidential and refuse to disclose remuneration policies or schemes, which was confirmed during the research carried out for the project (see Chapter 4). On the one hand, pay secrecy is connected with certain cultural taboos regarding the release of information about wages of other people. Employees do not normally reveal their remuneration or agree to disclose information on additional payment elements, such as bonuses, for example. On the other hand, for employers, it seems to be an intentional policy of 'exaggerated confidentiality' (Zielinska, 2010). It often occurs that the internal regulations on wages (regulations on remuneration) stipulate that the wages within the company are secret and employees are not allowed to disclose the amount of remuneration to anyone (although it has no legal basis, as the Labour Code contains no regulation on confidentiality of remuneration). Discussing pay levels can even be regarded by internal regulations as a violation of employee duties. The literature indicates that this policy is adopted partly to hide the practices of uneven and often discretionary remuneration, especially in case of more favourable pay of newly acquired employees (Walczak, 2009), although judicature recognises that old and new employees should earn the same if they have the same qualifications (Supreme Court 2007). The fight against discrimination in pay is more difficult because very few job advertisements (about 3.5%) include information on the proposed remuneration, particularly in the IT industry (TeamQuest, 2016).

The case law of the Supreme Court contributed significantly to the practice, especially the precedential verdict of the full court in 1993. The court held that trade unions' right to monitor compliance with labour law also includes the right to control employees' remuneration, but it does not cover the right to obtain information on an individual employee's salary without their consent. According to the court, the disclosure of the amount of remuneration without employees' consent can be regarded as a violation of personal rights and the information of individual salaries is not necessary to conduct trade unions' activity in the field of protection of both individual and group interests (Supreme Court 1993). Consequently, the labour law doctrine commonly confirms that each employee has the right to protect the amount of their salary as a personal right. Interference with the privacy of the worker in this regard can be done only with the consent of the employee or under express provision of the law (which is considered as circumstances excluding the illegality of the threat or violation of personal rights), for example, to the court bailiff (*Article 882 of the Code of Civil Procedure*) (Dörre-Nowak, 2005). Jurisprudence, on the other hand, admits that pay secrecy is not absolute, particularly referring to the obligation to disclose the level of all earnings, including the salary received at another employer in order to be granted the benefits from the social fund, which does not infringe worker's personal rights (Supreme Court 2002). According to current regulations, the benefits from the social fund shall depend on the social situation of the employee. This means that the law does not grant the benefits of the same amount to all employees and requires the income of the employee and her/his family be established (Court of Appeal 2013).

Therefore, whilst the state can demand pay transparency, the obligation to maintain the secrecy of wages remains on employers. According to the jurisprudence, disclosure by an employee to other employees of information on wages, even if they are covered by the confidentiality clause which aims to prevent violation of the principle of equal treatment and forms of discrimination concerning wages, may not involve negative consequences to the employee, including termination of employment, regardless of how the employee obtained access to the information. The prohibition of abuse by employers of confidentiality clauses, or payroll 'secrecy', does at least meets Cherradi's (2016) concept of anti-retaliation law, but pay secrecy is still permitted by the protection of trade secrets, the disclosure of which could jeopardise the essential interests of the company, for example, its competitiveness (Supreme Court 2011).

Lack of knowledge on remunerations makes it considerably more difficult for employees to pursue equal pay claims. In 2007, the Supreme Court referred to case-law of the Court of Justice of the European Union (CJEU) on discrimination and determined that whenever the pay system used by an employer is not transparent, it is the employer's responsibility to prove that it is not discriminatory. According to the Court, in case of differentiating the pay of employees performing the same work (for example, due to their different qualifications or length of service), the employer should prove that they used objective criteria and that these criteria were important for the performance of tasks assigned to the employees (Supreme Court 2007).

However, since it is the employee who is required to establish facts from which it can be presumed that there has indeed been discrimination, discrimination cases (in general, not just pay discrimination) account for merely 1% of all employment cases. In its recent judgement, the Supreme Court confirmed that an employee who claims violation of the principle of equal pay should 'indicate employees who are better paid although they are doing comparable work in order to set direction and allow the carrying out of a comparative analysis'. As a result, the burden of proving that objective criteria were used in the process of determining pay will be shifted to the employer (Supreme Court 2016). This is in line with the settled case law, according to which, if an employee accuses his employer of violation of anti-discrimination regulations, the employee should present circumstances giving rise to his unequal treatment claim (Supreme Court 2007, Supreme Court 2009, Supreme Court 2011). In disputes where an employee derives their claims from a breach of the prohibition of discrimination, the employee shall present the court with facts from which it can be presumed that the employee in question has been directly or indirectly discriminated, in which case the burden of proving that objective criteria were used to differentiate employees' compensation shifts back to the employer (Supreme Court 2005, Supreme Court 2006, Supreme Court 2007).

What follows is that an employee who derives their claims from regulations prohibiting discrimination in employment is required to present such facts that will make it possible to presume not only that the employee indeed receives less compensation than another person(s), but that the differences in compensation were due to a reason prohibited by the law. It is not until such facts are made plausible that the employer will be required to prove that such pay differentiation between the applicant and other employees stemmed from using rational and just differentiation criteria (Supreme Court 2016).

These circumstances lead to the conclusion that, in order for the principle of equal pay for work of equal or similar value to be actually realised, collective agreements or, in the absence thereof, remuneration rules, should include a system of wage determination based on job evaluation and a resultant pay scale that is gender-neutral in its operation (Walczak, 2009). This will improve pay transparency and will make it easier (or, in fact, possible) for employees to pursue pay discrimination claims before labour courts.

As mentioned earlier, public sector salaries are characterised by greater transparency. Wages for state employees are determined by the law. This includes persons employed in state budgetary units, state budgetary enterprises, state universities, as well as professional soldiers and officers specified by the law (**Law of 23rd December 1999** on **Wages in Budgetary Sector**). The remuneration of the employees covered by the multiplier is calculated in relation to the base amount, indexed annually, and the basis for determining the remuneration for the financial year for employees not covered by such a system is the salary from the previous year, indexed to average annual wage increases. Principles and elements of their remuneration are set out by the respective law and enactment legislation and, although allowed, negotiations are very limited.

The public sector is subject to regulations which guarantee disclosure of remuneration of certain people. Examples include the **Act of 9 June 2016** on the principles of determining the salaries of persons managing certain companies, or the **Act of 2003** on salaries of persons managing certain legal entities. The applicable regulations govern, for example, the wage-setting principles for members of management bodies and supervisory boards of companies controlled by the Treasury, local government authorities and associations thereof, as well as state and locally owned legal entities. They also apply to persons managing state-owned enterprises, state budget entities, or independent public healthcare institutions. The acts expressly provide that salaries in entities covered by the respective acts shall be made public, are not subject to personal data protection or trade secret protection, and shall be published in the Public Information Bulletin online.

Salaries of persons performing important public functions, such as councillors, heads of local communities, mayors, poviat[1] council members, voivodeship[2] board members, and commune, poviat and voivodeship treasurers shall also be made public. Pursuant to legislation regulating local government in Poland, such persons are required to submit declarations of financial assets which, in the part concerning salaries, shall be made official and published in the Public Information Bulletin. The case-law recognises that salaries of commune authorities (commune heads, mayors, and their respective deputies) do not fall within the ambit of privacy of persons performing these functions as they are connected with the public roles these persons play (Administrative Court in Wrocław 1997).

In contrast to the pay secrecy that holds for employees in the private sector, salaries of board members of companies listed on the stock exchange should also be made public. In this context, it is worth mentioning the *Code of Best*

Practice for Warsaw Stock Exchange Listed Companies, effective since 1 January 2016. Developed on the initiative of the Warsaw Stock Exchange, the document, although not mandatory, contains guidelines for companies listed on the stock exchange ensuring protection of the most important values developed in conjunction with the market and recommended by the stock exchange. As far as good practices are concerned, the document makes reference to salaries of board members and key managers, which should be published and is currently considered a fundamental principle of corporate governance. The document also recommends that all companies listed on the stock exchange adopt a remuneration policy, which will prevent salaries from being determined on an ad hoc basis, on an impulse, under the influence of current events, as a reaction to financial performance, or under pressure. It is recommended that companies develop a long-lasting, predictable and transparent pay policy covering all employees or at least members of executive bodies and key managers. The pay policy should encompass solutions helping to prevent any and all kinds or discrimination and may play a role in building an environment friendly to women and conducive to gender equality (Nartowski, 2016). That said, in 2015 more than 70% of the largest companies listed on the stock exchange (stock indexes WIG20, mWIG40, sWIG80) did not disclose salaries of their top executives. It is also worth noting that in 2015, the GPG among board members increased from 47% (year 2013) to 59% (PwC, 2016).

While analysing the issue of transparency in pay, attention must also be drawn to the recent changes of the Polish Labour Code which entered into force from 1 January 2017. Until then the conditions on remunerations for employers with at least 20 employees not covered by a collective labour agreement were obligatorily determined in the remuneration regulations. As indicated in Chapter 1, the content of the remuneration regulations is known to all employees, because both its introduction and each change must be communicated to the employees in accordance with the standard method used by the employer. The amendment to the Labour Code, introduced by the **Act of 16 December 2016** on improvement of the legal environment of business, raises the limit of employees that makes the regulation on remuneration mandatory. Since 1 January 2017, the regulation on remuneration is obligatory for employers with at least 50 employees not covered by a collective agreement. Smaller employers can introduce the regulation on remuneration, but it is more likely that for a certain number of them it is more probable to determine pay in individual employment contracts. It is interesting to note that limiting wage transparency in companies employing between 20 and 50 employees is considered to provide an improved legal environment for business, particularly when statistical data show the impact of transparent pay schemes on the GPG.

In the public sector, where most pay schemes are regulated by the law and, therefore, have greater transparency, the GPG reaches 3.9%, whereas in the private sector, where setting wages is left to employers and is less transparent, the gap is 17.9%. Although this change remains in accordance with *Commission Recommendation 2003/361/EC of 6 May 2003* (European Commission,

2003), concerning the definition of micro, small and medium-sized enterprises, it will not help to tackle the GPG. We should bear in mind the specifics of the Polish labour market, where 98.9% of enterprises are small enterprises, employing fewer than 50 employees, of which 95% are micro enterprises, employing fewer than nine employees (Central Statistical Office, 2014). There-fore, most of the private sector has no requirement for pay transparency, while individually negotiated pay and individualised pay systems lead to increased pay disparities between employees at similar levels that can result in a widening of the GPG (European Commission, 2013: G).

There may be unintended consequences for collective representation of employees in small enterprises. The amendment to the Labour Code requires employers with between 20 and 50 employees to introduce the regulation on remuneration on request of an enterprise trade union. Whilst this amendment is meant to strengthen the powers of the trade unions, in reality it is likely to intensify the already reluctant attitude of small employers towards the union movement (Legislative Council, 2016).

According to the European Commission, reducing the gender pay, earnings and pensions gaps is considered as one of five priority areas for 2016–2019. Strengthening pay transparency is one of the key actions to be taken to enforce the equal pay principle (European Commission, 2015). The Polish Ombudsman supports the introduction of the obligatory transparency of wages as the mea-sure to effectively tackle the GPG. The Ombudsman specifically referred to the *Recommendations of the European Commission* from 7 March 2014, pointing at disclosing the information of pay levels to the employees, obligatory report-ing by the enterprises, pay audits in big enterprises and the necessity to include the equal pay principle into collective agreements (Ombudsman, 2016). The Polish Ministry of Labour has commissioned the development of a methodology to assess the GPG and tools to measure it adapted to Polish conditions. The Ministry also engaged in the creation of the Polish version of the web-based gender pay analysis tool, 'equal pace' (Ministry, 2016) but there are no further legal measures planned.

Pay transparency in the UK

As Chapter 4 highlights, the UK has played a key role in developing case law on equal value and the role of job evaluation in making the GPG more transparent. However, there is no legal requirement for employers to undertake job evalua-tion and its practice remains limited largely to the public sector, where the majority of the case law emanates. Furthermore, the UK case law reinforces the arguments of US writers that transparency for collective bargaining purposes does not, of itself, lead to gender pay equality. The GPG has remained stub-bornly at around 19% in the UK and there is a view that reactive forms of anti-discrimination legislation, particularly in relation to equal pay, have done as much as they can but are unable to close the gap completely (Dickens, 1999; Hepple *et al.*, 2000).

The EqA 2010 was intended to move the equality agenda forward in the UK and contains more direct approaches to pay transparency for gender equality purposes. The first of these is what Cherradi (2016) describes as an anti-chilling approach. Prior to the legislation it was not unlawful for employers to insert a pay secrecy clause into employment contracts, which would leave employees who did disclose their salary details open to disciplinary measures or even dismissal for breach of contract. Section 77 of the EqA 2010 prevents employers from inserting such a clause into contracts of employment or preventing in any other way employees discussing their pay with each other. This clause also covers workers seeking to find a comparator for an equal pay claim and should, in theory, make finding an actual comparator easier.

The second legal initiative to promote pay transparency to reduce the GPG falls into what Cherradi (2016) described as an affirmative obligation on employers. Section 78 of the EqA 2010 requires private and voluntary sector employers with 250+ employees to report annually on the GPG in their organisation. Although these provisions were present in the original EqA 2010, they required secondary legislation to bring them in to force. The Conservative/Liberal Democrat government formed in 2010, just after the passage of the Act, decided to delay secondary legislation, preferring instead a voluntary approach to GPG reporting. In 2011 the government introduced a voluntary scheme, Think, Act, Report, which invited private and voluntary sector employers to commit to calculating and reporting their GPG. By 2015, although 250 companies had signed up to the scheme, only four companies actually published their GPG and, in most cases, this was reported as a single figure with no indication of how the figure had been calculated. The government produced three annual reports on the initiative before announcing in 2015 that it intended to bring into effect the original legislation under s.78 of the EqA 2010.

The Equality Act 2010 (Gender Pay Gap Information) Regulation 2017 came into effect on 6 April 2017 for private and voluntary sector employers. The first 'snap shot' date was 5 April 2017 and gave employers with 250+ employees 12 months to report on the GPG in their organisation as at the snap shot date. The regulations on how the GPG must be calculated are surprisingly detailed and require employers to report on six separate metrics:

- the difference in mean hourly pay rate between men and women;
- the difference in the median hourly pay rate between men and women;
- the mean gender bonus gap;
- the median gender bonus gap;
- the proportion of men and women who receive bonuses;
- the proportion of male and female employees according to quartile pay bands.

The inclusion of bonus pay, which must be separately reported on, is particularly important given it prominence in the case law as a major factor in gender pay discrimination. Another important factor is that the regulations

cover workers working on non-standard contracts, including zero-hours contracts, which have also been implicated in widening the GPG. However,
employers do not have to provide a breakdown of the GPG of part-time
employees, which is the factor associated with the largest GPG. Furthermore,
only 34% of the UK workforce is employed in workplaces with 250+ employees
(LRD, 2017) and smaller employers are more likely to have larger GPGs.
Employers must publish their report on their own websites and upload the
information to a dedicated government website.[3] There is no requirement for
employers to act to close reported pay gaps or even to provide a narrative
to explain them. The EHRC has powers to enforce the legislation or to take
pre-enforcement action with employers who fail to publish GPG data required
by the legislation.

It must be noted that s.78 does not include public sector employers. Instead
public authorities were partially covered under the *Public Sector Equality Duty*
(s. 149 of the EqA 2010). One problem of relying on the *Public Sector Equality
Duty* for pay transparency via GPG reporting is that the part of the Duty that
contains regulations for this purpose (the specific duties) is devolved to England, Scotland and Wales separately. In Scotland, public authorities with 150+
employees have been required to publish information on the percentage difference between men's and women's average hourly pay (excluding overtime) since
2013 and every second year subsequently. The limit has since been reduced to
employers with 20+ employees. There is an additional regulation that required
public authorities with 150+ employees to report on equal pay and occupational
segregation between men and women, disabled people and people from ethnic
minorities, again reduced to 20+ employees. In Wales the specific duties require
all public authorities to collect information on pay differences between people who
share a protected characteristic and those who do not and the causes of the
differences. Public authorities must formulate and publish equality objectives
and an action plan to address pay differences and, where it has not, it must
publish the reasons for its decisions not to. In England there were no specific
duties that addressed gender pay transparency in public authorities until the
government decided to bring into force mandatory gender pay audits in the
private and voluntary sectors. Following this decision the specific duties in
England were extended to include the same provisions as s.78 of the EqA 2010
that apply to private and voluntary sector employers. The only difference is a
slightly different snap shot date of 31 March. It must be noted that mandatory
pay reporting legislation does not cover Northern Ireland. There is similar legislation planned for Northern Ireland, but this has been delayed. The result is
that in the public sector in the UK there are very different requirements for
mandatory GPG reporting between the four main constituents.

There has been a mixed reception to mandatory gender pay reporting by
the TUC and trade unions in the UK. Whilst most of the trade unions welcome
additional steps towards pay transparency, their concern is in relation to the
weak enforcement mechanisms in the legislation. Enforcement falls largely to
the much reduced EHRC, who, the TUC argues, does not have sufficient

resources to adequately enforce the legislation (TUC, 2015). In their response to the government consultation, the TUC (2015) noted that, although the government were relying largely on employers wishing to avoid bad publicity and competition as a motivation for change, the greatest pressure for pay equality was still likely to come from employees and their trade unions. As such, they reiterate the point that internal reporting of pay transparency, to employees and the unions is an important aspect of the legislation. There are also concerns amongst unions and women's pressure groups that the 250+ threshold in the private sector (and public authorities in England) will mean that the regulations do not cover the majority of women employed in SMEs in the UK who are likely to have the biggest pay gaps (LRD, 2017). The response to the legislation will not be known until 2018 but, rather worryingly, a private sector survey of 145 employers (Totaljobs, 2016: 11) found that 51% of employers were not even aware of the legislation.[4] Emerging important academic research (Mortimore and Rees, 2017) indicates that HR professionals are taking a largely ambivalent, procedural approach to the legislation, citing weak enforcement for reducing its priority.

Pay transparency in Italy

Like Poland, the GPG in Italy is one of the lowest in Europe, but this is acknowledged to be, in part, an artefact of the low labour market participation of Italian women, particularly once they have children. Ballestrero (1992) notes that, although formal legal equality in Italy was established by Act 903 of 9 December 1977, by 1987 there was a general understanding that the legislation was not being implemented effectively. Ballestrero cites three reasons for the inadequacy of the early legislation: 'first, relatively few judicial rulings, secondly, uneven implementation in collective agreements and thirdly, an initial lack of institutional support, remedied by the establishment of a public equality agency between 1984 and 1987' (1992: 152). However, Ballestrero also notes that pressure from women's groups, trade unions and other progressives sought a change in the approach to equality legislation from a negative, formal approach to anti-discrimination to more substantive equality that requires a 'complex strategy…involving new ideas and legal mechanisms' (Ballestrero, 1992: 152). She argues that the **Act 125 of 10th April 1991** (125/1991) provided potential impetus for change. The Act provided a raft of proactive measures largely aimed at encouraging public and private sector employers and trade unions to work together to insert proactive equality measures into collective bargaining agreements 'because collective agreements are considered the best way to promote positive action' (Ballestrero, 1992: 155). The need for transparency was considered important to the success of social partnership working on proactive equality measures. Although company level collective agreements remain unpublished and difficult to access (De Simone and Rivara, 2006: 53), *Article 9 of the Act 125/1991* (now *Article 46 of the Delegated Decree 198/2003*) requires public and private employers with more than 100 employees to report on female and male employees in all occupations, specifically in relation to hiring, promotion, training, dismissals, retirement and pay at least every two years. The report must be sent to the Regional Equality Body (*Consigliera regionale di parità*) and to union representatives in the workplace. Following amendments by *Delegated Decree 5/10*, the Regional Equality Body is required to analyse and process this data, and send it to the National Equality Body, the Ministry of Labour and the Equal Opportunities Department of the Presidency of the Council of Ministers. If this requirement is not fulfilled, after a 60-day warning notice, companies are sanctioned with a financial administrative fine (100–500 euro). In the most severe cases, a one-year suspension of social-security contributory benefits may be applied.

In theory, the report should have the proactive effects anticipated in 125/1991 to allow social partners to monitor gender equality in companies and public authorities (Marino, 2010) and could be used by equality bodies and trade union representatives 'to tackle horizontal and vertical segregation, as well as the gender pay gap at the company level' (Plantenga and Remery, 2006: 38). However, there are a number of administrative and technical difficulties in interpreting the guidelines and drawing up the report in a way that is comparable across companies, or that disaggregates data for part-time workers and workers on non-standard employment contracts (Marino, 2010). The role of non-standard contracts in the widening of the GPG is important since De Simone and Rivara (2006) argue that young women are increasingly employed on poorly remunerated fixed-term contracts, in what they describe as 'contractual segregation' (p. 55). Importantly, given our finding from Italian case studies in Chapter 4, no information is recorded on individual bonuses or length of service (De Simone and Rivara, 2006). Furthermore, Marino (2010) highlights that, since the Italian labour market is largely made up of small employers, the legislation only covers a minority of Italian employees. Therefore, whilst in 1992 Ballestrero felt cautiously optimistic that the 'Act 125/1991 is full of great promises; only its actual implementation will determine whether these promises will be fulfilled' (1992: 156), by 2010 Marino argued that 'the legislation has been scarcely implemented: the collection and analysis of pay-related data is hampered by several obstacles'. As a result De Simone and Rivara argue that '[o]ften pay discrimination can be easily hidden, both in additional wages bargained at local or enterprise level and in the so-called *superminimo individuale*' (2006: 54).

Whilst 125/1991 represented an early, if somewhat unsuccessful, attempt at instigating what Cherradi (2016) describes as affirmative obligations for employers, there has been no attempt at anti-chilling approaches to pay transparency at the level of the workplace. Pay secrecy in relation to individual workers' pay remains protected by law in accordance with the Code on protection of personal data (*Delegated Decree 196/2003*). This legislation implements *directives 95/46/EC* and *2002/58/EC*, as well as to the decisions of the Privacy Authority concerning the processing of employees' personal data in the private sector (*Res. 23 November 2006, no. 53*) and in the public sector (*Res. 14*

June 2007). In addition, with specific regard to payslips (*Res. 25 June 2009, n. 325*), employers are required to deliver payslips in closed envelopes or folded-and-stapled sheets in order to prevent third parties from seeing their contents. The communication of this data to third parties needs to be approved by the employee.

There have been limited attempts to broaden the concept of pay transparency to encompass equal value by implementing gender-neutral job evaluation. The effects of vertical and horizontal gender segregation on the GPG persist, despite *Article 2 of Act 903/1977* which states that 'job classification systems applied for the purpose of determining remuneration shall adopt common criteria for men and women'. De Simone and Rivara (2006) argue that 'the neutral defini-tion of the occupational categories and/or of the jobs sometimes hides a de facto discrimination between men and women in the assignment of jobs and grades' (p. 50).

Conclusions

Despite the differences in industrial relations, legal systems and size of the GPG between our three countries, there are some remarkable similarities in relation to pay transparency. First, in all three countries pay transparency, or the lack of it, is problematic in relation to the GPG and prevents access to equal pay remedies. In all three cases a culture of secrecy in relation to pay, often bol-stered with legislative claims to data protection, hinders transparency in rela-tion to the full extent of the GPG. Second, neither collective bargaining nor anti-discrimination legislation have succeeded in making the GPG more trans-parent. Third, voluntary initiatives in the private sectors of Poland and the UK have largely been ineffective. Fourth, SMEs, which employ the majority of employees in all three countries, are exempt from any attempts at legislative attempts to improve pay transparency in organisations. Where there have been some attempts in the UK and Italy to adopt proactive legislative approaches towards transparency, there are some similarities and some differences. There is little European conceptual research or literature on pay transparency that helps us explain the similarities and differences between our three countries, but there is some useful US literature, which we have drawn upon in this chapter.

Cherradi (2016) distinguishes between anti-chilling, anti-retaliation and affir-mative obligations as policy options for improving pay transparency. Of our three countries, only the UK has introduced anti-chilling legislation. Poland has some anti-retaliation measures in place, but Poland and Italy have counter-productive privacy legislation in place, which works against pay transparency. Both the UK and Italy have legislative measures requiring employers to proac-tively report on GPGs, but these work in different ways. In the UK, s.78 of the **Equality Act 2010** is specifically designed to encourage employers to make their GPGs transparent to the public generally, with the intention that bad publicity and competition amongst employers will motivate action. The requirements for collecting, analysing and publishing GPGs are very specific, but enforcement mechanisms are weak with no penalties for failure to comply. It is too early to assess the success of this legislation, but emerging research suggests that, as Fung *et al.* (2004) argue, simply requiring employers to publish information may not automatically lead to the changed behaviour anticipated by legislators unless equality officers, trade unions and women's groups use it to press for change.

In Italy, 125/1991 introduced transparency amongst many different workplace gender equality dimensions, with the main intention of encouraging social partners to include the information in collective bargaining. However, the broader coverage of the legislation means that interpreting the guidelines is open to variation, possibly failing the comprehensibility test suggested by Fung *et al.* (2004) as a criterion to change behaviour. Therefore, although there are greater penalties for failure to comply, in practice the law is not widely adhered to.

Although not covered in the US literature on pay transparency, our analysis includes the role played by horizontal gender segregation in obscuring the GPG. Horizontal or occupational segregation continues to be a significant contributory factor in the GPG in all three countries, even though the concept of equal value is established in European law. The impact of horizontal segregation on the GPG and the concept of equal value is largely obscured in Italy and Poland because of claims that collective bargaining structures automatically result in pay equality.

There is a greater acknowledgement of the concept of equal value in the UK, where national collective agreements in the public sector have included job evaluation that has exposed the extent to which the undervaluing of feminised occupations contributes to individual cases of pay discrimination and GPGs (see Chapter 4). The UK case demonstrates that collective bargaining need not inherently result in obscured GPGs. However, it does mean that social partners need, first, to accept that, even in collectively bargained pay structures, occupational segregation is likely to give rise to gender pay inequality, followed by a willingness to act decisively to expose it. But, as Fung *et al.* (2004) suggest, this would require social partners to face up to the ways in which their current interests might mitigate against doing this. For employers, it will mean accepting that closing the GPG will be costly, since trade unions are unlikely to accept levelling down of men's pay. For trade unions, it will mean accepting that securing bonuses and a pay premium for male-dominated occupational groups of workers that are not similarly secured for feminised occupations does lead to pay discrimination. In short, pay transparency in relation to the GPG is as much about social partners being transparent to themselves and to each other about their real commitment to closing the GPG and pay equality as it is about simply publishing information.

Jurisprudence

Judgment of the Supreme Court of June 9, 2016, III PK 116/15, Lex no. 2057629.

Judgment of the Court of Appeal in Szczecin of January 24, 2013, III AUa 674/12, Lex no. 1293046.

Judgment of the Supreme Court of May 26, 2011, II PK 304/10, OSNP 2012, no. 13–14, pos. 171.

Judgement of Supreme Court of January 21, 2011, II PK 169/10, Lex no. 1130823.

Judgement of Supreme Court of August 18, 2009, I PK 28/09, Lex no. 528155.

Judgement of Supreme Court of February 22, 2007, I PK 242/06, OSNP 2008, no. 7–8, pos. 98.

Judgement of Supreme Court of January 9, 2007, II PK 180/06, OSNP 2008, no. 3–4, pos. 36.

Judgement of Supreme Court of June 9, 2006, III PK 30/06, OSNP 2007, no 11–12, pos. 16.

Judgement of Supreme Court of May 24, 2005, II PK 33/05, Lex no. 184961.

Judgment of the Supreme Court of May 8, 2002, I PKN 267/01, OSNP 2004, no. 6, pos. 99.

Judgment of the Administrative Court in Wroclaw of May 6, 1997, II Sa/Wr 929/96, ONSA 1998, no 2, pos. 54.

Judgment of Supreme Court of July 16, 1993, I PZP 28/93, OSNCP 1994, no 1, pos. 2.

Notes

1 A poviat is a second-level unit of local government and administration in Poland, equivalent to a county or a district in other countries.
2 A voivodeship is the highest level of local government and administration in Poland, corresponding to a province in other countries. Presently there are 16 voivodeships in Poland.
3 https://genderpaygap.campaign.gov.uk/.
4 No details are available on the representativeness of the sample.

References

Ballestrero, M. V. (1992) 'Legislation in Italian Equality Law Act 125 of 10 April 1991 (the Positive Action Act)' *Industrial Law Journal* 21(2), pp. 152–156.

Central Statistical Office (2014) *Działalność przedsiębiorstw niefinansowych w 2013 roku* [*Activity of Non-Financial Enterprises in 2013*]. Warsaw.

Cherradi, S. (2016) 'Pay Transparency Laws: Vogue, Mirage, Miracle, Untested Theory, Needed Remedy, Conspiracy or Cynical Plan?' *EEO Insights* 8(1), pp. 7–44.

Colella, A., Paetzold, R. L., Zardkoohi, A. and Wesson, M. J. (2007) 'Exposing Secrecy' *Academy of Management Review* 32(1), pp. 55–71.

De Simone, G. and Rivara, A. (2006) 'Italy' in *Legal Aspects of the Gender Pay Gap: A Report by the Commission's Network of Legal Experts in the Field of Employment, Social Affairs and Equality between Men and Women*. Available from: www.bmfsfj. de/blob/84378/2c4b9336adae0232daa97bd00eb38719/nl-dezember-06-kom-equal-pay-da ta.pdf (accessed 18 April 2018).

DelPo Kulow, M. (2013) 'Beyond the Paycheck Fairness Act: Mandatory Wage Disclosure Laws – a Necessary Tool for Closing the Residual Gender Wage Gap' *Harvard Journal on Legislation* 50(2), pp. 385–435.

Dickens, L. (1999) 'Beyond the Business Case: A Three-Pronged Approach to Equality Action' *Human Resource Management Journal* 9(1), pp. 9–19.

Dörre-Nowak, D. (2005) *Ochrona godności i innych osobistych dóbr pracownika* [*Protection of Dignity and Other Employee's Personal Rights*]. Warsaw: CH Beck.

Eisenberg, D. T. (2011) 'Money, Sex and Sunshine: A Market-Based Approach to Pay Discrimination' *Arizona State Law Journal* 43, pp. 953–1020.

Eisenberg, D. T. (2012) 'Walmart Store v Dukes: Lessons for the Legal Quest for Equal Pay' *New England Law Review* 46, pp. 229–273.

Estlund, C. (2009) 'Just the Facts: The Case for Workplace Transparency' *Stanford Law Review* 63, pp. 351–407.

Estlund, C. (2014) 'Extending the Case for Workplace Transparency to Information about Pay' *UC Irvine Law Review* 4, pp. 781–799.

European Commission (2003) 'Commission Recommendation of 6 May 2003 concerning the definition of micro, small and medium-sized enterprises' (notified under document number C(2003) 1422) (Text with EEA relevance), (2003/361/EC).

European Commission (2013) 'Report from the Commission to the European Parliament and The Council on the application of directive 2006/54/EC of the European Parliament and of The Council of 5 July 2006 on the implementation of the principle of equal opportunities and equal treatment of men and women in matters of employment and occupation', COM(2013) 861 final. Available from: http://eur-lex.europa.eu/legal-content/EN/TXT/?uri=celex:52013DC0861 (accessed 28 March 2018).

European Commission (2014) 'Commission Recommendation of 7 March 2014 on strengthening the principle of equal pay between men and women through transparency, COM(2014) 1405 final'. Available from: https://publications.europa.eu/en/publication-detail/-/publication/b8668ea5-a69a-11e3-8438-01aa75ed71a1/language-en (accessed 28 March 2018).

European Commission (2015) 'Strategic Engagement for Gender Equality 2016–2019, Brussels, 3.12.2015, SWD(2015) 278 final'. Available from: https://ec.europa.eu/anti-trafficking/sites/antitrafficking/files/strategic_engagement_for_gender_equality_en.pdf, (accessed 28 March 2018).

European Commission (2017) 'Pay Transparency in the EU: A Legal Analysis of the Situation in EU Member States, Iceland, Liechtenstein and Norway'. European Network of Legal Experts in Gender Equality and Non-Discrimination.

European Parliament (2012) 'European Parliament resolution of 24 May 2012 with recommendations to the Commission on application of the principle of equal pay for male and female workers for equal work or work of equal value (2011/2285(INI)). P7_TA(2012)0225'. Available from: www.europarl.europa.eu/sides/getDoc.do?pubRef=-%2F%2FEP%2F%2FTEXT%2BTA%2BP7-TA-2012-0225%2B0%2BDOC%2BXML%2BV0%2F%2FEN&language=EN (accessed 28 March 2018).

Figgart, D. M. (2001) 'Wage Setting under Fordism: The Rise of Job Evaluation and the Ideology of Equal Pay' *Review of Political Economy* 13(4), pp. 405–425.

Fung, A., Weil, D., Graham, M. and Fagotto, E. (2004) 'The Political Economy of Transparency: What Makes Disclosure Policies Effective?' The Ash Institute for Democratic Governance and Innovation John F. Kennedy School of Government, Harvard University, working paper OP-03–04. Available from: https://ash.harvard.edu/files/political_econ_transparency.pdf (accessed 28 March 2018).

Gilbert, K. (2005) 'The Role of Job Evaluation in Determining Equal Value in Employment Tribunals: Tool, Weapon or Cloaking Device?' *Employee Relations* 27(1), pp. 7–19.

Gilbert, K. (2012) 'Promises and Practices: Job Evaluation and Equal Pay 40 Years On!' *Industrial Relations Journal* 43(2), pp. 137–151.

Guidelines (2016) *Close the Deal, Fill the Gap: Closing the GPG – Guidelines for the Social Partners*, June 2016. Available from: www.fillthegap.eu/sites/default/files/attach ment/product/Guidelines%20for%20the%20social%20partners.pdf (accessed 28 March 2018).

Hepple, B.Coussey, M. and Choudhury, T. (2000) *Equality: A New Framework Report of the Independent Review of the Enforcement of UK Anti-Discrimination Legislation.* Oxford: Hart.

Jaszcz, Ł. (2016) *Trendy w wynagradzaniu w 2016 roku* [*Trends in Remuneration in 2016*]. Available from: http://wynagrodzenia.pl/artykul/trendy-w-wynagradzaniu-w-20 16-roku (accessed 12 February 2017).

Legislative Council (2016) 'Opinia Rady Legislacyjnej przy Prezesie Rady Ministrów z 21 września 2016 r. o projekcie ustawy o zmianie niektórych ustaw w celu poprawy otoczenia prawnego przedsiębiorców' [The Opinion of the Legislative Council at the Prime Minister of 21 September 2016 on the Draft Law Amending Certain Laws to Improve the Legal Environment of Business], RL-0303–30/16. Available from: http://radalegislacyjna.gov.pl/dokumenty/opinia-z-21-wrzesnia-201 6-r-o-projekcie-ustawy-o-zmianie-niektorych-ustaw-w-celu-poprawy (accessed 28 March 2018).

LRD (2017) 'Will Employers Finally Start to Mind the Gap?' *Labour Research* 106(3), pp. 9–11.

Marino, S. (2010) 'Addressing the Gender Pay Gap: Government and Social Partner Actions – Italy' Eurofound. Available from: www.eurofound.europa.eu/observatories/ eurwork/comparative-information/national-contributions/italy/addressing-the-gender-p ay-gap-government-and-social-partner-actions-italy (accessed 28 March 2018).

Mas, A. (2016) 'Does Transparency Lead to Pay Compression?' Princeton University and NBER Working Paper, February. Available from: www.princeton.edu/~amas/papers/ transparency.pdf (accessed 28 March 2018).

McCrudden, C. (1993) 'The Effectiveness of European Equality Law: National Mechan- isms for Enforcing Gender Equality Law in the Light of European Requirements' *Oxford Journal of Legal Studies* 13(3), pp. 321–364.

Ministry (2016) 'The answer from 8th April 2016 to the letter of Ombudsman from 19th March 2016, DAE.III.6103.6.2016.AG/MMI'. Available from: www.rpo.gov.pl/sites/defa ult/files/Luka%20p%C5%82acowa%20-%20odp%20MRPiPS%2C%208.04.16_0.pdf (accessed 28 March 2018).

Mortimore, H.and Rees, L. (2017) 'HR, Employment Solicitors and the Application of the Gender Pay Reporting Law'. Paper presented at the British Academy of Management Annual Conference, 5–7 September 2017. Warwick University.

Nartowski, A. (2016) *Dobre praktyki spółek notowanych na GPW 2016* [*Best Practices of Companies Listed on the Warsaw Stock Exchange 2016*]. Available from: www.gp w.pl/pub/GPW/files/PDF/Podrecznik_DPSN_2016_9_03_16.pdf (accessed 28 March 2018).

Newell, A. and Reilly, B. (2001) 'The Gender Pay Gap in the Transition from Communism: Some Empirical Evidence' *Economic Systems* 25(4), pp. 287–304.

O'Neill, B. P. (2010) 'Pay Confidentiality: A Remaining Obstacle to Equal Pay after Ledbetter' *Seton Hall Law Review* 40(3), pp. 1217–1256.

Ombudsman (2016) 'The letter to the Minister of Family, Labour and Social Polity from 19th March 2016 on differences in pays between men and women, XI.816.9.2016. KWŻ'. Available from: www.rpo.gov.pl/sites/default/files/Do_MRPiPS_ws_roznic_w_ wynagrodzeniach_kobiet_i_mezczyzn.pdf (accessed 28 March 2018).

Plantenga, J. and Remery, C. (2006) 'The Gender Pay Gap. Origins and Policy Responses. A Comparative Review of Thirty European Countries'. The co-ordinators' synthesis report prepared for the Equality Unit, European Commission. Final Report, July. Available from: www.bmfsfj.de/blob/84376/9376ec6e2d947e81235cb7247ff76792/ nl-dezember-06-eu-expert-group-gender-pay-data.pdf (accessed 28 March 2018).

PwC (2016) *Wynagrodzenia zarządów i rad nadzorczych największych spółek giełdowych w 2015 roku* [*Remuneration of Management Boards and Supervisory Boards of the Largest Listed Companies in 2015*]. Available from: www.pwc.pl/pl/pdf/wyna grodzenia-zarzadow-2015-raport-pwc.pdf (accessed 28 March 2018).

Ramachandran, G. (2012) 'Pay Transparency' *Penn State Law Review* 116(4), pp. 1043–1080.

Risher, H. (2014) 'Pay Transparency is Coming' *Compensation and Benefits Review* 46 (1), pp. 3–5.

Rosenfeld, J. (2017) 'Don't Ask or Tell: Pay Secrecy Policies in U.S. Workplaces' *Social Science Research* 65, pp. 1–16.

TeamQuest (2016) 'Ile zarabia sąsiad, czyli plusy i minusy ujawniania listy płac'. Available from: https://teamquest.pl/blog/208_ile-zarabia-sasiad-czyli-plusy-i-minusy-uja wniania-listy-plac (accessed 28 March 2018).

Totaljobs (2016) *Gender Pay Gap 2016*. Available from: www.totaljobs.com/insidejob/ gender-pay-gap-2016/ (accessed 28 March 2016).

TUC (2015) 'Gender Pay Gap Reporting: Response to the GEO Consultation, September 2015'. Available from: www.tuc.org.uk/sites/default/files/GeenderPayGapReporting. pdf (accessed 28 March 2018).

Walczak, K. (2009) 'Regulamin wynagrodzeń a zasada tajności indywidualnego wyna grodzenia za pracę' [The Regulation on Remuneration and the Principle of Secrecy of Individual Remuneration], *Monitor Prawa Pracy no. 3*.

Wright, A. (2011) 'Modernising Away Gender Pay Inequality? Some Evidence from the Local Government Sector on Using Job Evaluation' *Employee Relations* 33(2), pp. 159–178.

Zielinska, E. (2010) 'Poland' in P. Foubert, S. Burri and A. Numhauser-Henning, *The Gender Pay Gap in Europe from a Legal Perspective (including 33 Country Reports)*. European Commission. Available from: www.equalitylaw.eu/downloads/3857-the-gen der-pay-gap-in-europe-from-a-legal-perspective-including-33-country-reports-pdf-4-246 -kb (accessed 28 March 2018).

Conclusions

Hazel Conley, Donata Gottardi, Geraldine Healy,
Barbara Mikołajczyk and Marco Peruzzi

Comparative research is always a challenge. It might be thought that researching the GPG in countries covered by the same EU legislation and principles would make the task much more straightforward. In theory this is the case, however, countries of the EU retain their own political systems, national institutions and have different interpretations of EU legislation. The analysis carried out in this book, based on the reflections and outcomes achieved in the project 'Close the Deal, Fill the Gap', focused on the way that pay is ordered and structured in the three countries, Italy, Poland and UK, and in different sectors within those countries to enable a wider understanding of the GPG from the perspective of two contradictory forces: the arguably centralised EU imperative to reduce the GPG against the alternative imperative for increasingly decentralised collective bargaining and industrial relations. Given this context, the challenges begin to become clear when we remind ourselves of some of the key difference between the countries with respect to bargaining and the GPG.

The literature is unclear on the link between collective bargaining and pay equity. Pillinger's (2014: 4) ETUC study provided a valuable overview of national level unions which were shown to have been instrumental in fighting for and implementing legislation to improve pay transparency, for example through company level pay audits, pay surveys, equality plans and income reports. Nevertheless, the issue of union wage premium is less certain with the contraction of unionisation in the private sector. Wage premium has generally been associated with high union density, wide coverage of collective bargaining, multi-unionism, union characteristics and gender composition of the workforce (Achatz et al., 2005; Addison et al., 2017; Forth and Millward, 2002; Elvira and Saporta, 2001). Thus, it is evident that the union pay premium will vary between countries, and within countries. Where there is a positive relationship we would expect to see high collective bargaining coverage and low GPG; this certainly holds good for Italy (80% collective bargaining coverage and 5% GPG), but not for Poland, which also has a low GPG (8%) but a very low collective bargaining coverage (15%), much lower than the estimated coverage in the UK (26.3%). Thus at the country level, we cannot presume that the relationship between collective bargaining and pay equity will be strong.

Moreover, we see different complexities in analysing the negotiated agreements themselves. In both the Italian and the Polish cases, it is evident that not only is collective bargaining legally binding (unlike the UK) but also that the agreements themselves are available for analysis. Again we may find differences and limitations in the content of the agreements, but the legally binding nature of collective bargaining in Italy and Poland leads to a level of transparency particularly at the sectoral or industry level agreements, which is unavailable in the UK. A key factor here is that the agreements work at regional and sector level in Italy and Poland. Again the UK is the outlier with some collective agreements operating at sector level (e.g. universities, rail, health) but others more likely to have been decentralised to the level of the enterprise (e.g. to a particular bank in the UK financial sector). Thus we find greater decentralisation in the UK than in either Italy or Poland, resulting in greater fragmentation and more local negotiation. The UK has gone further down the decentralisation road in its neo-liberal journey than Italy and Poland, including decentralisation resulting from the increased privatisation of previously public sector segments of operation. In the context of austerity, we should not be surprised to see further decentralisation in Italy and Poland and an increasing challenge to unionisation and a decline in the strong collective bargaining context of Italy. In this respect, we wondered if the UK was holding a mirror up to Italy and Poland's decentralised future.

The case studies in this book show the huge differences between the countries and very importantly *within* the countries. We show that the relationship between pay and sector is strong in Italy and Poland but less so in the UK where enterprise level is more important. Thus we find that while a number of the solutions we propose for trade unions rely on union involvement, in the UK, the role of employers becomes very important in the context on non-unionised workplaces. Thus whilst we have offered guidelines in the Appendix, these guidelines need to be interpreted according to the national, sectoral and organisational context.

Notwithstanding the differences between the countries, we notice some common themes with respect to gender, confirming as we have argued elsewhere that there is a universalism in the way women are treated in the workplace (Kirton and Healy, 2013). There was a general need to raise awareness of the GPG by unions and employers and in workplaces, at sectoral level and during the negotiating processes. There is a danger that lack of awareness leads to an implicit acceptance of the status quo. Moreover, the GPG is often considered as a 'women only' issue, benefiting only women and therefore of interest only to women. While women bear the brunt of the negative effects of the GPG, for example in all three countries they are more likely to be in poverty as they age and they certainly suffer a gender pensions gap, the highest being in the UK. Therefore, while equal representation of women on union and management negotiating and decision-making teams is important, this is not enough: our study has highlighted the importance of men and women being sufficiently knowledgeable to identify and challenge stereotyped and indirectly discriminatory regulatory schemes for such schemes to be acknowledged and eradicated in legislation, policy, collective bargaining and decision-making processes.

Moreover, we also saw the value of external forces through new alliances, which potentially add power and support to the social partners. British trade unions, for example, have already started to work with some women's organisations such as the Fawcett Society to challenge the government on budget cuts that have disproportionately affected women's jobs and women's access to welfare and public services. Alliances of this sort can also help trade unions widen their scope of representation of their women members beyond traditional collective bargaining agendas.

Gendered conceptions of work–life balance emerged from our study as a barrier to women's development. This was illustrated in the way that stereotyping consistently emerged in the analysis of collective agreements with respect to a gendered conception of work–life balance. Work–life balance measures are designed to be used by women to balance work and family burdens but may lead to women working part-time, refusing overtime or avoiding occupations or promotion at work that demand longer working hours. Rather than promoting a perspective of equal roles and sharing of care between the parents, instead the unintended outcome is to give little support for working fathers and to reinforce the traditional 'breadwinner' models. If work–life balance arrangements do not lead to an equal sharing of family burdens between men and women, they can hardly intervene in the 'vicious circle' characterising women's careers, by horizontal and vertical segregation and the resulting gender time/pension/pay gaps. Our study supports work that exposes the perils for women of certain kinds of flexibility (see for example Charlesworth, 2013).

One of the major topics addressed by the research concerned the awarding of performance/productivity-related pay elements. In the Italian and Polish context, the analysis highlighted that the vast majority of company agreements use work attendance as the sole or one of the criteria for the awarding of the above-mentioned pay elements. Moreover, it was observed that this occurs independently of the sector concerned or of whether it is a male-dominated sector or not. The consequence of prioritising work attendance as the sole or one of the criteria for the awarding of performance-related pay elements impacts on the gender time gap and leads to a worsening of the GPG. This worsening is exponentially increased if – as in the Italian context – reductions of tax rates and/or of social security contributions are applied to such pay elements in order to incentivise a rise in the percentage of pay linked to productivity, in accordance with the EU policy guidelines. Nevertheless, the national social partners involved in the project explained that the employees themselves often request the criterion of work attendance as they reckon it is capable of measuring their performance impartially and objectively. The important point here is that all criteria used in the calculation of bonuses should not only be transparent and subject to negotiation, but also free of indirect gender bias. However, the use of the criterion of work attendance can imply an indirect discriminatory effect to the detriment of women, due to the gender time gap deriving from the above-mentioned uneven distribution of family burdens. Our research suggests that including some types of leave, such as maternity leave and parental leave, in the measurement of work attendance can be a corrective measure capable of reducing the discriminatory impact resulting from the use of such criterion. In the Polish context, for example, if only a short pre-maternity leave is provided (six weeks before the delivery only since 2013, increased from two weeks), the short maternity leaves means that women are forced to use sick leave during the final months of their pregnancy if the conditions of their work results in their incapacity to work. In the UK, an employer should record any pregnancy-related sickness absence *separately from other sick leave*, so that pregnancy-related sickness absence is ignored as absence and is not used to the person's disadvantage, e.g. for disciplinary action, dismissal or redundancy or in attendance calculations. It is also the case that in order to foster an even distribution of family burdens, any paternity-related leave should also be taken into consideration in corrective measures.

The economic analysis of the case studies demonstrated that the GPG also derives from the individual negotiation or awarding of bonuses, given by the company on a discretionary basis, with a lack of transparency and no room for union social partners to control and take action on them. Besides, the analysis of case studies revealed that, even when the company agreement regulates productivity bonuses, companies may use separate – and not negotiated – systems of productivity remuneration for the highest positions in the company hierarchy, based on a subjective assessment of the employee's expertise and capability of achievement specific targets. Confronting the secrecy around discretionary payment is a challenge for the social partners, yet discretionary pay accounts for a significant proportion of the pay gap in certain sectors, e.g. finance, and is intensified at higher levels of the hierarchy. Collective agreements should aim to include transparent criteria on which individual productivity will be evaluated and bonuses will be paid, and push for equality audits with respect to bonuses. In this regard, a previous evaluation of job requirements could also help in determining the criteria useful for evaluating workers' performance and workers' productivity on a transparent and more objective basis. This draws attention to the key importance of an analytical job evaluation and, in a second step, of an analytical evaluation of skills, performance and productivity, both carried out on a gender-neutral basis.

As shown by a UK case, job evaluation is a key instrument for implementing the concept of 'work of equal value', and it is therefore important for enabling a comparison between different jobs in context of intra-occupational gender-based horizontal segregation, to the purposes of the principle of pay equality, as regulated by art. 157 TFEU and by dir. 2006/54/CE. As a second step of a process built on an analytical job evaluation, performance and productivity evaluations can be conducted on a gender-neutral basis thereby improving transparency and ensuring the awarding of productivity bonuses avoids the indirect discriminatory effect deriving from the use of the criterion of work attendance. Key questions arise when identifying which level of collective bargaining should take action in this field of regulation. The UK model provides a good example for company-level decentralised systems, whereas the Belgian model can provide an example of good practice for member states characterised by a nationally centred system of collective bargaining (as well as a good example of legislative support of the social partners' action on this topic, see Loi 22 April 2012, '*Loi visant à lutter contre l'écart salarial entre hommes et femmes*'). By similarly providing gender-neutral criteria for career progress, social partners can work to overcome the issue of vertical segregation. Once again, such criteria could be introduced by collective agreement, with a bilateral gender-balanced committee responsible for monitoring its implementation. This may be most likely in Italy, but in all three countries, the underrepresentation of women at senior levels should be a matter of concern and for action. In order to break the entrenched nature of gender segregation and the GPG across hierarchies, social partners should promote targets for women's representation at higher levels of organisations. Targets alone are not sufficient and should be linked to equality audits, skill development and flexible work. Our cases suggest that there is much work to be done by social partners in improving women's representation.

Moreover, job design may also be a means to challenge existing occupational segregation and facilitate opportunities for women to move through job hierarchies. It is recognised that this is particularly important in sectors, such as financial services, where men dominate the more lucrative (both with respect to base pay and to bonuses) jobs. Linked to job design, it is crucial that women are encouraged to access training and skills development to enable them to break into better-rewarded positions. Alone, this is not sufficient. Social partners must promote access to development resources and for all jobs to be advertised with job flexibility in hours and conditions as a means to break the dominant male culture in some jobs that acts as a barrier to women's application and acceptance.

Finally, arguably, transparency in pay is one of the key aspects in the fight against the GPG. On the one hand, there should be transparency in the communication of payments schemes, compensation strategies and practices so that there is a common understanding. More controversially, transparency should enable employees to be able to compare their salaries and to understand where the possible differences may come from. Only the awareness of the existence of pay differences between men and women can result in actions undertaken by the employees and by the social partners themselves.

On the other hand, public policies should incentivise and support employers' virtuous practices to the purpose of encouraging transparency by requiring GPG mandatory reports and/or by granting specific benefits (such as tax reductions, or additional points in public procurement procedures) for companies that meet certain targets in the assessment of the GPG carried out in accordance with the regulations on mandatory reporting.

Our work has revealed examples of where social partners may independently collect pay data – for example through a trade union membership questionnaire asking members for their pay details, as in the UK case study 'Transport and Salaried Staff Association /Network Rail' – as a comparison with the data reported and published by the company in accordance with the law (if present and applicable). The resulting data was successfully used to persuade employers to negotiate better pay structures where data indicates that women in their organisations are likely to suffer pay inequality. Social partners could ensure such transparency is granted also along the supply-chain of a company by negotiating 'social clauses' in company agreements making the respect of certain transparency standards (or of certain low GPG rates) a condition of sub-contracting.

In Italy, despite being introduced in 1991 and currently stated by Art. 46 Delegated Decree 198/2006, mandatory reporting on men and women employment conditions for public-owned and private companies with 100+ employees has proved to be ineffective to the purpose of detecting an actual GPG: as the wage data that companies are required to present are too aggregated, meaning that any assessment on the GPG and its causes is difficult to conduct.

While there are no legal requirements for employers to publish reports on gender pay equality in Poland, in April 2017 the UK introduced legislation on the publication of the GPG that can provide a useful example also for the other member states, Italy included. The Equality Act 2010 (Gender Pay Gap Information) Regulations 2017 require companies (with 250+ employees) to publish detailed information on pay. As we saw in Chapter 6, the reporting requirements are detailed. Specifically, a relevant employer must publish: the difference in mean pay between male and female; the difference in median pay; the difference in mean bonus pay; the proportion of male and female relevant employees who received bonus pay during the period of 12 months preceding the relevant date; and the numbers of male and female relevant employees employed by the relevant employer. Chapter 4 reports on the outcome of GPG reporting regulations with respect to its three case studies in rail, local government and financial services. It is evident that transparency of the GPG is only a first step. Some 1,500 organisations did not initially comply by the deadline for reporting and, as we go to press, it is not clear precisely what sanctions will apply to those firms that do not comply. The EHRC has stated that they will be held to account and large fines are likely. It is clear that much work needs to be done to eliminate the GPG and that transparency alone is not the solution. However, the publicity that has resulted from the large GPGs revealed through the reporting mechanism will put much pressure on organisations to properly audit and explain the reasons for their GPGs.

The differences between the countries are stark and reflect not only the importance of small GPGs, but equally the importance of fair pay and the two do not necessarily go hand in hand. In the Polish case, the generally low levels of pay do lead to a low GPG, but this does not necessarily mean that workers are fairly paid. In the UK case, there is genuine concern that the gains that have been achieved in employment rights through membership of the EU may be lost as a result of Brexit. Unions and concerned politicians are working to ensure the retention of those rights that have had a positive effect on women's and men's employment. The current contemporary European environment is in flux, not just in the UK but also in the governments of Italy and Poland, which underlines the importance of the involvement of social partners in the overall context of EU employment. Our book is about the GPG, but of course our concern relates to the overall fairness of pay systems and the amount of wages received. Our cases indicate that transparency is important but not sufficient. Rather transparency needs to be part of a complex package of initiatives drawing on EU and state regulation, joint regulation and voluntary initiatives ensuring equality audits and attacking the myriad of inequality regimes that make up gendered organisational culture and practices. In all three countries, a gendered culture permeates systems and practices to the detriment of women and reflects a universalism in the gendered treatment of women that is still to be confronted and overcome. The current economic and political uncertainty does not necessarily bode well for gender equality. However, we would like to end on an optimistic note. As we go to press, the anger expressed by women across national boundaries about the resilience of sexism and the significance of reclaiming a feminist identity may well be countervailing forces from below to ensure that EU policy and practice become more aligned and strengthened, leading to more equitable employment conditions.

References

Achatz, J., Gartner, H. and Gluck, T. (2005) 'Bonus or Bias? Mechanism of Sex Specific Wage Compensation' *Kolner Zeitschrift Fur Soziologie Und Sozialpsychologie* 57, p. 466.

Addison, J. T., Portugal, P. and Vilares, H. (2017) 'Unions and Collective Bargaining in the Wake of the Great Recession: Evidence from Portugal' *British Journal of Industrial Relations* 55(3), pp. 551–576.

Charlesworth, S. (2013) 'Enterprise Bargaining and Women Workers: The Seven Perils of Flexibility', *Labour & Industry: A Journal of the Social and Economic Relations of Work* 8(2), pp. 101–115.

Elvira, M. M. and Saporta, I. (2001) 'How Does Collective Bargaining Affect the Gender Pay Gap?' *Work and Occupations* 28, pp. 469–490.

Forth, J. and Millward, N. (2002) 'Union Effects on Pay Levels in Britain' *Labour Economics* 9, pp. 547–561.

Kirton, G. and Healy, G. (2013) *Women and Union Leadership*. London: Routledge.

Pillinger, J. (2014) *Bargaining for Equality*. Brussels: ETUC.

Appendix

Closing the GPG: 11 guidelines for the social partners

In a time when a higher collective bargaining decentralisation and an increase of the percentage of pay linked to productivity are prompted, what is the role to play for the social partners in tackling the GPG? What are the problems to solve, the possible gender bias to bear in mind, and the issues to deal with in collective bargaining in order to fill the gap?

Guideline no. 1: *Improving awareness and knowledge, building networks, testing experimental cases*

The GPG is not a 'women only' issue: gender stereotypes need to be overcome and the role of men in caring burdens increased. An hourly GPG does not reveal the part-time, maternal, precarious, promotion and pensions penalties: the full extent of the problem is recognised only if the lifetime earnings of men and women are taken into consideration. The topic also implies a reflection on the job, performance and productivity evaluation in new forms of work organisation. To this purpose, social partners should organise training and sensitising activities with experts, including experimental pilot cases. When appropriate, and with no overlapping of roles, social partners should also build networks with organisations promoting gender equality.

Guideline no. 2: *Mainstreaming pay equality in collective bargaining by training negotiators and promoting leading cases*

Social partners could enhance the quality of company agreements that directly or indirectly deal with pay equality by adopting mainstreaming actions aimed at sensitising on the topic (for example, organising a day devoted to pay equality in negotiation), training negotiators and supporting them with glossaries, models, best practices. In this regard, social partners could test the following guidelines in pilot cases, and promote these experimental company agreements as leading examples. The social partners should require a balanced representation of women on both sides in the negotiation of company agreements. At least one member must be an expert in gender discrimination.

Guideline no. 3: *Ensuring legal correctness and avoiding gender stereotypes in terminology*

When negotiating or revising company agreements, the social partners should use a legally correct and gender-neutral terminology as well as foster paternity-related rights. A gendered naming of professions is to be avoided. Parental leave must not be (re)named as 'optional maternity leave': besides raising a question of legal correctness, this can perpetuate a gendered social image of work–life balance that eventually confirms the GPG. The same effect results when there is not an equal support of paternity-related leave. This occurs, for example, when company agreements that award productivity bonuses according to work attendance do not consider paternity-related leave among the gender corrective measures aimed at preventing gender bias.

Guideline no. 4: *Avoiding ambiguity and gaps in the regulation of the criteria for the awarding of productivity bonuses*

Ambiguity and regulatory gaps are often the conscious result of compromise in the negotiation of a collective agreement. However, they can leave room for unilateral/informal company practices that can eventually introduce indirect or direct discriminatory measures. For example, if a company agreement provides an all-round distribution of a productivity bonus, this does not prevent the company from reducing the amount of this bonus in the case of employees taking parental leave. This situation could be avoided if the company agreement included a specific provision on this aspect.

Guideline no. 5: *Avoiding (or minimising the impact of) work attendance in the choice of criteria for awarding productivity bonuses*

The choice of work attendance as a criterion for awarding productivity bonuses is anachronistic: the development of new forms of work organisation makes it less possible to measure workers' performance and productivity by merely referring to the length of time worked and to the amount of hours or days actually worked. Teleworking, smart working and the digitalisation of work require other criteria of measurement, such as workloads and performance standards.

Due to the gender time gap deriving by an uneven distribution of care burdens, the choice of work attendance can also have an indirect discriminatory impact on women's wages. Such impact is intensified if reductions of the tax rate and social security contributions are applied. This can be partially limited by gender corrective measures aimed at excluding maternity, parental and paternity leave from the calculation of work absences. The company agreement should clarify this aspect with a specific provision. Company agreements could also distinguish between short-term and long-term sick leave, depending on whether the national legal framework provides an anticipated/extended maternity leave in the case of risks in pregnancy and/or a paid leave connected with childcare in the case of a child's sickness.

Guideline no. 6: *Ensuring equal treatment between long-term/fixed-term employees and full-time/part-time employees*

In accordance with the EU and national framework enshrining the principle of non-discrimination between part-time workers/fixed-term workers and full-time/permanent workers, company agreements cannot provide separate and different criteria for these categories of workers as far as the awarding of productivity bonuses is concerned (for example, an all-round distribution for permanent full-time workers and an awarding of such bonus proportionally with the hours actually worked for fixed-term and part-time workers). In the case of part-timers, this can also imply indirect discrimination on grounds of gender.

Guideline no. 7: *Negotiating a gender-neutral job evaluation system*

The undervaluation of job requirements typically connected to female skills and abilities results in an underpayment of those jobs that in a company are mainly carried out by women. This can be neutralised by re-scaling job positions on the basis of a gender-neutral job evaluation (JE), which is a key instrument for implementing the concept of 'work of equal value' and for enabling a comparison between different jobs in context of intra-occupational gender-based horizontal segregation. JE could be implemented through a collectively negotiated process, with the establishment of a bilateral/gender-balanced committee responsible for monitoring its implementation. In nationally centred collective bargaining systems, this might require a process of review of job classification systems adopted at sectoral level. The clarity associated with a gender-neutral JE will also provide a firm foundation for the development of transparent bonus systems.

Guideline no. 8: *Negotiating the criteria for measuring and evaluating workers' performance and productivity, and for awarding bonuses*

Social partners should address the complexity and potential dangers of discretionary bonus systems and ensure that 'objective' criteria are free from bias. To this aim, performance and productivity criteria need to be spelt out clearly and jointly determined. This could imply a collectively negotiated process and the establishment of a bilateral/gender-balanced committee responsible for monitoring their implementation. Three main positive outcomes are: the company would be accountable for the awarding of any productivity/performance-related bonus; such awarding would not be exclusively based on a measurement of work attendance but would nevertheless be transparent and impartial; greater transparency and fairness may finally result in better employee morale/productivity.

Guideline no. 9: *Breaking the promotion barrier*

Vertical segregation can be overcome by providing gender-neutral criteria for career progress, which could be introduced by collective agreement, with a bilateral gender-balanced committee responsible for monitoring their implementation.

Job design, flexible work in hours and conditions, access to training and skills development, specific conditions for women returning from maternity leave, promotion of targets for women's representation at higher levels of organisations with equality audits should be considered a means to challenge existing occupational segregation and facilitate opportunities for women to move through job hierarchies and break into better-rewarded positions.

Guideline no. 10: *Fostering transparency in the company and along its supply chain*

Social partners should negotiate a procedure aimed at providing company level reports with very detailed information on pay, such as the difference in mean and median pay between male and female workers, the difference in mean bonus pay, the proportion of male and female employees who received bonus pay during the period of 12 months preceding the relevant date, and finally the numbers of male and female employees employed. Each calculation should be based on a specific measurement method stated by the company agreement. Social partners could ensure such transparency is granted also along the supply chain of the company by negotiating 'social clauses' in company agreements making the respect of certain transparency standards a condition of sub-contracting.

Guideline no. 11: *Use proactive, reflexive forms of legislation as a lever for negotiation*

The law, specifically reflexive legislation, should be used as a proactive *lever* to further negotiation, to 'mainstream' pay equality into organisations, thereby potentially reducing the amount of pay discrimination and subsequent legal cases. Specific duties required in the public sector could play a pivotal role to this purpose.

In the meantime, social partners should lobby the government for improvements in the regulatory framework and for making the law effective in reducing the GPG. In this regard, they should call for the government to deal with the topic from a lifetime perspective.

Index

legal correctness 175; legislation
leverage in negotiation 177; negotiator
training, promotion of leading cases
and 174–5; network building 174; pay
equality, mainstreaming of 174–5;
performance and productivity,
measurement criteria for 176–7;
productivity bonuses, awarding of
175–6; promotion barrier breaking 177;
testing experimental cases 174; transparency and GPG 145, 149–51, 174–7;
work attendance in award of
productivity bonuses 175–6
Gunnarsson, Å. 25
Gunnarsson, Å., Schratzenstaller, M. and
Spangenberg, U. 25

Hastings, Sue 109
Healy, G. and Ahamed, M. 101
Healy, G. and Kirton, G. 119
Healy, G., Bradley, H. and Forson, C.
32, 130
Healy, Geraldine xv, 1–7, 90–113, 114–44,
167–73
Heery, E. 17
Hepple, B., Coussey, M. and Choudhury,
T. 156
hourly work, GPG and 3, 13, 16, 23, 44,
46–7, 52–5, 73, 85, 101–105, 111n6, 157,
158, 174
Hyman, R. 115

incapacity at work, compensation for 73
inequalities, awareness of 123–5
inequality regimes 114; effects of 138–9;
gender bias and 127
international shipping company,
remuneration regulation in (case study)
79–82
Intersectoral Agreement on Productivity
(24 April 2013) in Italy 67n1
Istituto Nazionale di Previdenza Sociale
(INPS) 14
Italy 1–2; Act 125 of 10th April 1991 (125/
1991) 9, 159–60, 162; Article 2 of Act
903 (1977) 161; case law in 11–13; cases
cited 33; collective agreements 10–11;
collective bargaining 24, 168; Constitution, Articles 36 and 37 of 9–10; 'contractual segregation' in 160; Delegated
Decree 81 (2015) 10, 14; Delegated
Decree 196 (2003) 160–61; Delegated
Decree 198 (2006) 9, 10; Delegated
Decree 198 (2006), ineffectiveness of

172; employment relationship in 24;
family burdens, fiscal allowances for
14–15; institutional players and actions,
multiplicity of 9–10; interdisciplinary
analysis of decentralisation and GPG in
4, 38–68; key variables compared to
GPG in 32; Law Decree 148 (2011) 11;
legal framework in 3, 9–15, 172;
National Social Security Institute 14;
pay transparency in 159–61, 162; Privacy Authority 160–61; reconstruction of
concept of equal pay in 8; Regional
Equality Body *(Consigliera regionale di
parità)* 160; regulatory framework
9–11; *'superminimo individuale'* in 160;
tax and social security framework
14–15; wage system 13
Italy, interdisciplinary analysis of decentralisation and GPG in 4, 38–68; affirmative action, question of equality and
65–6; anti-discrimination practices 43,
51, 61; basic wage threshold, gaps in
38; bonus determination methods 40,
43–4, 51–2; bonuses, interface with
logic of 62; collective agreements, legal
certainty and validity of 40–41; company case studies, analysis of 42–56;
Confederation of Workers' Trade
Unions (CISL) 43, 51, 61, 68n17; Consolidated Law on Income Tax (TUIR)
41–2; contractual classifications, differences in 47; contribution performance
index 51–2; Corporate Social Responsibility (CSR) approach 57; corporate
welfare, experiences of 38; corporate
welfare, link between GPG and 67;
corporate welfare, reconciliation
between work and family life 60–61;
discrimination, direct or indirect 39, 41,
42, 47, 65–6; exchange, related critical
issues and 63–6; full-time work, GPG
and 45, 53; gender discrimination and
criteria for awarding productivity
bonuses negotiated in second-level collective agreements (case study 1) 39–42,
66–7; General Confederation of Labour
(CGIL) 43, 61, 68n17; horizontal segregation, problem of 38, 50, 66; hourly
work, GPG and 54; Intersectoral
Agreement on Productivity (24 April
2013) 67n1; Labour Union (UIL) 43, 61,
68n17; legislative context 59–60; Legislative Decree 151 (2015) 67n2; metal-
work sector company (case study 3)

negotiator training, promotion of leading
cases and 174–5
network building 58, 118–19, 120, 125,
139, 174
Network Rail (UK) 105, 107, 124, 172;
impact of Fair and Transparent Pay
Project on 109–11
Newell, A. and Reilly, B. 151
night work, compensation for 73
Nowakowska-Małusecka, Joanna xvi,
8–37
Nunin, R. 13

Oaxaca, R. 46
Office for National Statistics (UK, ONS)
92, 111n6, 140n6
O'Grady, Frances 117
Oliver, L., Stewart, M. and Tomlinson, J.
93, 94
O'Neill, B.P. 146
O'Reilly, J., Smith, M., Deakin, S. and
Burchell, B. 3
Organisation for Economic Cooperation
and Development (OECD) 19
organisational practices to raise awareness
126–7
overtime work, compensation for 72
Özbilgin, M.F. and Woodward, D. 99

parental leave 170
pay equality, mainstreaming of 174–5
pay policy secrecy in Poland 70
pay setting, gender bias in 132–5, 138–9
pay transparency 167; conceptualisation of
146–51
performance/productivity-related pay
114–15, 169; gender bias in awards of
132–5; measurement criteria for 176–7;
regulation of 43, 46
Peruzzi, Marco xvi, 1–7, 12, 38–69,
114–44, 167–73
Pillinger, J. 141n15, 167
Pillinger, J., Schmidt, V. and Wintour, N.
141n15
Plantenga, J. and Remery, C. 2, 160
Poland 1–2; additional annual salary and
bonuses 30–1; birth grant and allowance 29; bonuses, rules for awards in
31; business, Act of 2016 on legal
environment of 155; care allowance
29–30; case law in 23–5; cases cited 34;
Central Statistical Office 156; Code of
Civil Procedure (Article 882) 152; collective bargaining in 23, 24, 168;

Constitution (1997), equality and non-
discrimination in 21; discrimination
cases in 153–4; employment relationship in 24; equal pay principle, individualistic context of 23; Equal
Treatment Act (2010) 21–2; Family
Benefits Act (2003) 29; focus on post-
communist development in 8;
Government Plenipotentiary for Equal
Treatment 129–30, 141n12; guardianship allowance 29; Illness and Maternity Benefits Act (1999) 25;
interdisciplinary analysis of decentralisation and GPG in 5, 70–89; jurisprudence in 24; key variables
compared to GPG in 32; Labour Code
1975 (as amended) 21; Labour Code
(from 1996) 21–2, 24, 27–8, 29, 31;
Labour Code (from 2017) 155, 156;
Law of 23rd December 1999 on Wages
in Budgetary Sector 154; legal framework in 3, 21–32, 172; Legislative
Council in 156; maternity arrangements
in 170; maternity benefit 28–9; Minimum Wage Act (2002) 22; National
Labour Inspectorate 27; Natural Persons Income Tax Act (1991) 25;
Ombudsman for 156; parental allowance 30; pay transparency in 151–6,
161–2; Polska Klasyfikacja Działaności
(PKD) 75; pregnancy, maternity leave
and parental leave 26–7; problem of
GPG in, serious nature of 88; Public
Information Bulletin 154; regulatory
framework in 21–3; Retirements and
Disability Pensions Act (1999) 26;
salary determination in, Acts of 2003
and 2016 on 154; secrecy about wages
in 151–2, 152–3, 154–5; sickness benefit
27; Social Dialogue Council 22; Social
Insurance System 25; Supreme Court in
12, 21, 24–5, 34, 146, 152–3, 162; tax
and social security framework in 25–6;
transparency issue in 24–5; unions in,
lack of awareness by 124; unions in,
women's underrepresentation in 118;
wage system 24–5; Wages in Budgetary
Sector Act (1999) 25; Warsaw Stock
Exchange Listed Companies, Code of
Best Practice for (2016) 123, 154–5
Poland, interdisciplinary analysis of
decentralisation and GPG in 5, 70–89;
academic positions and salaries 85–7;
anti-discriminatory provisions in CLAs